RESTLESS PURSUIT

Discovering the Pathway to Purpose in Your Life

Marlon T. Perkins, Sr.

Scripture taken from the King James Version of the Bible.

Scripture quotations marked (CEV) are taken from the Contemporary English Version®, Copyright © 1995 American Bible Society. All rights reserved.

Scripture quotations marked (NIV) are taken from the Holy Bible, New International Version®, NIV®. Copyright © 1973, 1978, 1984, 2011 by Biblica, Inc.™ Used by permission of Zondervan. All rights reserved worldwide. www.zondervan.com The "NIV" and "New International Version" are trademarks registered in the United States Patent and Trademark Office by Biblica, Inc.™

Scripture quotations marked (GNT) are taken from the Good News Translation (GNT) in Today's English Version- Second Edition Copyright © 1992 by American Bible Society. Used by Permission

ISBN: 978-1-6847-0473-6 (sc)
ISBN: 978-1-6847-0472-9 (e)

Library of Congress Control Number: 2019907100

Lulu Publishing Services rev. date: 06/18/2019

*To all those who sincerely long to find and fulfill their life's calling,
and to—*

*Shurla, the wife of my youth;
Thank you for joining me in this journey.*

*Marlon, Jr. and Reba Marlayna, my beloved son and daughter,
Thank you for filling dad's quiver. (Psalm 127:5)*

*Daddy and Madea (both deceased),
for giving their children the indispensable gift of loving parents.*

*Marcellus, Maurice (deceased), Marsha, Gloria, Michael
(deceased), Madeleine, and Chris (deceased),
For giving me a sense of belonging.*

*Drs. Roland and Susie Hill,
for providing <u>incessant</u> motivation to write.*

*Leanne Ebsen, my friend and former church clerk,
whose "11th Hour" editorial assistance gave the necessary push to
finish this project (Thank you from the bottom of my heart!)*

*Most of all to—
Jesus,
for giving me life and a purpose for living it,*

This book is lovingly dedicated.

Contents

Acclaim for Restless Pursuit: xi

Foreword..xv

Preface xvii

Introduction...xix

Part I: Beginnings

Chapter 1   Telltale Signs... 1

Chapter 2   Broken Dreams...13

Chapter 3   The Way Forward..45

Chapter 4   Mr. Sheely 63

Part II: Middle Passage

Chapter 5   First Light..73

Chapter 6   School Daze...92

Part III: Decisions Determine Destiny

Chapter 7   Answering Destiny's Call............................... 131

Chapter 8   From Acorn to Acorn: the Anatomy of Purpose 162

Chapter 9   Potholes in the Road 178

Chapter 10   Go to Your Destiny..212

Endnotes..225

To live *with* purpose
is to live *on* purpose.
-AUTHOR

Acclaim for Restless Pursuit:

It has been a privilege and a pleasure to have a life-long friendship with Pastor Perkins. Meeting as young men in high school, at the crossroads of uncertainty and dreams of greatness, I encountered an intelligent and focused student, one who was serious about his future and dedicated to achieving his goals. Our friendship has strengthened over the years, and I have witnessed his growth and faithful commitment to spreading the Word of God.

In his honest and inspiring work, *Restless Pursuit*, Pastor Perkins reveals his journey to answer Destiny's call. Being one of the lucky few, I know the seeds of *Restless Pursuit* date back over 20 years. *This* is the book Pastor Perkins was born (in Christ) to write. It is the culmination of lessons learned from a prayerful heart and a patient spirit.

In *Restless Pursuit*, Pastor Perkins gives us each the gift of understanding that God has a grand and unique purpose for us all. He challenges us to look at our lives and see the moments God has revealed glimpses of His purpose for us.

It is with great personal joy and anticipated excitement for every reader that I commend this book. May it lighten your path in Christ and help bring forth the person God called you to be. I continue to be proud and impressed by my brother's life—and his work. God bless!
-Steven C. Watkins, friend

After working closely with Pastor Perkins for several years in Des Moines, IA, building a ground-breaking job training organization, I'm not surprised that his book, *Restless Pursuit*, is filled with insights on how you can realize your full potential in life. Using good humor, biblically-centered examples and stories from his own journey, Pastor Perkins weaves a heartfelt narrative that should inspire all readers to discover their pathway towards a more meaningful life!

- Paul Turner, Regional Organizer
   South and West Industrial Areas Foundation
   (Nation's longest standing organizing network)

Restless Pursuit is a wonderful, practical, and very timely publication. Pastor Perkins does an awesome job developing the concept of purpose from a biblical perspective. We are witnessing a society that has lost its identity and direction. This book helps to place the focus back on where direction is derived, from the Word of God.

-Dr. Paul Day, Senior Pastor
Oak Gardens Church
Dallas, Texas

Restless Pursuit is a beautifully written, engagingly captive piece of work. The author, Pastor Marlon T. Perkins Sr., uses a personal narrative approach to take readers into a deep search for identifying meaning and finding purpose in life. Perkins skillfully builds suspense and develops our appetite and interest for deeper knowledge and understanding of life's purpose, as he takes us on an intense journey of clarification and process.

Restless Pursuit successfully presents avenues for navigating what Perkins ably describes as the "potholes" of life, leaving one thirsting for a sequel to an intriguingly revealing masterpiece. A well-chosen selection of notable quotes and relevant Bible verses add to the profundity of the work, inspiring all to pursue meaning in spiritual relevance and guidance as pathways to discovery and fulfillment of one's calling and life's purpose.

~Theodora Jn Baptiste, Ed.D.
Educator/Youth Empowerment Specialist

There is something refreshing and optimistic about the words of Pastor Marlon T. Perkins, Sr., in his work *Restless Pursuit*. This is his story – his journey – his purpose. And yet, the wisdom and love contained in this memoir reveal how each of us has a path to a higher purpose – a higher calling – a higher consciousness. If you are on that journey to the truth, Pastor Perkins' poignant and Bible-centered instruction lets us all know that the Kingdom of Heaven cometh not by observation, but by God's quiet, still voice within our soul.

Judge Penny L. Willrich (Retired)
Superior Court of Arizona, Maricopa County

In a world of constant consumption and aimless pursuit, Marlon Perkins places a stake in the ground on the importance of the Creator-God's desire for you to know and fulfill His purpose and will in your life. Clarity of pursuit will be discovered through the author's personal journey and spiritual insights. Read this and be encouraged, really encouraged. Get this book! It will clear up life's fog about meaning and purpose.

Ivan L. Williams, Sr. Director, Ministerial Association
North American Division of the Seventh-day Adventist Church

Foreword

For over 40 years as a pastor, professor, and seminar presenter, I have watched parishioners, students, and people in the larger society search for purpose in life. These varied professional positions have allowed me to observe up close and personal the mental agony of hundreds drowning in the ocean of a purposeless life. But I have also observed the ecstasy, energy, and excitement of those who have found their purpose in life and are now living "on purpose".

Pastor Marlon T. Perkins, Sr., is one of those people that I have personally observed as he searched for and discovered his purpose in life. I was his pastor for seven years while he was a teenager growing up in Memphis, Tennessee, and it has been my privilege to serve as his mentor for over twenty-five years now. I fondly refer to him as my "son" in the ministry, and since those teen years I have walked with him for much of his purpose-full journey. In 2011, he accepted an invitation to serve as my successor as senior pastor of Living Waters Worship Center of Seventh-day Adventists in Dallas, Texas. He is the church's second pastor.

Restless Pursuit: Discovering the Pathway to Purpose in Your Life, is his well-written, open, and honest invitation for readers to journey with him in his personal and private path to purpose. I've discovered, though, that this book is more than a journey; it is a journal that unveils the process to finding purpose in life. In this unique book, Marlon moves flawlessly from the narrative of his life to instructional lessons aimed at helping you, the reader, discover your own purpose. Throughout the book, he skillfully weaves stories, illustrations, anecdotes, and wise sayings that unpack what he has discovered on the journey to purpose.

Marlon unabashedly states that the purpose of this book is "to awaken within the reader God's unique purpose for *their* life." He helps the reader understand that true purpose can only be discovered in a relationship with God. With the heart of a pastor and the passion of a crusader, Marlon lays out a clear path to discovering your purpose. *Restless Pursuit* is a book whose time has come. It is a book that will allow you to peer into your own life and peel away the layers that keep you from seeing your purpose and reaching your destiny.

Join Marlon on his journey to purpose. I promise you that the wisdom you discover in this book will assist you on your path to purpose—and the arrival at your destiny!

Dr. Roland J. Hill
Stewardship and Wealth Creation Consultant
Huntsville, Alabama

Preface

Great masses of people awaken every day to a purpose no more inspiring than paying the bills, saving for a bigger house or boat, or desperately hoping that their retirement years won't be filled with the drudgery of a survival-based employment. For others still, they face a daily plight against starvation, disease, homelessness, or other harsh realities that simply eclipse any notion of personal value or self-actualization.

One Christian author insightfully observed, "In the hearts of all mankind, of whatever race or station in life, there are inexpressible longings for something they do not now possess. This longing is *implanted* in the very constitution of man by a merciful God, that man may not be satisfied with his present conditions or attainments, whether bad, or good, or better. God desires that the human shall seek the best, and find it to the eternal blessing of his soul...It is God's design that this longing of the human heart should lead to the One who alone is able to satisfy it. The desire is *of* Him that it may lead *to* Him, the fullness and fulfillment of that desire. That fullness is found in Jesus the Christ, the Son of the Eternal God... '*for **in Him** dwelleth all the fullness of the Godhead bodily.*'"[1]

Restless Pursuit: Discovering the Pathway to Purpose in Your Life will offer you a fresh, practical, and biblically-centered guide to understanding the timeless issue of meaning and purpose in life. Presented in first-person narrative form, this book builds upon the firm notion that God has a *central purpose* for your life and that you can trust Him to reveal and fulfill it.

Whether you find yourself struggling with picking the right college, making a career change, parenting, what life holds for you in retirement, or anything in between, all of these decisions require a strong foundation in your purpose. You will be inspired, engaged, and equipped to discover and pursue your own God-given purpose, and you will see clearly the critical link that exists between your earthly pursuits and your eternal destiny.

Pastor Marlon T. Perkins, Sr.
Mansfield, Texas
May 1, 2019

Introduction

I once took a course in college entitled "1968: The Way We Were." It surveyed some of the momentous events which took place that year and how they made American history, events such as the Tet Offensive in Vietnam, the assassinations of Dr. Martin Luther King, Jr. and presidential candidate Robert F. Kennedy, the Poor People's March on Washington, D.C., that summer, and so on. Even Elvis Presley, after a break from his musical career, staged a highly rated comeback concert at the NBC studios in Burbank, California, that aired in December of that year. 1968, it seems, was a year of unparalleled social and political upheaval in America, and for that reason it easily rivals any year of the 1960s as the single-most controversial year of that decade.

On March 24 of that year, eleven days before the assassination of Dr. King in Memphis, Tennessee, a "medium-sized" family in the Walker Homes subdivision of southwest Memphis was experiencing its own change. The Perkins family was comprised of six children—three girls and three boys— and thus resembled a soon-to-be famous television family, *The Brady Bunch*. It was about to have its first addition in seven years, and also its seventh child. That child would be me.

The number seven is a special number in the Bible. Strangely enough, I have always felt special. My birth occurred at 6:40 p.m on a Sunday evening, just twenty minutes shy of—you guessed it—"seven" o'clock. I felt special— not just because I was raised with a lot of love by my family, nor because of the many accomplishments I have achieved thus far in life. By "special" I mean that since my early teen years I have had a strong sense of *purpose* about my life, as if I were predestined for a special purpose. The most frustrating thing throughout my teenage years was that I just didn't know *what* that purpose was. As a matter of fact, I would not discover that purpose until I was twenty-one years old and a senior in college...but more about that later.

As a teenager, that sense of purpose—a sense of *destiny*—was always in the back of my mind. It haunted me. Back then, I thought it was just an overly sensitive conscience. My mindset as a teenager was one of concern that I'd offend others or that others would reject me due to my words or actions. But in my latter years, I have come to recognize that this was the voice of God. It was this "Voice" that kept me from getting involved in some things that definitely would have derailed my life's course.

I'm not suggesting that I was a saint as a teenager, for I experienced some of the same temptations my peers faced: sex, skipping classes, the desire to be socially popular, etc. I've always felt, however, that God gave me pimples and plain facial features as a teenager as a way of keeping me unattractive to members of the opposite sex. Add to this the fact that I had (and still don't) absolutely no rhythm (African-Americans call it "soul") when it came to dancing, and what you had was an academic nerd who couldn't *buy* a date in high school. (It's interesting: maybe what we see as an "affliction" is actually a *gift* from God to protect and deflect us from distractions as He grows and guides our development into His spiritual son or daughter?)

What I did have, however, was *purpose*. Although I didn't know exactly what that purpose was, what I did know was that it was a driving force in my life so potent as to propel me to academic and leadership excellence throughout junior high and high school. It was also a moral force that made me constantly aware that certain behavior was not only wrong but that my life *could be* significantly altered if I engaged in this behavior. This moral compass would continue to guide me throughout college, graduate school, and into young adulthood, despite occasional mishaps along the way.

My purpose in sharing portions of my life with you in this book is simple: to awaken within you God's purpose for *your* life, and to encourage you to pursue it with all the passion that God's Spirit can muster within you. Through all of the stories and colorful anecdotes I share in this book I hope that you, by the guidance of the Holy Spirit, will come to discover your own pathway to purpose. It begins, simply, with God instilling within you an instinctive and unshakeable conviction that He has summoned you to fulfill some purpose in your life that is in accordance with His Divine will. In his book, *In Pursuit of Purpose*, Dr. Myles Munroe puts it this way: "There is something you came to this planet to do that the world needs in this generation. Your birth is *evidence* that your purpose is necessary."[2]

I want to add one more thought before I conclude this introduction. I want to clear up any confusion about God's ultimate purpose for everyone. That's right, *everyone*! The Apostle Peter was emphatic when he wrote, "*The Lord is not slack concerning his promise, as some men count slackness; but is longsuffering to us-ward, **not willing that** any **should perish, but that** all **should come to repentance**"* (II Peter 3:9, emphasis added). Although it is quite evident in Scripture that everyone who has or will live since the time of Adam up to the second coming of Christ will not go to Heaven, this in no way implies that God *wills* certain individuals to eternal damnation. His desire, rather, is for everyone to receive the sin-pardoning grace and gift of eternal life that is found in Jesus Christ. This is God's universal purpose for every soul.

But there is another component to God's universal purpose or will for our lives; namely, what we *do* with our lives *before* we go to Heaven. Jesus makes an interesting statement while relating a parable in Luke 19:13: "… *Occupy till I come.*" In this parable, Jesus stresses in no uncertain terms the need for faithful exercise and investment of our God-given gifts—for Kingdom purposes. For sure, God calls us to discipleship and to discipling others for His Kingdom. Soul-winning is part and parcel of the Christian life. Yet in a broader sense I believe that Jesus is speaking to the whole sphere of one's life, to the vocations, endeavors, and purposes that we pursue in our lives. How we *occupy our lives on earth* is equally important as when we someday will occupy the New Jerusalem.

God *does* have specific purposes for our lives as we occupy this earth until He comes.

He *does* want each of us to come into relationship with Him so that we might discover how we can better understand and develop the innate talents and skills with which He has gifted us.

He *does* desire that we serve His purposes in such a way that we might experience a meaning and fulfillment in our personal lives which would otherwise be unimaginable to the human senses.

The world is in dire need of men and women, young and old, whose purpose-directed contributions to the material and spiritual welfare of humanity will be of such benefit so as to lift the senses beyond the earthly and plant them in the Heavenly. How we occupy *now* is equally important as when we occupy *then*.

If somehow this book awakens within you a sense of "specialness" about your own life, and evokes within you a strong desire to seek and to fulfill

God's design for *your* life so that you too can begin experiencing a sense of personal fulfillment that will withstand the most severe trials and setbacks one can face in life, then this book will have served its purpose.

"Those who follow Him are not now or ever the helpless victims of environment or circumstances…circumstances can always be turned into providences because God uses circumstances to bring about His own overruling purpose, [so] that you can have a life and live a life in which nothing goes wrong, and in which all the disciplines of life are allowed to shape and mold you into the person God has in mind to make, made after His own image, in complete harmony with His all-ruling will."[3]

> *"But as many as received Him, to them gave he power to become the sons of God, even to them that believe on His name."*
> (John 1:12, KJV)

Let the pathway to purpose begin!

PART I

Beginnings

Excerpt from Psalm 139*
(A Psalm of David)

You have looked deep into my heart, LORD,
and you know all about me.
2 You know when I am resting
or when I am working,
and from heaven
you discover my thoughts.

3 You notice everything I do
and everywhere I go.
4 Before I even speak a word,
you know what I will say,
5 and with your powerful arm
you protect me
from every side.
6 I can't understand all of this!
Such wonderful knowledge
is far above me.

7 Where could I go to escape
from your Spirit
or from your sight?
8 If I were to climb up
to the highest heavens,
you would be there.
If I were to dig down
to the world of the dead
you would also be there.

⁹ Suppose I had wings
like the dawning day
and flew across the ocean.
¹⁰ Even then your powerful arm
would guide and protect me.
¹¹ Or suppose I said, "I'll hide
in the dark
until night comes
to cover me over."
¹² But you see in the dark
because daylight and dark
are all the same to you.

¹³ You are the one
who put me together
inside my mother's body,
¹⁴ and I praise you
because of
the wonderful way
you created me.
Everything you do is marvelous!
Of this I have no doubt.

¹⁵ Nothing about me
is hidden from you!
I was secretly woven together
deep in the earth below,
¹⁶ but with your own eyes
you saw
my body being formed.
Even before I was born,
you had written in your book
everything I would do.

17 *Your thoughts are far beyond*
my understanding,
much more than I
could ever imagine.
18 *I try to count your thoughts,*
but they outnumber the grains
of sand on the beach.
And when I awake,
I will find you nearby.

*Contemporary English Version

1

Telltale Signs

What is past is prologue.
—William Shakespeare

My mother impacted my life significantly and was *the* spiritual "driving force" in my childhood. Instead of calling her "mother," or "mom," I've always known her as Madea. Madea is a term of endearment used in many African-American families to refer to a matriarch of the family, usually one's mother or grandmother. Some say the word Madea is a hybrid term to mean "Mother Dear." Again, all I know is that from the start, I've known her simply as Madea. And I loved her dearly.

> *You were born with and for a purpose.*
> – Dr. Myles Munroe

My earliest memories of childhood go back to when I was three years old. Trust me, I know how old I was because I have a vivid memory of some of the events of my life at that age—events that have been verified by members of my family.

For instance, I remember the strong attachment I (still) had at three years of age for my milk bottle and the sadness I felt at its "mysterious" disappearance. For months Madea and my older sister Marsha had been trying to wean me from it, but I just wouldn't give it up. Finally, it came up missing and Marsha told me that the garbage man had come and taken it away. One day she and I were at the *Nite-n-Day*, a local convenience store a few blocks from our home. Marsha said that I suddenly broke away from her and ran out of the store toward a garbage truck nearby, begging the garbage men to give me back my bottle! She caught up to me before I ran too far, and spent some time consoling me. Oh how I was attached to that bottle! It was a deep heartfelt bond within my little soul.

First Steps

Before I went to kindergarten at age five, my younger brother Chris and I rode along with Madea every day as she would drop off our older brothers and sisters at their school. I was thrilled at the prospect of going to school, and couldn't wait until the day came when I too could go to school!

After we returned home, I would grab my make-believe textbooks, which were simply some old books I had gathered from around the house. I'd put them in my book bag, an old, worn-out leather satchel, and head off to my make-believe classroom in the den. I would sit down on the ivory-colored brick hearth, open my books, and begin talking to myself as if I were a teacher instructing his students. I would happily sit in my private school for extended periods of time. I didn't mind because I simply loved the idea of being in school.

As I opened my books (and they were the same books I looked at every day), in my mind

> *Even a child is known by his doings, whether his work be pure, and whether it be right.*
> – Proverbs 20:11

I pictured myself learning great things—like how to spell my name—and going off to great places—like anywhere beyond my front and backyards. It's amazing how creative the imagination can be. True enough, after I entered school, one of my favorite times of the day was simply staring out of the window, completely spellbound by the thoughts in my mind. To this day, I am still at home with my thought world. Sometimes this can get me into trouble.

Once, when I was dating a girl in college, we were driving along the highway and everything was quiet. We weren't mad at each other; I had just slipped off into my thought world and for a moment I was completely lost to everything around me—including her! Finally, she began making light conversation to break the deafening silence, jolting me back into the present. Before I knew it I retorted rather coldly, "You're invading my thoughts!" That really hurt her feelings and she quickly apologized for having "invaded my thoughts." These words had flown out of my mouth so fast I was shocked at myself for having said them. I apologized for being so rude to her.

During my preschool years I was consumed with studying. One day while Madea was hanging clothes on the clothesline in the backyard, I came up to her with my book satchel in hand. "Marlon, where are you going son?" she asked. "I'm going to school," I replied, and walked away briskly. Madea didn't take me seriously. After a few moments, as she recounted, the Holy Spirit spoke distinctly to her and said, "he's serious! You better go after him." She stopped hanging the clothes and ran after me. Sure enough, I had started walking up the street in the direction of the school.

Still, my preschool years were filled with warm memories and carefree days of playing in the yard, going to (pretend) school, and watching my favorite television programs like *Sesame Street*, *Zoom*, *The Electric Company*, and a whole host of cartoons. My all-time favorite TV program (even into adulthood) was *The Six Million Dollar Man*. Chris and I would lay in front of the television set in our parents' bedroom at seven o'clock on Sunday nights to watch this show. That's right, we managed to take over our parents' bedroom—which they allowed, knowing that this was the highlight of our week. Afterwards, we would sometimes go outside and jump off the front porch, pretending as if we were jumping off a ten-story building. We even made funny noises to mimic the "bionic" sounds made whenever Steve Austin, the show's main character, used his bionic strength. You would have to know the show—intimately—to know what I'm talking about.

The Mind (and Heart) of A Child

Like any other boy, three or four years old, I had my share of red fire trucks and big-wheeled scooters. To this day I remember the last time I saw my red, racy fire truck before it was smashed. Since I could actually sit in the truck and pedal it around, I loved to drive it up and down the street in front of our home, pretending that I was driving a car. Imitating my parents, I would drive my little truck up our driveway and park it like they parked their cars.

> *Some people see things as they are and say 'Why?' But I dream things that never were and say, 'Why not?'*
> – George Bernard Shaw

In retrospect, that little red truck looked so small parked in our big driveway, but to me it was the biggest, coolest thing on four wheels...until the day I parked it right behind Madea's car as I ran into the house to get a quick drink. My parents had warned me about leaving the truck in the driveway, but they just didn't understand how cool it felt to park my *own* car just like they parked theirs. As I sipped my drink my eyes got as big as the moon as I heard "*BAMM!*" "*CRUSH!*" and my heart sank faster than the Titanic. Madea, who was leaving in the car, must not have seen my truck parked behind her as she backed down the driveway. In those few minutes that passed after I entered the house, I had completely forgotten that I had left my truck parked behind her car. I ran outside, afraid to look at what was surely complete demolition. As I ran down the porch and looked down the driveway, there lay my truck, bent up like a crushed soda can. Madea scolded me for having parked it out of eyesight, but even then I felt that deep down inside she was very sorry for running over my favorite truck.

For minutes I stared at the wreckage in total shock and disbelief. I just could not accept seeing my truck in any shape other than shiny and in mint condition. I can't remember now, but I'm sure I must have burst into tears then. Finally, Madea told me to pick it up and dump it in the wooded area next to our home, which I did. In the days and months that followed, I watched that truck rust and weeds grow up around it. For years after the incident I could still see portions of the rusted truck whenever I dug down deep enough through all of the growth that had accumulated around it. Even into my adulthood, whenever I returned home I looked at that wooded area and thought of my red fire truck.

Another thing I remember doing before I entered kindergarten was *ironing* my own clothes. I became a neat freak at an early age. For instance, afros were in style for African-Americans in the seventies. The bigger the afro, the more attractive you were supposed to look. The only problem was, it was difficult

> *Great minds have purposes, little minds have wishes.*
> – Washington Irving

to keep your 'fro nice and even. If, for example, I leaned my head against something or inadvertently rubbed my hand through my hair, it would immediately get messed up. I would then have to go through the time-consuming task of re-combing my hair and patting it down to make it look neat and even on all sides. The crowning act to all of my preschool hair jobs was to put in the famous "Perkins Part," a parting line placed along the left side of the head. All the men in our family wore it; my older brothers

Marcellus, Maurice, and Michael often did it for Chris and me and eventually taught us how to do it ourselves.

I especially remember getting the Perkins Part on my fifth birthday, March 24, 1973. This was a milestone for me because it meant that I would now be eligible to attend school in the fall of that year. And that fifth birthday was a special one. I was excited the entire day, until the celebration officially took place that evening. I took a bath and dressed in a green jumpsuit complete with a color-matching turtleneck shirt and dress shoes. My brother Michael combed my hair for me and put in the Perkins Part. I then walked out into the living room along with my brothers and sisters and waited for Madea to bring in my cake. She had baked a double-layered chocolate cake, my favorite at the time. It was decorated nicely and had five candles in the middle. The candles were lit, the lights were dimmed, and everyone sang "Happy Birthday" to me. A picture was taken of Chris and me standing side by side behind the coffee table on which sat the cake, with my arm draped over his shoulder and his arm wrapped around my waist. We both smiled gleefully, and it seemed as if Chris was as excited as me. Despite occasional sibling rivalry in our early years, we remained close. After all, we were the babies of the family. I will talk more about this relationship later.

> *May our sons in their youth be like plants that grow up strong. May our daughters be like stately columns which adorn the corners of a palace.*
>
> — Psalm 144:12

My official transcript from Memphis City Schools declares that I entered kindergarten at Walker Homes Elementary School on August 21, 1973. The day for which I longed had finally come.

Your Past – A Preview of Your Future

Concerning the story of one's life, what I have come to understand is that oftentimes the channels of one's attitude and behavior – *telltale signs* of character development – are laid early in life. They are a preview of what is to come. This is why I have taken the time to describe some of the details of my early childhood. As you reflect over your own life, perhaps you will discover this to be true. Think about some of your own attitudes and behaviors now, your own idiosyncrasies. Are not some of them traceable to early childhood experiences?

Some who read this book are either parents already or will some day have children of their own. Do you view your child as someone whom God has destined for a certain purpose, someone for whom God has a life plan? I believe that a child's life takes on a deeper dimension of meaning in the eyes of his parents when it is looked at from the viewpoint of God. This is why it is so important that we dedicate the lives of our children to God early in life, if possible. By doing so, we acknowledge that life itself is special and is to be directed to the end of serving God. The Bible declares that

> *The potential possibilities of any child are the most intriguing and stimulating in all creation.*
> – Roy L. Wilbur

"*Lo, children are an heritage of the Lord, and the fruit of the womb is His reward*" (Psalm 127:3). When God called the Old Testament prophet Jeremiah into the prophetic ministry, He let him know in no uncertain terms that His call was one of destiny: "Before *I formed thee in the belly I knew thee; and* before *thou camest forth out of the womb I sanctified thee, and I ordained thee a prophet unto the nations*" (Jeremiah 1:5).

I draw particular emphasis upon the word "before." Isn't it simply amazing that God would pick a certain man *before* he was even a "gleam in his father's eye" to perform a certain task in life? There was nothing necessarily special about Jeremiah's life. He was from a small town named Anathoth (Jeremiah 1:1), located approximately three miles to the northeast of Jerusalem, and he was born into a "pastoral" family; his father Hilkiah was a high priest. Other than that, there is nothing else in scripture noteworthy of his lineage. Yet God told him unequivocally that He had destined him for a purpose even *before* he was conceived in his mother's womb. To me, this is absolutely astounding. In other words, this man's life was special *before* he was even born!

From this point forward you can never look at your life or the life of another person in the same light. You don't have to have your name placed prominently in books, or to have made some ground-breaking discovery in any field of learning, or to be CEO of some powerful corporation for you to consider your life a success. We can view success from essentially two perspectives – the world's and God's. I believe that God acknowledges *faithfulness* as a prerequisite for success. By faithfulness I mean *a willingness on the part of the believer to surrender his or her life completely to the will and way of God.* We must view ourselves as clay in the hands of the master Potter, molded after the fashion of His own desires. This form of surrender is not easy and is not necessarily done only once, for you will find yourself spiritually on the altar of sacrifice many times throughout your life. Again, this is the only guarantee of success.

Stop and reflect for a moment. When you think of your own childhood, what were some activities you enjoyed most? Did you enjoy working with your hands—like building things, throwing things, destroying things—or were you more introspective and self-absorbed—a daydreamer? Did you like being around other kids or did you prefer to be alone? Do you still have any friends from your preschool or middle school years? In group activities of any sort, would you consider yourself a leader or a follower, someone who would take initiative or someone who would prefer to be told what to do? Whatever your present occupation, did you have any childhood premonitions that you would one day be involved in such an occupation? For example, I've heard that some ministers know as early as five or six years of age that they are *called* into the ministry. I am also told that people who desire to become doctors know as early as middle school that that's what they want to be in life and therefore set out, mentally and academically, to achieve this goal. Think about it—we rarely see people determining at age thirty or forty that they want to become a doctor.

> *In my experience, the problems of people's past impact them in one of two ways: they experience either a breakdown or a breakthrough… past hurts can make you bitter or better—the choice is yours.*
> – John Maxwell

My point in asking these questions is this: *one can often trace the seminal elements to his or her life's calling back to early childhood experiences.* I know that I can, and you will see why later on. Therefore, if you are trying to figure out where God is leading in your life by way of either occupation or specific ministry, why not spend some time reflecting on your childhood, on some of the things you did then that brought you the greatest joy? Even if they were somewhat mischievous, are there any positives that you can extract from these otherwise negative experiences and say to yourself, "If I were to direct this same mentality in a positive manner, who knows what I might be able to accomplish?" After all, God has turned many a person from profligate to preacher, from misfit to missionary, and from sluggard to success.

Turn Your Pain Into A Promise

For some, however, the memories of your childhood will not be pleasant but rather painful, perhaps because they have been marred by some traumatic experience, such as emotional, physical or sexual abuse, or perhaps the death of a loved one. Despite painful experiences early in life, I have found that God *still* has ways of showing us His love and care for our lives and will use people, experiences or both during the painful times to do this. If you will dig deep enough into the recesses of your memory, you will find these people, places or events.

> *The deepest craving of the human spirit is to find a sense of significance and relevance. The search for relevance in life is the ultimate pursuit of man.*
> – Dr. Myles Munroe

Whatever joyful times you can recall, no matter how brief they may have been in frequency or duration, Jesus is certain to have been there. These pleasant experiences may constitute the only light in otherwise dark and despondent situations, but this light is strong enough to cast shadows, in the midst of which you will find Jesus. The Bible declares reassuringly in Lamentations 3:22-24; *"It is of the Lord's mercies that we are not consumed, because His compassions fail not. They are new every morning: great is thy faithfulness. The Lord is my portion, saith my soul; therefore will I hope in Him."*

Yes, God is there. Whatever our childhood experiences, good or bad, God has been there for us and longs to show us how if we will let Him. With God at the helm of your life, you *are* a son or daughter of destiny.

Parental Guidance Suggested!

I wish now to turn my attention to parents. The greatest feat you will ever accomplish as parents is to model, daily, a Godly lifestyle in front of your children and lead them to the feet of Jesus. A word of caution, however: you don't have the power to "make" Christians of your child(ren). This is a work reserved solely for the Holy Spirit (John 6:44). But you *can* walk righteously before them, and you *can* let them see the beauty of Jesus within you. Perhaps the second greatest feat you can accomplish, and one that closely parallels the first, is to help your child recognize that God has a purpose for him or her, and inspire within them the desire to see and to fulfill this purpose—whatever it may be. It really doesn't matter whether your child becomes a construction worker or a cardiologist, a patient homemaker or a professional home designer, just as long as the work to which they put their hands is a part of God's plan for their lives. "*Whatsoever thy hand findeth to do, do it with thy might*" (Ecclesiastes 9:10). With a sense of Divine purpose in life, it is difficult to settle for less because that purpose becomes a driving force in your life.

Here's why. When I graduated from high school, I became gainfully employed for the first time in my life—at McDonald's. After a little coaxing from one of my best friends, Tyrone, I went and filled out a job application. Tyrone was working for McDonald's at the time. I still recall the excitement I felt when I received a call from Della, the store manager, requesting an interview with me, and the indescribable feeling of awe I felt when she offered me a job right after the interview was completed. The feeling of accomplishment I had upon receiving that first job easily rivaled any other achievement—academic or otherwise—I had attained in high school.

> *When God created you, He built into you all the natural necessities for performing and fulfilling your purposed assignment. Everyone possesses natural inherent traits that are required for their purpose.*
> – Dr. Myles Munroe

Nevertheless, I did not have any grandiose ideas of building a career at McDonald's. I knew that I was not destined to flip hamburgers for the rest of my life! So I maintained the perspective that this job was simply a stepping stone, propelling me further along the path to discover what I was truly fit for in life. That's what purpose does for you: it helps you prioritize things in your life so that you can be able to say "no" to the good and "yes" to the best. And, yes—having a job at that age was a *good* thing.

Promising Prospects

As a parent, do you honestly view your child as promising, as a person with God-given talent that needs to be developed and employed for His purposes? If so, great! If not, then why not? There is a text that is often quoted and as equally misunderstood: *"Train up a child in the way he should go: and when he is old, he will not depart from it"* (Proverbs 22:6). This text is often quoted as the premier authority on the justification for "disciplining"—being interpreted, "spanking"—children or hauling them off to church every weekend. Indeed, there is the need for properly disciplining children for disobedience as well as regularly exposing them to religious instruction and worship services. However, these are not the *only* interpretations of the text. In the King James Version of the Bible, the margin reference for the phrase "in the way he should go" reads "in his way." In other words, we can properly interpret this verse to read, "Train up a child *in his way.*"

Does "in his way" mean that as parents you should give free reign to your child's impulses and urges? I think not. What the phrase "in his way" does suggest, however, is that each child born into this world possesses certain natural traits of character that will eventually manifest his or her *bent,* or direction (way) in life.

> *We have all been placed on this earth to discover our own path, and we will never be happy if we live someone else's idea.*
>
> — James Van Praagh

The German composer Ludwig van Beethoven was destined to be what he was – a virtuoso of musical composition and not the Bob Vila of home construction! And vice versa. So often parents get caught up in their own high expectations of their children, so rather than trying to figure out what their child's natural bent is, they try to bend the child in the direction of their own preconceived notions of what he should be. As you can imagine, this would be like trying to fit a square peg in a round hole. In some cases, it just wouldn't work and if it did it would require a lot of pressure and "hammering" into place. The result would be a tight squeeze, and the unnecessary strain placed upon the child could some day manifest itself in suppressed rage and frustration aimed at *you* the parent.

Roots & Wings

Study your child. Take special note of his or her temperament and disposition. As best as you can, try to expose your child to a broad, balanced educational environment, with a view toward a symmetrical development of character. Your job is to give him two things: roots and wings. Give him the "roots" of a Christian home filled with an abundance of love, laughter, and learning. When the roots sink deep into the spiritual soil of your child's life, they will be a stabilizing force during the tempestuous times he is sure to face in life. Give him the "wings" of self-confidence (hopefully rooted in firm reliance upon God) that will one day allow him or her to leave the nest of your home with the solid assurance that he or she can face life without child-like dependence on you. This is not to suggest that you necessarily force your child to pack his bags and leave your home on his eighteenth birthday! With a proper balance between the "roots" and the "wings," there can be a healthy transition for your child from teenager to young adult. I know—it happened to me.

When we were teenagers, Madea did not want Chris or me to work outside of the home. By "work" I mean gainful employment. She felt that after we finished high school we would have the rest of our lives to work. She desired, instead, that we enjoy our teenage years free from as many adult responsibilities as possible. So, our summers were always filled with baseball, football, basketball, and just about anything else we could find to work off all our youthful energy. This is not to say that we didn't have household chores to do, for we had our share; we just weren't employed outside of the home.

> *Example is not the main thing in influencing others – it's the only thing.*
> – Albert Schweitzer

This may or may not be what's best for your child and as a parent you will have to make that determination. All I remember is that in less than four months—from the time I graduated from high school in May 1986 until the following September—I went from having no job to working two jobs, one on campus and one at McDonald's. This was in addition to taking twelve credit hours of collegiate work. From what I recall, I made the transition relatively well, and I enjoyed working immensely. In fact, with the exception of my freshman year, I paid all of my "cost of living" expenses in both college and graduate school on my own and successfully pursued and attained all the student loans and scholarships necessary to complete my educational path. I take great delight in that I was able to bear so much responsibility so quickly in my early adulthood. I credit that to my mother's profound wisdom and loving concern for her growing sons, as well as my father's occasional prodding to "be your own man."

Again, it's about roots and wings. Madea worked hard to lay a good foundation of honesty, integrity, and individual responsibility in the lives of her children, thus the "roots," and when it became time for me to leave the nest of our home and soar into young adulthood, I was able to do so relatively well.

A second experience in my life that reflects this concept of roots and wings happened on my wedding day. My wife Shurla and I were married in Bermuda, her native country. Her Uncle Carlyle, an ordained minister, administered the wedding vows. After he pronounced us husband and

> *For I know the thoughts that I think toward you, says the Lord, thoughts of peace and not of evil, to give you a future and a hope.*
> — Jeremiah 29:11, NKJV

wife, we walked down from the platform to greet our parents. Shurla's parents were seated in the front pew on our left, and Madea was seated in the front pew on our right. Daddy was unable to attend due to health problems at the time. As I hugged Madea, I immediately became overwhelmed with emotion. Tears filled my eyes. At that precise moment, the roots that Madea had nurtured within my soul were now taking wing as I began my new life with Shurla. I felt immensely satisfied and joyful—joyful for the fact that, deep within my soul, I felt *prepared* to accept the responsibility of helping to establish my own home. I took great joy in knowing that Shurla and I would be going to our own home when we returned to the U.S., and that God had blessed me with a job that would allow me to meet all of our household expenses without any outside assistance.

I was also grateful that I could truly call Shurla my *wife* in every proper sense of the term without the ghost of some past relationship still lingering in my mind. In other words, I felt like a man, and at that moment I was profoundly grateful that God had blessed me with such parents. I knew that all of this was directly attributed to my God-fearing home; I was simply the product. Because of the roots of such an upbringing, that day I was able to soar into married life. Praise God from whom all blessings flow!

The telltale signs of our lives are often revealed during childhood. Parents and mentors, may you view your children or those who you mentor as "diamonds in the rough," and may your guidance in every facet of their lives be of the highest order.

2

Broken Dreams

What happens to a dream deferred?
Does it dry up
Like a raisin in the sun?
Or fester like a sore—
And then run?
Does it stink like rotten meat?
Or crust and sugar over—
like a syrupy sweet…

—Langston Hughes

Much has transpired from the days of watching *Sesame Street* and playing pretend school. I would not be where I am today were it not for the upbringing and guidance I received as a child. As good as my parents were to all eight of their children, our home, unfortunately, would be marred by the sting of divorce. This traumatic experience would profoundly affect every member of our household and would prove to be life altering. One positive for Chris and me was that we were too young to understand what was really going on. The only explanation I have for that is that God somehow shielded our delicate emotions from much of the severity of the ordeal. For the most part, this seventh child had pleasant childhood experiences and felt free to explore much of what his imagination would allow.

Journey Into the Unknown

I still recall that Saturday morning, July 5, 1975, when we left Memphis. It was a bright and warm summer day, with a gentle breeze cool enough to temper the otherwise hot and humid southern climate. I was seven years old. Normally, we would be getting ready to go to church, but on this day we were preparing to leave home—leave Memphis. Daddy and Madea were separating.

During what would be the final hours of my parents' marriage, you would have thought that there would have been a lot of yelling, arguing and threatening going on. But that was not the case. In fact, I recall so clearly the calm demeanor of my father. What sticks out most in my mind is the image of him sitting on the edge of their bed, in his pajamas, watching television. And all the

> *The greatest use of life is to spend it for something that will outlast it.*
> – William James

while Madea was right there, in his presence, finishing her packing. From what I remember, he did not try to interrupt her.

As he recounted this event many years later, he didn't believe she was really serious. She would be back eventually, he thought. After all, she had left him once before for five months in 1954 and had traveled all the way to Florida with Marcellus, Maurice and Marsha, who was barely a toddler. This time she would be taking with her my sister Madeleine, who was fourteen at the time, me, and Chris, who would turn six within a couple of days. We were the only children of the eight still at home. Now we would be leaving for Elizabethtown, Kentucky, to stay with my eldest sister Marsha, who was in the Army and stationed at nearby Fort Knox.

Madea, as she related to me in later years, had packed little by little all that week leading up to our day of departure, and worked all through the night on Friday night. After a brief period of sleep, she got up on Saturday morning and continued packing. She said Daddy had asked her several times that morning if she were going to church, to which she replied "No." He asked her the same question again, and finally she said, "No, Junior (as she called him), I'm leaving you." As it turns out, Madea had already made arrangements with my Aunt Rose, the widow of Daddy's brother Randolph, to drive us to Kentucky. I remember Aunt Rose as having the brightest smile of almost any person I'd met. This weekend Aunt Rose had made arrangements for someone to keep her children while she drove us to Kentucky. I'm not quite sure what she expected to see as she drove up to our home with a U-haul trailer attached to her car. I'm sure she was surprised to see everything so peaceful, but obviously chose not to comment. There was no way that she was going to give the appearance of taking sides.

A Father's Tale

To better understand some of the factors which contributed to my parents' marital demise, you would have to go back a few years. Daddy, named Ousley Perkins, Jr. was born in Memphis to Ousley and Evelyn Perkins in 1927. Like me, he was born into a large family with eight other siblings. My grandfather Ousley (whom his grandkids called "Big Daddy") worked a variety of jobs and my grandmother was a homemaker. They were both hard

> *We know what we are, but know not what we may be.*
> – William Shakespeare

workers, and my grandfather was an avid reader. He especially enjoyed the law and hoped, vicariously, that his son Ousley, Jr. would one day become a lawyer. Things were tight financially for the family, as was the case with many poor families during the Great Depression, so Daddy started his own shoeshine business as a pre-teen.

Daddy was good at his craft and soon had a thriving business going. He made enough money to help out at home, and used some of his extra money to buy clothes and shoes for himself. He developed the habit of being a neat dresser at an early age. He grew to be a handsome young man with sterling features and brown-colored, baby-smooth facial skin. He was a ladies' man, and one who was well-acquainted with the street life of inner-city Memphis. After some formal training as a boxer, he developed a reputation as a good street fighter, one who wasn't afraid to defend himself, his family or friends at a moment's notice. He dropped out of school after the eighth grade, though he would later complete his GED as an adult. Nevertheless, Daddy excelled at basic mathematical computations, a gift that would later help him to excel as a top-flight salesman at a local car dealership.

He served a short stint in the U.S. Army toward the end of World War II and was honorably discharged. He worked a variety of jobs thereafter until 1951 when he landed a position with the U.S. Postal Service, a job he would hold until 1969 when a serious back injury at work forced him to retire. Even after back surgery, the pain he experienced in his lower back was so severe that it prevented him from working full-time for the next four years.

By 1973, he finally felt strong enough to work again and began working as a salesman at the Oakley-Keesee Ford dealership in Memphis, where he became very successful. Though only a five-year-old at the time, I distinctly remember some of the new cars Daddy would bring home from time to time. They were "demo" cars that the salesmen were allowed to drive. Our family was tremendously blessed financially during the time that Daddy sold cars.

Daddy continued to work there until 1975, when his mother's failing health prompted him to take a year off from work to care for her. Earlier that year, my grandmother Evelyn (whom the grandkids called "Big Mama") had come to live with us because of her failing health. Later that same year, Madea had left him and moved to Kentucky, while Big Mama continued to stay in the family home under Daddy's care until she moved in with my Aunt Ernestine. Then Daddy was able to return to Oakley-Keesee in 1976 and worked there until 1978, when his back problems again forced him into early retirement and he depended on disability and his Post Office pension for support thereafter.

Simply A Country Girl

Billie Gloria Smith, Madea, was born on May 3, 1931, to Josephine Smith-Green in Jackson, Mississippi. Josephine settled in Canton, Mississippi, some twenty miles northeast of Jackson. Madea was one of several children born to Josephine. She, however, was born out of wedlock. At birth, Josephine reportedly called her step-great grandmother, Margaret Boone-Smith, and told her, "I

> *There is surely a future hope for you, and your hope will not be cut off.*
> – Proverbs 23:18, NIV

don't want this child and I'm gonna leave her here in this hospital. If you want her, you better come and get her." And that's just what "Grandma Maggie"—as Madea affectionately referred to her—did, walking the nearly 20 miles from her farm home in nearby Ofahoma to the hospital in Jackson to get Madea.

Grandma Maggie was the second wife of Madea's biological great-grandfather, Clint Smith, and was well-acquainted with Josephine Green, as she had been living on the homestead with Clint and Maggie up until the birth of Madea. Although Madea would live sporadically with her mother, she still claimed that it was Grandma Maggie who raised her, gave her abundant love and attention, taught her about the love of God, and schooled her in the virtues of being a woman. As for Madea's father, he was a light brown-skinned Black man nick-named "Ben". He had a fine grade of hair, deep brown penetrating eyes and overall good looks. In reality, he looked almost White. His great-grandfather was indeed a White man who had fought for the Confederacy during the Civil War. From the little I know of "Ben," he was considered a ladies' man, which is what probably attracted Grandma Josephine to him.

My grandfather never openly acknowledged Madea as his daughter, and from the day of her birth until the day she died he never had any contact with her in a fatherly manner—directly or indirectly. On one occasion, when she was a girl, the two happened to attend the same gathering at a friend's home. As Madea entered the door, her father was standing nearby. She heard someone say, "Hey [Ben], isn't that your daughter Billie?" Madea said he quickly dismissed the question and didn't bother to look her way. She, too, decided at an early age to dismiss him as a father. As it turns out, my grandfather would marry several months after Madea's birth and raise a rather large family with his wife, with whom he remained married until his death in 1996.

> *Purpose is the most valuable treasure you can find because it takes you beyond temptations, misunderstandings, the unfaithfulness of family and friends and even death itself.*
> – Dr. Myles Munroe

Despite this negative experience in her early life, she nevertheless found peace of spirit on Grandma Maggie's small farm in Canton. There she attended to her daily chores, played with her other siblings and cousins, and made the mile-and-a-half trek to her little schoolhouse—which is still standing today! She also learned the old Negro code of behavior: when "grown folks" were talking, children were to be seen and not heard. Oftentimes she and her cousins would sneak under the front porch and listen to the grown folks gossip. As hard as they tried to refrain from snickering, it would inevitably burst into small laughter, enough to be heard by the adults sitting above them and evoke their immediate wrath.

One of her favorite pastimes was walking through a nearby wooded area around the farm. By today's standards, that would be considered dangerous, but not so for Madea. She found solace in those woods. There she developed her own relationship with the Jesus whom Grandma Maggie spoke so intimately about. She would unburden the woes of her heart to Him, talking as if He were physically walking by her side. Her eyes would sometimes fill with tears as she spoke of her experiences, but she would always leave those woods refreshed and strengthened, for no doubt she had met with God. Madea would later tell me that Jesus became real to her—intimately real— during those early years.

She also would pretend to be a preacher there in those woods. She found an old tree stump that would serve as her platform, and she would fling her arms demonstrably and bellow from the depths of her stomach as she mimicked the Negro preachers she saw in church on Sunday mornings. By her own estimate, she could really preach, and she would preach her heart out to her attentive "parishioners"—the nearby tree stumps, bushes, vines and crickets. Occasionally, a few of her cousins and friends would be guests. She thought she would become a preacher, until the Lord spoke to her one day and told her that her mimicking was actually blasphemous to Him. She said she felt so badly after that incident that she immediately gave up the desire to be a preacher.

> *When God measures man, He puts the tape around his heart – not his head.*
> – Guideposts

For all intents and purposes, Madea was simply a country girl. When she turned thirteen, Grandma Maggie felt that it was time for her to move on to bigger and better things, for she concluded that their small community offered no attractive future for a young but poor Black girl. Madea had recently completed the eighth grade, and Granda Maggie thought that Memphis would present her with better opportunities. Madea had an aunt who lived there, and so at age thirteen she found herself moving to the big city. It was a painful departure for her, for she greatly loved her great grandmother, not to mention the fact that Grandma Maggie's health was now failing.

The next six years would find Madea mostly doing domestic work in Memphis, cleaning the homes of well-to-do (predominately White) families. There was really no time for school, and living with her aunt necessitated that she work to earn her keep. At age eighteen, she met and befriended Victoria Perkins, a young Christian girl who happened to be one of my father's sisters. It was through their friendship that Daddy and Madea met—the young and handsome city boy and the pretty, young country girl—and the two were wed about a year later on May 5, 1950.

Cracks in the Foundation

Their two backgrounds couldn't have been more different. Daddy practically grew up amid the hustle and bustle of one of the Mid-South's largest cities and Madea grew up on a small farm in southwest Mississippi. Daddy was very much a "ladies' man" and Madea simply wanted a family and "a house with a white picket fence." Daddy was very keen to the ways of street life; Madea, by her own admission, was simply naïve. He told her that he wanted to settle down and was ready to start a family with her. Madea reckoned that since he came from a Christian home and was a hard worker, he was sincere. Grandma Evelyn, his mother, was a devout Seventh-day Adventist Christian. She had raised her children according to biblical principles and faithfully attended weekly worship services, which were held on Saturdays. Madea would join the same church, which only added to her desires that she and Daddy could share the same spiritual values and raise their own children accordingly.

> *A man's conscience, like a warning line on the highway, tells him what he shouldn't do – but it doesn't keep him from doing it.*
> – Frank A. Clark

Their marriage, however, was challenging from the beginning. Daddy was a solid provider for the family, and sometimes worked two and three jobs to make ends meet. The first eleven years of their marriage, between 1950-1961, produced six children: Marcellus, Maurice, Marsha, Gloria, Michael, and Madeleine. I, along with Chris, would be added in 1968 and 1969, respectively. But Daddy had other "relationships," some before and after their wedding, which had a devastating impact upon their marriage. To begin, his first child, my eldest sister, was born just several months after he married Madea. Daddy would go on to father four other children during the first six years of their marriage. To protect the privacy of my other brothers and sisters, I have chosen not to reveal their identities. Despite the deep pain and obvious humiliation of these affairs, Madea, by steadfastly clinging to the grace, strength, and forgiveness she found through God, remained a faithful and dutiful wife.

There would be a period in their marriage, however, when there was relative peace and tranquility. That period began in 1960 when Daddy was baptized and joined the Mississippi Boulevard Seventh-day Adventist Church. Madea had always been a faithful attendee, along with our growing family, but now Daddy joined the spiritual circle. His faithful support of the church would have a marked influence upon our church and our family. The next decade in our family life would be unmarred by infidelity and characterized by fervent devotion to God. My sister Madeleine, born in 1961, was the first child born into this tranquil period. What's interesting is that her recollections of her early childhood—as far

> *Our deeds determine us, as much as we determine our deeds.*
>
> – George Elliott

as the tranquility within the family is concerned—differs somewhat from those of her five predecessors—Marcellus, Maurice, Marsha, Gloria and Michael.

Because I was so young when my parents' marriage began to unravel, and therefore have no substantial context in which to place their struggles, I have asked my older siblings to share some of their individual reflections of our family life, both good and bad, leading up to our parents' separation and divorce. Although younger than me, Chris, too, had a clear memory of our departure from Memphis, and wanted his recollections included here as well. My hope is that their reflections will provide a clearer context for this defining event in our family's history. Interestingly, you will notice some similarities between their testimonials, which proceed in order from the oldest, Marcellus, to the youngest, Chris. Two testimonials are not present: Maurice's, because he was deceased at the time I requested these testimonials, and Michael's, who though now is deceased but was alive when the testimonials were requested, respectfully declined to comment.

IN THEIR OWN WORDS

Marcellus's Story

We lived in a nice, comfortable, three-bedroom, one-bath home with a big backyard. Our home was situated on a hill. Daddy and Madea had one bedroom, all three boys slept in one room, and the girls slept in the other room.

Our days consisted of getting up around 5:30 or 6:00 a.m. Daddy allocated everyone about fifteen minutes to get themselves ready for the day, then we would generally have worship and Daddy would read from the Bible. On Mondays we would all recite a verse that we had learned from the previous week. On Wednesdays we'd each expound on the meaning of our various verses. Then, on Thursday or Friday evenings, which was the Sabbath, we'd each try to learn a new Bible verse for the following week. We would open our devotion times with prayer, starting with me, the eldest, on down to the youngest. Daddy would add a few more words we would then leave for school, generally by 7:00 or 7:30a.m.

We had a very talented family. I was the singer of the family. Marsha and Gloria were honor roll students. Maurice was perhaps the most charismatic one of us all, as he had a way of winning people's confidence. But he was also the most mischievous one of us all. He and I would tease the girls a lot, pulling their hair locks and things like that. Maurice was the worst between the two of us because he would terrorize the girls!

The quiet one of the whole bunch was Gloria. Michael and Madeleine were active in church, along with the rest of us. Then came Marlon and Chris, the babies. Overall, we were perceived very well as a family. Actually, many of our peers admired our family very much. We presented ourselves with dignity and grace. Our family engendered a lot of respect from church members and the community as well.

Prior to Marlon being born, Madea had a miscarriage; quietly, I had hoped she wouldn't have any more children. She took the miscarriage hard. One day when I was about sixteen years old, she opened up to me about it. She broke down in tears. She took the loss very hard for some time afterwards. It was as if she had lost a part of her own self. I hated to see Madea cry, and I tried my best to comfort her. "Maybe something was wrong with the baby," I told her. "Maybe God in His wisdom knew what was going on. Whatever the purpose, there was a reason why you had a miscarriage. You didn't do it on purpose." But she still took it hard. I tried to reassure her further by telling her that she could always have more kids. It was also very hard on me because I couldn't completely understand what was going on or how Madea felt. It wasn't until after she was pregnant again, this time with Marlon, that the depression finally went away. All of us got excited again about having another addition to the family...

Daddy and Madea argued a lot, it seems. This was one of the most frustrating aspects of my upbringing. I didn't think that couples should act that way towards each other. They were rough on each other, although it seemed like Madea would end up getting hurt the worst. Our house was full of confusion [at times] because of the tension that existed between them.

Fridays were different because of the Sabbath, which brought a change of pace in our weekly activities. We always cleaned the house on Fridays in preparation for the Sabbath, church attendance, and the guests we would have over to our home for dinner after church. After I started dating, I especially made sure the house was clean on Fridays to impress the girls who would come over after church.

It seems like after I left home for college things began to change and deteriorate between Daddy and Madea. I couldn't wait to get away from home, as I was ready to start making my own decisions. Daddy wasn't as regular in church attendance and relaxed some of his strict behavior; he wasn't as tough on the younger kids—Madeleine, Marlon and Chris—as he was on the rest of us. Daddy became a car salesman, making a lot of money and meeting a lot of people. Consequently, temptations came his way. I remember Madea telling me later that she stayed in their relationship until the Lord told her it was time to go. When they separated, in a way I was sorry to see this happening to them but in the long run I knew it was for the best. I got tired of seeing them argue. After I left, it seemed like the "innocence" was gone in our family.

Marsha's Story

My earliest memories of our family go back to when I was three or four years of age. Daddy and Madea would take us to the Cotton Carnival and The Mid-South Fair every year. After Daddy joined the church, we attended church services regularly as a family and we enjoyed our Sabbath afternoon meals together as well. We spent a lot of time around Daddy's parents, "Big Daddy" and "Big Mama", and our cousins.

For some reason, Maurice sticks out most in my mind because I consider him to have been my protector. I was the first girl to be born behind Marcellus and him; he looked after me and took good care of me. Whenever Madea had a baby, Aunt Bonnie—Madea's sister—would come over and take care of us until Madea got better. I don't recall either Gloria's nor Michael's birth, both of whom came after me, but I do remember Michael as a baby, and I vividly recall Madeleine's birth. After she was born, she was the brightest spot in the entire family because we all thought she was the most beautiful, talented child among the children. We all were very proud of her.

Madea took time and special care with us as children, as she taught us how to count money, how to count numbers, and she seemed to always have some kind of workbook. To keep us entertained, she would take worn out sheets and make stuffed animals. We had a shade tree in the front yard, and oftentimes Madea would take a blanket and spread it under the tree to make a "pallet," as they call it. She would sit and read Bible stories to us, and a lot of other kids in the neighborhood would come over to sit and listen in too. To me, her whole world revolved around her children.

As siblings, we were not allowed to fight or fuss at each other, no matter how old we got. Daddy instilled a strong sense of family in us. We were not allowed to go "against" one another, because Daddy taught us that when all else failed, you would still have your family. We truly did love each other and would express this love through hugs and kisses. Others marveled at our strong affection for one another. Although the boys had their own room and the girls theirs, at night we would all get together in one room and just talk. We were very sheltered and provided our own entertainment...

I watched Daddy and Madea's relationship deteriorate after Daddy hurt his back while working as a postal worker. He was a staunch churchgoer at that point in his life. He truly believed in visiting and ministering to the needs of the sick and the poor, and he taught us to do the same. But after his back surgery, he became bitter toward the church because of what he felt was a lack of attention shown to him by the members. Daddy felt that, while he was strong and was up and about, he had given his all to the church, only to be treated insensitively by the same church when he was disabled. To his credit, Daddy took his church commitments seriously. He was a hard worker for the church. But when he became ill with back problems, no one came over to the house to say, "Bro. Perkins, is your family hungry? Is there anything I can do for your family?" There were many times during his illness when we didn't have much in our home; however, he taught us that no matter what, you don't let anyone know what is going on in your household.

When he felt better, Daddy began working for Oakley-Keesee Ford, selling cars and making a lot of money. In my opinion, he became enticed by a lot of things that were going on in the world around him: money, women, and "the good life." Sure, we had more money in the family then, and everything took on a better mood, so it seemed. But in reality, it wasn't. The money only masked deeper problems that were taking place in my parents' marriage...problems that would eventually affect us all. (Satan is such a deceiver!)

Before, we had a sense of togetherness, pride, integrity, and hard work. What did we have now? It felt like everything we had, as a family, was disintegrating around us. I went off to college for a while, dropped out, and then I joined the Army.

When Madea separated from Daddy, I was stationed at Ft. Knox, Kentucky. She had talked to me about leaving him a lot. I would ask, "Where are you going? What are you going to do?" "I don't know," she would say. "The Lord will take care of me." She was a staunch believer.

This was on my heart—a lot. I would ask myself, "Where is she going? I really don't want her to come here." I prayed to the Lord about it: "Lord, I really don't want to take care of my mother. I really don't want her to come here with the kids." I didn't want them to come and live with me because I didn't love or care about them; that wasn't the case. I loved my mother and siblings dearly! It's just that I was so young myself and I was really just getting started in life. I was only 21 at the time. I knew that this would be a lot of responsibility to take on, and I felt overwhelmed by the prospect of it all. And I didn't want Daddy to feel like I was being disloyal to him. I felt torn inside.

Looking back, I knew then that the Lord was moving on my heart to take them in and that I couldn't be disobedient to Him, no matter what. I now know that regardless of a person's decisions, God's Will will be done!

I tried to be neutral, as I thought that any child should be. Did I think that they would get back together? I had hoped that they would, but I can't actually say that I visualized them getting back together. I just hoped that they would for the sake of the entire family. Their separation was never announced. It just happened. They stayed separated for two years and eventually Daddy sought a divorce.

Over time, both Daddy and Madea were able to come together for the sake of the children, at weddings, births of grandchildren, deaths, or even to participate in holidays together. We were still a family, and I think that's admirable.

Gloria's Story

There were six of us, three boys and three girls. I thought we had the most perfect family. And everyone who asked Daddy how many kids he had always said so too.

When I was quite small, maybe three or four years old, I felt like Daddy delighted in me. He used to always laugh at me and have fun with me. But as I got older, he became sterner and required more things of me, so it seemed.

We were all kind of shocked when we found out that Madré (as I affectionately referred to her in my adult years) was pregnant with Marlon. Madeleine was the baby of the family at that time. Just prior to her pregnancy, Madré had a miscarriage, and though I didn't fully understand it at the time, I could tell that she felt very sad about it. Madré, though, never looked back and said very little about it. When I found out she was pregnant again, I wondered whether this one would be born or not. And then it became time for her to go to the hospital…

We were excited about the birth of Marlon and I couldn't imagine a baby being born after all these years. When Madré went into the hospital, it felt like she stayed forever. Mrs. Rita Jones [a neighbor and friend of Madré] came over to take care of us. I said, "I'll be glad when my momma comes home because I like her cooking better." Now that I look back on it, that was a very heroic thing for Mrs. Jones to do, to be in somebody else's home when the kids only liked their own mother's cooking, and to continue to cook for them no matter what they said about it. She was wonderful!

Daddy and Madré argued a lot, it seemed. I noticed that Daddy would often leave late at night, around 10:30 p.m. or so and would say, "I need to make a little run, I'll be back. I'm going to take care of some business." That was his main thing to say, "I'm going to take care of some business." And he would leave. I would go to sleep, but he was always there in the morning when I got up, even though he had been gone all night. I sort of knew he would come back by 6:00 a.m. or so.

I blamed Madré a lot for their breakup because at the time I thought, "It's your job to make your husband happy." When I became older and got married myself, I understood differently. I realized that a woman can't make a man happy; he's got to be happy all by himself.

Daddy did not believe her when she said that she was leaving for good. He thought that she would leave, but would eventually come back after she realized how hard it would be to make it on her own with no job and three children. As it turns out, we spent the 4th of July [1975] together and on July 5, Aunt Rose drove up and packed Madré, Madeleine, Marlon and Chris into her little car. Madré turned to me and asked, "Do you want to come Gloria?" Daddy and I were standing on the front porch. I said, "No, I want to stay here with Daddy. I'm not going." I was in college at the time. So, she got in the car and left.

I went back to school in August. I would come home from time to time and Daddy would cry about how Madré had left him and took his whole family. He seemed so lonely. I'd massage his back. Then I would go back to school. Sometimes he would have other women there. Then I understood what Madré was going through in their marriage. I found out years later that she would sometimes get phone calls from other women who would taunt her about being with Daddy. I didn't like the fact that she had to endure not only him staying out late at night but also having these other women calling her home and taunting her.

As I've said, after they separated, I blamed Madré. I never hated her, per se, but I disliked her very much. Once, I wrote her a letter that was very hurtful to her. Again, at the time I didn't see the total picture of their marriage—I just blamed her for its breakup. In my letter, I asked, "Madré, why don't you go back to Daddy? You know you hurt him and hurt the whole family. This is not right. The children should be raised with their own father, but you've taken them away. Daddy is sad and he wants his family back." I also told her, "If you don't go back to Daddy, I never want you to speak to me again." It's a good thing that Madré was a good mother because she ignored the part about never speaking to me again. In reality, I probably would have been hurt if she never spoke to me again.

Madré never stopped writing me and would tell me, "I will always love you." She would even call from time to time. My greatest surprise came at my college graduation; she came, and so did Daddy. Daddy bought me a used car as a graduation gift. Madré bought me a sewing machine. I thought that was so special that it just broke my heart. I thought to myself, "She does love me!"

By the time Daddy and Madré divorced I had a marriage of my own. I came to understand that it would be difficult for Madré to live with a man who was unfaithful to her. From that point on I never asked her to return to Daddy again. He simply had been with too many women. It didn't matter to me that Daddy remarried. I just hoped that he would be happy.

Madeleine's Story

I thought that we had a pretty cohesive family unit. We did everything together. We were encouraged to be together, to be supportive of each other. Family values were instilled in each of us pretty intensely in that we were taught to be more concerned about how family members thought and felt more so than other people. In other words, we were taught to be kinder to our own family than we would be to a stranger. We were taught to never put anyone else above a member of our family.

Our family life was very regimented, I thought. There was a certain way that we were required to answer the telephone, for instance. It was really embarrassing to me as kid, because when people called, they would tease me for sounding so formal. I remember having to answer the phone, "Perkins residence, Madeleine speaking." Daddy would sometimes call home several times in a day just to see if we would answer the phone correctly. We all went to church on Sabbaths. On Fridays, it was real peaceful in our home. From the time we got home from school we'd start playing church music. There would be good smells from the kitchen because Madea would be cooking her Sabbath dinner, trying to get it done before the Sabbath came at sunset. I remember the boys used to get all their shoes shined, would iron their clothes, and everybody would be running around Friday afternoon getting prepared for Sabbath.

Marcellus was the first in our family to go to college. I remember when Marcellus made his first trip home from college, Daddy called a family meeting. Daddy said to him, "Come on son, share with your younger brothers and sisters what you've learned in college so they can get ahead in life. They can benefit from your education." I put Marcellus on the spot, of course, by asking a variety of questions.

I remember the times I had with Madea as a little girl, as I was the youngest in the family, at least until Marlon came along. We'd get everybody else up and off to school, and sometimes we'd come back home and Madea would cook either T-bone steaks or lamb chops and we'd drink Tab sodas. Or she would pack the two of us a lunch and we'd go on a picnic. We'd catch a bus and go downtown to the Mississippi River, sit on the banks and she would talk to me about a lot of different things. I really enjoyed those special times we spent together. We'd then go back home before all the other kids returned home from school and she'd begin preparing dinner.

I think that my experience as a child was different from everybody else's because I was the first child of us all born into a Christian union between Daddy and Madea. Prior to my birth, Madea was a faithful member in the church and Daddy wasn't, until he joined the church in 1960, a year before I was born. During that year, Daddy apparently transitioned into more of a Christian man, meaning that he had stopped his running around in the streets, cussing, fighting, drinking and being with other women. Perhaps his previous behavior is what brought tension into the home and made everybody feel as if they were on edge. But, again, as for my experience, I was born into a peaceful period in our home. So, all I knew from the onset was unity—us being together as a family, doing things together as a family, and having our parents' marriage intact.

As for other family activities, I thought it was kind of ridiculous, some of the stuff Daddy had us to do, stuff like how we were supposed to answer the phone, and the studying. I thought it was a bit extreme, especially when I got out more and started being around other people. Other kids, it seemed, got rewarded for getting C's, but Daddy's philosophy was, "You're not average. You don't get C's." We got disciplined for getting C's. If you got a B you still kind of got yelled at. Daddy would be like, "It's not good enough, pull it up to an A. You need to push for excellence." His real push was for that—excellence. I didn't have much of an appreciation for it then, but when I look at it in retrospect, I think the structure we had in the home had a huge part to play in who we became as people...

There was a general excitement over Marlon being born. Our family resembled the "Brady Bunch" clan, as there were three boys and three girls. There was competition between the boys and girls because the boys wanted Madea to have another boy and the girls wanted another girl. I remember the night Madea was in labor; we kept calling the hospital back-to-back. It got to the point where the operator came on the phone and said, "Are these the Perkins kids again? Y'all need to stop!"

I remember when Daddy began working for Oakley-Keesee Ford, selling cars. He made quite a bit of money. He was all tied up in work and stopped going to church. He started going to cocktail parties and hanging out. Then we started getting a lot of phone calls where the person on the other end would hang up once someone in the family (other than Daddy) answered. Then it progressed from hang-up calls to different women saying stupid stuff like, "I got your man. He's gonna be mine."

I remember one phone call specifically when this woman called Madea and told her "I'm gonna tear your playhouse down." I got on the extension phone and we were making kind of a joke out of it. Madea told her, "Oh, you don't have to tear my playhouse down. You can have it. As a matter of fact, you can have all seven or eight of the kids. You can take it all if you want it." We thought that was kind of a big joke.

At that time, I didn't fully understand all of the ramifications of what was happening. The phone calls started a lot of arguing and dissension between Daddy and Madea. Then, they just started going in separate ways.

After one particular argument between the two of them, Madea looked like she was in a trance. She calmed down and went into the backyard and cried. We talked about it a little bit. I don't remember what we said to each other, but we talked about it. This is what I remember as the last major event that took place between the two of them, because after that Madea said that she was leaving. She told Marsha about it, and Marsha started sending her some money each month, so she could prepare for it, and Madea saved it.

The day we left Memphis was on a Saturday. Daddy didn't believe she was going to leave. He was sitting and watching cartoons. He had gotten so disrespectful that he had started watching TV on the Sabbath. [The rest of us] were all still trying to keep the Sabbath, but he did whatever he wanted to do on the Sabbath. He said, "y'all ain't going anywhere…your mama's just going through a phase. When she gets down the road, y'all will be back next weekend."

I thought to myself, "He's sad." I was sad for him because I thought that he wasn't dealing with reality. We were really leaving! At that moment I wanted to say to him, "Don't let this happen. Do something!" But I didn't know how to articulate that to him, so I just kinda hugged him good-bye and I think I told him that I still loved him. Years later, he told me that I [had actually] told him, "I love you, but I feel like I need to go with my mama because she has two young kids, and she's going to need some help with them. You will be okay." And then we left. That was it.

In Kentucky, Madea tried her best to get a job. She said, "I don't want to be on welfare, and I don't want food stamps." She was too proud for that. She wanted to work but it got to a point where she had to take government assistance for a while. But then she changed her mind again.

"Nope, I'm not gonna do this," she said. She was adamant about wanting to work, so she worked for a short time.

If there was anything positive that I could say came out of our parents' divorce, it was how Marlon and Chris turned out. With our parents separated, it was more beneficial for them in that they didn't have to deal with the confusion of a divided household.

Chris's Story

I was happy when Daddy and Madea separated. They argued a lot and even as a child, I sensed that our home was not harmonious. The one bright spot out of living at Fairhope was that Madeleine, Marsha, Michael, and Gloria gave me a lot of attention and love. Daddy was a good father, but I seldom recall him spending time with me individually the way our older brothers and sisters did. Nor, at that time, did I recall Madea taking out a great deal of time. She was there for me, though, just not often, not at Fairhope. I cultivated a relationship with Madea after we moved away.

When I realized that Madea and Daddy were going to separate, I cannot fully explain it, but I was very excited. I didn't understand what separation and divorce were all about back then, but I knew what peace was. It was not peaceful in our home and I wanted peace. I looked forward to moving because I wanted a chance to start all over and make some friends on my own. The separation made me happy because I wanted away from Fairhope and from the negative atmosphere of that home.

Moving to Kentucky was one of the brighter spots in my life. Since I didn't have the experience of being in a harmonious home and feeling comfortable with both parents and the overall government of that household, to me their divorce made sense and brought about a much longed-for change in my life.

*It's so odd…I remember distinctly the good feeling I had
as I went to the shed in the backyard to get a suitcase we were
going to use for our move to Elizabethtown. It's as if the Lord
spoke to my heart as a child and told me that my life would be
much better now that we were moving.*

There was a marked difference between the Ousley Perkins, Jr., who had

> *Let this mind be in you, which was
> also in Christ Jesus…"*
> – Philippians 2:5

turned so devout in 1960 and the Ousley Perkins, Jr., who now had become enthralled by all the trappings that money and recognition on the job brought. As aforementioned, his personal devotion in spiritual things had waned and consequently so had his church attendance. His mind had turned, instead, to worldly things. He began keeping company with worldly-minded men, and this led him back down the slippery slope of temptation. No matter how much he may have tried to explain away his behavior, the consequences were unmistakable.

For Madea, it must have been difficult for her to watch her husband transform before her very eyes, especially after having enjoyed several years of marital and family harmony. As for Daddy, only God knows the battle that was being waged in his heart and mind. *"So do not make any hasty or premature judgments before the time when the Lord comes [again], for He will both bring to light the secret things that are [now hidden] in darkness and disclose and expose the [secret] aims (motives and purposes) of hearts. Then every man will receive his [due] commendation from God."* (I Corinthians 4:5, *Amplified Bible*)

A Difficult Decision

Meanwhile, Madea was facing her *own* internal battle. The cup of her patience had been filled to the brim and she was now entertaining thoughts of separating from Daddy again. This time, however, there seemed to be a delay, not because of external reasons, such as illness in the family or monetary concerns, for she had reached a point where she was willing to throw caution to the wind and just leave, depending on the Lord to once again provide for her. No, this time the delay was *internal*. In her own words, the Hand of God was upon her and He was telling her "not yet."

For several years she struggled with this. No matter how strong her commitment was to the Lord, to Daddy and to family unity, the increasing tension between her and Daddy was beginning to take its toll. She sought solace in extended seasons of prayer and Bible study. It was not unusual for one of my older siblings to awaken in the middle of the night and find the glow of light from one of the living room lamps casting an ambient shadow down the hallway. Madea would be sitting in a chair, reading her Bible and praying, sometimes silently and sometimes in hushed tones. Many times she had simply prayed for Daddy's safety, not knowing his whereabouts.

Our home was the last one on our side of the street and was bordered on its west side by a wooded area. Just as she had done as a girl, in those woods near her farm home down in Canton, Madea often retreated to our backyard or took a walk through that wooded area so she could have a "little talk" with the Lord. Often on these special journeys our family dog, Rex, whose black fur was streaked with lines of white, accompanied her. Rex was a smart dog and ferociously loyal to our family. His bark always made him seem bigger than his actual size, so as to keep visitors to our home honest. Our family felt secure with him around, and he was as much a part of our family as parent or child. He seemed to know when Madea needed quietude during one of her prayer seasons, which could be marked by anything but silence. She used these times to pour out her heart to God, to express as freely as she could the deepest sentiments of her heart. Finally, her answer came. As she would later recount, the Lord told her "it was time to go."

> *Adversity introduces you to yourself.*
> – Author Unknown

But where? When? How? These were all questions which needed to be answered, but Madea felt assured that God was leading. It must have been a strange mixture of excitement, anxiety and perhaps a small dose of fear that gripped her, for she felt that God was leading her into completely uncharted waters along the journey of her life.

It should be comforting to know that we need not fret over the direction of our lives. As He did with Jeremiah and countless others of His servants, God will reveal His purposes to us—*in His own time*. We must remember that God did not part the Red Sea until the children of Israel actually *arrived at* the Red Sea. God did not simply tell Moses that He wanted him to build a sanctuary for His presence. He *gave* Moses the *exact* specifications for the building. I am told that some missions are so secret for military pilots that they are not given the exact coordinates for their destination until they are actually in the air. If you are not clear as to the direction or purpose of your life, fear not: as you go, you will receive.

> *Once you are really challenged, you find something in yourself. Man doesn't know what he is capable of until he is asked.*
> – Kofi Annan, former United Nations Secretary-General

I'm not sure what Madea's exact thoughts were at the time. Did she hope that by separating from Daddy he would be forced to come to grips with his lifestyle and restore their marriage? Or did she separate knowing fully that divorce was inevitable? Only time would ultimately reveal which of these two thoughts would prevail, but for now the decision was simply made to leave.

Madea contacted Marsha and told her of her plans, and that she desired that they remain secret. She also asked if she could come and live with her. Marsha was hesitant. As Marsha told me years later, she really didn't want to have to be responsible for her mother and three of her younger siblings. She felt that her life was already full and, besides, *she shouldn't have to be responsible for them,* so she thought. She eventually came to feel that it was God's Will, nonetheless.

The time came for us to leave. We said our good-byes to Daddy. It was all so surreal to me at the time. Madea, Madeleine, Chris and I all climbed into Aunt Rose's car and left. Driving down the highway, Madea and Aunt Rose talked. No doubt mixed feelings filled her thoughts. With only an eighth-grade education, how would Madea provide for three kids? The thick darkness of the night outside so appropriately describes this experience. We drove throughout Saturday night.

It is hard to write about how I felt during these moments, primarily because I was so young and much of my memory has faded. What I do know is that we were leaving home…leaving Memphis…leaving Daddy and all that we knew up until that point to be family life.

The Aftermath

In this chapter, I wanted to share with you the experiences of my family life at this stage because they so profoundly impacted each member of my family. Although Chris and I were too young to fully comprehend all that was going on between our parents, we certainly felt the final result—the break-up of our family and the end of its innocence.

Today, there is extensive research surrounding the social, economic and emotional effects of divorce upon children. Eighteen years ago *TIME* magazine ran a feature story on this issue. The article, written by Walter Kirn, profiled the research of Judith Wallerstein (now deceased), a former therapist and university professor who chronicled her research in a ground-breaking book entitled *The Unexpected Legacy of Divorce*. While alive, she was one of few experts whose research on the effects of divorce upon children spanned more than three decades, a point worth noting when you consider the high divorce rate in America and the inescapable *long-term* societal impact this must have. Kirn summed up her book by stating:

> *It is not because things are difficult that we do not dare, it is because we do not dare that they are difficult.*
> – Seneca

> "The harm caused by divorce is graver and longer lasting than we expected. For America's children of divorce—a million every year—unfinished business is a way of life. For adults, divorce is a conclusion, but for children it's the beginning of uncertainty. 'Where will I live?' 'Will I see my friends again?' Will my mom's new boyfriend leave her too?'"[4]

These questions, as pondered by children of divorce, give many of us insights into some of the emotional trauma and insecurity faced by them. The article continues:

> "Children of divorce suffer depression, learning difficulties and other psychological problems more frequently than those of intact families…*[They] take a long time to get over*

divorce. Indeed, its most harmful and profound effects tend to show up as the children reach maturity and struggle to form their own adult relationships. They're gun-shy. Expecting disaster, they create disaster...

Children of divorce follow a different trajectory for growing up. It takes them *longer.* Their adolescence is protracted and their entry into adulthood is delayed. Children of divorce need more time to grow up because they have to accomplish more: they must simultaneously let go of the past and create mental models for where they are heading, carving their own way. Those who succeed deserve gold medals for integrity and perseverance. Having rejected their parents as role models, they have to invent who they want to be and what they want to achieve in adult life. This is far beyond what most adolescents are expected to achieve."[5]

Each of us—from Marcellus on down to Chris—suffered psychological and emotional trauma from the divorce. By now, you've read the accounts of my siblings with regard to our home life as chronicled earlier in this chapter, giving their own perspectives of our family life and the breakup of our

> *Life is not a dress rehearsal.*
> – Dr. John Maxwell

parents' marriage. The relationship difficulties that persist into adulthood, that Dr. Wallerstein's research reveals, were evident in our family.

For my brother Michael, although he declined to share his perspective, the pain of our family breakup revealed itself early on his life. After he graduated from high school, just a few months before Madea left Daddy, he briefly attended college, but dropped out and joined the army.

For a while, he was stationed in Kentucky at the Fort Campbell Army base, not far from where we lived near Fort Knox. His stint in the military opened up to him a world that was hitherto completely foreign to him: alcohol and drug abuse. He used alcohol and drugs as a way to cope with the intense pain he felt with Daddy and Madea's breakup. Remember, we were a close family who had strong familial *and* spiritual bonds.

While growing up, Michael was a conscientious young man, considered by many to be the quintessential "choirboy." He had developed early in life a love for God and obedience to His Word. And he was very active in our home church. Now, his path had taken a definite turn; the values of personal devotion to God and abstinence were placed aside. For more than a decade he struggled to find a direction for his life and fell into drug abuse, which almost cost him his life on more than one occasion. He never turned his back on God completely, but the Devil dogged his steps continually, using his own faults and our parents' breakup as the emotional ropes by which to try to hang him.

Finally, God would miraculously bring about a breakthrough in Michael's life, freeing him from the alcohol and drug abuse that had held him captive for so long. Although his first marriage ended in divorce, he would remarry and enjoyed over thirty years of marriage, until his untimely death due to cancer in 2015. He remained close to us all.

> *You are today where your thoughts have brought you; you will be tomorrow where your thoughts take you.*
> – James Allen

In my own young adulthood, I experienced difficulty early on while dating Shurla, who eventually became my wife. As our relationship developed and our thoughts turned toward marriage, I struggled with the feeling that no matter how hard I would try to be a good husband to Shurla and a good father when we were blessed with children, our marriage would—like my parents—end up in divorce. I felt as if I had a huge emotional monkey on my back. I desperately sought to find a reason for these feelings. "Maybe there is something wrong with Shurla," I thought. For a while, my internal conflict strained our relationship. Although she couldn't understand why I felt the way that I did, thank God Shurla didn't give up on me. Like Michael, I too would have a breakthrough in my thinking, and this monkey was finally lifted from my emotional back.

Lessons Learned

Why is the recounting of these experiences so important? Because I want you to see two essential things: 1) a traumatic, life-changing event can happen to anyone at any time in their life, especially during their early years; and 2) God *will* continue to work out His purposes in the life of an individual *despite* these traumatic experiences—*if they will allow Him to do so.* "*Blessed be the God and Father of our Lord Jesus Christ, the Father of mercies and God of all comfort, who comforts us in all our affliction, so that we may be able to comfort those who are in any affliction, with the comfort with which we ourselves are comforted by God. For as we share abundantly in Christ's sufferings, so through Christ we share abundantly in comfort too"* (II Corinthians 1:3-5, *ESV).*[6]

In a moment I will share a personal experience that Madea had, after we arrived in Elizabethtown, which illustrates this second principle. But first I want to address the impact of traumatic experiences in *your* life.

Man's accidents are God's purposes.
– Sofia Hawthorne

What do you do when your dreams are shattered? Broken dreams can occur early in life, or later in life. Whatever stage in a person's life they may happen, the outcomes are the same: discouragement, disillusionment, fear, and doubt that things will ever get better.

For all intents and purposes, our family life as we knew it was over— gone! My father's hopes and dreams of keeping his family together, despite his worldly living—shattered! My mother's hopes and dreams of having a family and "a house with a white picket fence"—shattered! The emotional well-being of my older brothers and sisters—shattered! I could list countless other aspects of the Perkins family dream that were left in the dust as we drove off that Saturday morning in July 1975.

For me, I was too young to know what my purpose in life would be, or how this experience would ultimately impact the direction of my life. What about you? What traumatic experiences have you had in your life that may be still impacting you today?

Often, the Devil uses such experiences early in life and attempts to derail us from fulfilling God's purpose for our lives. You can go all the way back to Adam and Eve to find illustrations of this. Although Adam and Eve were created in a fully-matured state, at least physically, they were still "young" in life. It was God's ideal that they would continue to grow mentally and spiritually, throughout eternity. Yet in Genesis 3, we see that the Devil comes to tempt Eve a short time after her creation. His purpose was to undermine God's ideal for her life, cut off her future prospects, and ultimately destroy her. Speaking of Satan' tactics, Jesus said in John 10:10, *"The thief cometh not, but for to **steal**, and to **kill**, and to **destroy**: I am come that they might have life, and that they might have it more abundantly."*

The same could be said for the life of Moses as well as Jesus Himself.

While both men were infants, laws had been passed that called for Jewish male children to be killed in their infancy (see Exodus 1 and Matthew 2). Both were men of promise, men of purpose—God's purpose. The Devil orchestrated conditions so as to attempt to destroy them before they even got started in life. He does this to countless lives.

This leads me to the second point mentioned above: God continues to work out His purposes in your life *despite* these traumatic experiences. *"I press toward the mark for the prize of the high calling of God in Christ Jesus"* (Philippians 3:14). God was working in the lives of each member of my family—including my parents. Like so many breakups of today, our lot could have been much bleaker. For instance, what if there weren't any family members available to open their home to Madea and us kids? Worse yet, what if they refused to open up their homes and take us in? Then what?

> *Being confident of this very thing, that He Who has begun a good work in you will complete it until the day of Jesus Christ.*
> – Philippians 1:6, NIV

Would we have been forced to live in a temporary shelter? Who knows?

Arrival in Kentucky and A Chat with God

We stopped for breakfast early Sunday morning. For Chris and me, this consisted of doughnuts and milk. When we arrived in Elizabethtown, Madea called Marsha. As we drove through the small town, it bore no resemblance to the city-scape of Memphis, to which I was accustomed. Except for the main highway, most of the off roads were paved with gravel. Today, Elizabethtown, Kentucky, is still a relatively small city compared to the average U.S. city, although it has become much more contemporary in its overall landscape. In 1975 however, in my seven-year old mind, Elizabethtown seemed like Hickville, USA.

We drove off the main highway onto a gravel road leading up to the trailer park community where Marsha lived. There were several such communities sitting side by side as we drove down the dusty road. Years later, Madea and I talked about this experience. I think her own reflections paint a better picture than I could ever attempt to, and it illustrates so profoundly how God was still working on our behalf.

Marsha did not want me to come [to Kentucky] because she was afraid for me. She wanted to tell me to stay in Memphis, but that wasn't what the Lord wanted either. When I got there, "Mack" and "James" [pseudonyms for two of Marsha's friends] had had a little squabble that previous night because "Mack" had drunk too much liquor and it brought out the worst in him. So when I got there, Marsha was standing in her doorway, wringing her hands. Rose had driven me up there, and promised to stay until noon, which would have given me some moral support. But when she saw what she thought was a bad situation, she got out of there real fast and left me there. That upset me very badly.

So there we were. "James" was on the couch asleep in the living room. "Mack" and another young man named "Carl" (pseudonym) were in the back room asleep too. Marsha told me what had happened the previous night. Satan said to me, "You've fallen into a den of dope addicts! They're gonna kill you and your children too." I was very upset. I was more concerned about what might happen to you all (Madeleine, Marlon and Chris) than I was about myself. So, in a little while, "James" woke up. He didn't look like a thug; he looked like a nice, normal, sweet young man. After that, "Mack" woke up, and after they introduced themselves, he apologized and explained to me what had happened and why they were sprawled out all over Marsha's home. He was so sorry. He explained that he drank but couldn't hold his liquor. He promised to never drink around me, and he didn't. He didn't look like he was a crook either. "Carl" woke up and he looked like an innocent young man as well. I was still very much upset. I didn't take them at face value. The Holy Spirit said to me, "Let's go for a walk."

So, the Lord and I walked and we talked. I said, "Lord, what am I going to do?" I couldn't go back. I'd burned my bridges behind me. I felt like the children of Israel at the Red Sea: I couldn't go forward and I couldn't go backward. The Holy Spirit spoke to me, "Be still. I am in control." I said, "Lord, *what am I going to do?*" The Lord spoke to me again just as clearly, saying, "I was here before you got here. Tomorrow will be better than today." This was Sunday, the day we arrived. Monday morning, when the sun arose, it arose with healing in its wings!

A friend of Marsha's, Jewel, came for a visit. She was a wonderful person. We got acquainted, and I shared with her a little bit of my plight. Here I was in a small town with three children and no job, and a broken marriage. Finally, Jewel said, "I'm gonna take you downtown and get you set up. Everything is gonna work out, it's gonna be alright." I didn't know what she meant.

We went downtown to the welfare office. Fortunately, I was able to get government assistance without any problems. This would help with household expenses, as Marsha functioned like a "husband" in that she was the family's main breadwinner. She was so unselfish in providing for our family that she would feel bad if she took just five dollars to spend on herself.

Soon it would be necessary for us to get our own home. We were staying with Marsha, who actually was renting from "Mack" and "Harold" [another friend of Marsha's]. We were short on money. One day Jewel told me, "You are going to get a big check from the government in about three or four months." This was July. In October of that year (1975), I got a check in the mail for $240. That was a lot of money back then. Several weeks later, I had a dream one Wednesday evening. In the dream, I saw our mailbox as it stood in front of our home…the lid was opened halfway. Inside I saw three brown envelopes sitting on top of each other. Each of them had a check inside.

I awoke the next morning thinking that was an interesting dream. That following Saturday I went to church. When we came home, I noticed that the lid on the mailbox was opened halfway – just like it was in my dream three nights before. I got out of the car and walked up to the mailbox. When I opened it, there were three brown envelopes inside – just as I had seen in the dream – and each contained a check for $240. That was a total of $720. In a little more than a month we had received $960 in lump sum payments from the government. Needless to say, we had a big Christmas that year!

Not long after we arrived in Elizabethtown, we moved into a bigger trailer home, thanks to the money from the government, a little further up the street from Marsha's home. We were the only Black family on our street.

We needed a car. So I went down to Radcliff [KY] and paid $500 down on a car, in cash. Then I prayed about it. I said, "Now, Lord, if you don't want me to have this car, you use a technicality to get me out of it." That's exactly what the Lord did. I filled out an application and Marsha co-signed for it. Then [the car salesman] wrote me a letter and told me that I could not have the car, since there was a possibility that Marsha (who was in the Army) might get called overseas. They thought I was a bad risk and denied my application.

"So what?" I thought. Nevertheless, I believed this to be the "technicality" I had prayed to the Lord about, so I didn't argue it further. Later, the Lord explained to me clearly why He didn't want me to have a car. That explanation came to me as I rode with Hosea to church one Saturday night. The roads seemed so dark, windy and hilly. It seemed to me as if the people in Elizabethtown drove crazily. As I thought about the driving conditions that night, the Holy Spirit spoke to me and said, "Look around you. *You* wouldn't last ten minutes trying to drive around this town. But don't I always see to it that you get to where you need to go?" This thought sank into my mind, and then I relaxed. From that point forward I didn't worry about my transportation needs in Elizabethtown.

The Ultimate Healer

So, I hope you see from these stories that God is the ultimate healer of broken dreams, disappointed hopes, and haunting fears. Events and occurrences in themselves are not always good, but "...*we know that all things work together for good to them that love God, to them who are the called according to his purpose*" (Romans 8:28). Healing doesn't always come instantaneously or overnight. More often than not, it occurs over a period of time, which would certainly be the case with our family. What is important to remember, nonetheless, is that healing *does* take place. God's words to the prophet Isaiah ring with encouragement: "*When thou passest through the waters, I will be with thee; and through the rivers, they shall not overflow thee: when thou walkest through the fire, thou shalt not be burned; neither shall the flame kindle upon thee. For I am the LORD thy God, the Holy One of Israel, thy Savior...*" (Isaiah 43:2, 3)

3

The Way Forward

"With malice toward none..."—Abraham Lincoln

Our new life in rural Kentucky was relatively easy for Chris and me, although Madeleine had a slightly different viewpoint, which I will explain in a moment. But Chris and I adapted fairly well to our new surroundings.

Boys Will Be Boys

> *There is nothing in the world so inspiring as the possibilities that lie locked up in the head and breast of a young man.*
> – James Garfield

As stated earlier, we lived in a trailer park community not too far from the Fort Knox Army base where Marsha was stationed. Chris and I were "blessed" with very active imaginations. We created our own entertainment. In the mid-1970s there weren't as many options, media-wise, for entertainment, so Chris and I played outside a lot. We would re-enact our favorite scenes from cartoons, *The Three Stooges* sitcom, or *The Six Million Dollar Man*, which was still our favorite television show.

I liked to be the show's main character, Steve Austin, or the main character of any other show that Chris and I enjoyed watching together for that matter. This should give you a clue into my general character. I had the more dominant personality between the two of us. As I was older (by only sixteen months), Chris looked up to me and gladly played the bad guy role when we played together. This is not to say that we didn't switch roles occasionally; he just gave in to my wishes more often than I did to his. At the time, I was seven years old and he was six. I had a slightly bigger body build than him. My temperament was more serious than his at times, whereas in contrast Chris was much more upbeat and funny. His light-hearted temperament remained the same into his teenage years and eventually into adulthood. As an infant, however, Chris had been sickly and because of this was constantly under the watchful eye of Madea. In time, his frail constitution strengthened and Madea felt comfortable letting him venture more outside of the house. We played together often, before and after our move to Kentucky. Chris looked up to me so much that Madea and others said he used to call me "*The* Marlon."

Two trailers down the street from us lived a young Caucasian married couple with two small kids, a boy and a girl, who were slightly younger than Chris and me. We played with them so much that Madea said that we began to imitate the dialect of their long, Southern drawl. The road which led into our trailer park was made of gravel, as were the side roads which led into different portions of the overall community. This meant that there was a lot of dirt and dust around. Chris and I and our two friends constantly played in the dirt, so much so that the four of us developed sores on our legs, knees, and elbows.

"I Just Fought 'Em Tooth and Nail"

This was late 1975-76, just a few years removed from the assassination of Martin Luther King, Jr., and although much of segregation in the South had begun to be dismantled by then, racism was still alive and well. The irony of it all is that Chris and I were somewhat insulated from this racial hostility. Madeleine, on the other hand, had a different perspective on the racial climate in rural Kentucky at this time. She was fourteen years old when we moved there, and was getting ready to go into high school. She certainly was more sensitive to certain social norms, racially speaking, than Chris and I were. While interviewing her for portions of this book, she had the following reflections to share about her school experience in Kentucky:

School was different for me in Kentucky. I kinda got into being a teenager, being in school, signing up for classes and thinking the whole experience was something out of a book, like some

Jack London novel. The environment was strange; culturally-speaking, I felt they were kinda "behind" at times. People had talked about racism, you heard about racism, but at that point I didn't think that I had actually experienced racism, or if I had, I wasn't aware that I had. I noticed that people began making a difference [between themselves and me] because of the color of my skin. I simply didn't have an awareness of it until I got to Kentucky.

In school, White people, I thought, were blatant in their thinking that Black people were inferior to them. I had come from taking advanced placement classes at my Memphis school to this little rinky-dink rural high school and they were trying to tell me that I couldn't take chemistry, physics nor advanced placement English—you know, all of this [stuff]. I just fought 'em tooth and nail. I ended up taking it anyway and they were like, "Well, you know you're not gonna be able to pass. You don't have the capacity for advanced placement classes." So, of course, they made me work harder to get A's and B's in those classes. It was silly. I was in the Principal's office probably every other day. I had never had a problem in school until then. I was told that I was "uppity" and that I was "out of my place" and that I thought I knew too much for my own good. The Principal—who I thought was a redneck—said to me one day in his slow, Southern drawl, "I oughtta just put your name on [my office] door. You're up here more than me." I felt like some of the teachers said a lot of stupid stuff to me and I didn't take guff from anybody. I just never allowed people to talk to me any kind of way that they wanted to. And I would get sent to the Principal's office because the teachers thought I was insubordinate, incorrigible.

One of my teachers had a real stereotypical view of Black people, that most Black people didn't have their fathers around and were on welfare, and so on. I think I felt a little bad about it because, at that time, we were not with Daddy, although that had not [in actuality] been our experience. I was not even aware of this stereotype until then. I started making up a lot of lies and told her that I had a bunch of brothers and sisters and that all of us had different fathers. I remember this teacher came to our house one day. At the time, we were living in a double-wide trailer home, which was considered a luxury accommodation around those parts. The teacher was really impressed with how neat and clean it looked. Then everyone came out to greet her, and, to her surprise, spoke intelligently. Needless to say, our actual family did not match the lies I had created for her. She would later ask me why I told her all that stuff. I told her that I thought she was stuck on her stereotypical views of what she thought I (and other Blacks for that matter) was about, where I came from and where I was going; I just decided I would continue to feed her nonsense. I thought she felt superior to Blacks anyway. So, that was my experience with the public school system in rural Kentucky in 1975-76.

A Different Perspective

Madeleine's perspective on the racial climate she faced in her school reflects a deeper dimension to our family values. Daddy and Madea both raised us to be confident in ourselves, to understand that our lives were *inherently* valuable, and to stick together as a family. Madea took it a step further and always encouraged us to take things in stride, to maintain a Christ-like attitude

> *He who cannot forgive others breaks the bridge over which he himself must pass.*
> – George Herbert

and to trust in God to give us the mental outlook that was needed to weather the storms of life. She would fondly quote the Bible verse, *"Owe no man anything, but to love one another..."* (Romans 13:8).

Neither Daddy or Madea harbored racist views in our home. This is not to say that they didn't experience their fair share of racial abuse. Remember, they both lived during the Civil Rights Era in the South. They both knew what it meant to be viewed as second-class citizens in a racially charged culture. They were accustomed to being addressed by some of their Caucasian counterparts as either "boy" or "girl" (even as adults) or, worse yet, "n_ _ _ _r". Nevertheless, they never viewed themselves as second-class citizens. They proudly exercised their right to vote and developed their *own* political ideologies. Especially Daddy. He loved to stay on top of current events and was an avid reader and viewer of the news. He was a fighter, and *this* attitude he passed on, mentally speaking, to his children. It has served us well.

Daddy and Madea simply didn't allow any bitterness from these experiences to infect how their children fundamentally viewed people that were different from them. They taught us to show respect for ourselves and for others as well along with forgiveness. Knowing who you are in Christ determines how well you relate to others, especially within a society that may be adversarial to you at times.

> *Nothing on earth consumes a man more completely than the passion of resentment.*
> – Friedrich Nietzsche

Back to Memphis

Madea made the decision to return to Memphis in early 1976, but would not make the trip until that summer. Madeleine, Chris and I had completed one full school year in Elizabethtown. For reasons that she did not fully understand, Madea felt impressed by the Lord to return to Memphis, and she decided to do so. My sister Gloria and her husband D.C. (now deceased) drove up to Elizabethtown to get us.

Gloria managed a new apartment complex in a northern suburb of Memphis called Raleigh. At that time, the north side of Memphis was undergoing development. Our apartment complex was barely three years old and situated in a very nice, quiet, middle-class neighborhood, with lots of kids for us to play with. For a while, we moved in with Gloria and D. C., which was quite a challenge. For a family on welfare, we lived very comfortably.

Gloria and D.C. were newly married and still enjoying the post-honeymoon bliss of early married life. All of a sudden, they were "bombarded" with four relatives in their beautiful but small two-bedroom, one-bath apartment. I'm sure they were inconvenienced at times, especially with two rambunctious boys who, from time to time, managed to break something. As a kid, I didn't think of any such inconveniences. I was simply happy to live in a beautiful apartment, enjoy three square meals a day and simply enjoy the warmth and love of my family. Besides, I had bigger issues to deal with—like making new friends. At least Chris and I had each other. We were virtually inseparable, like peanut butter and jelly, salt and pepper, or cookies and milk.

A New Beginning

Eventually, Gloria leased us a three-bedroom, one-and-a-half bathroom apartment one building down from hers. I still remember the day we got the keys. There was not a stick of furniture in the home, not even carpet. All of the floors were laminate, and there were no window treatments. To a small child, our apartment felt like a mini-house. Chris and I had fun walking up and down the hallway, hearing the echoing sound of our feet and voices in the hollow home. The apartment was brand new; not a soul had occupied it before. The white walls were clean, the kitchen and bathroom fixtures were bright and shiny, and the

> *Both riches and honor come from you, and you rule over all. In your hand are power and might, and in your hand it is to make great and to give strength to all. And now we thank you, our God, and praise your glorious name.*
> – I Chronicles 29:12, 13, ESV

smell of all-things-new permeated the place. Madea and Madeleine seemed pleased too.

Finally, Madea called us all back to what would be her bedroom. It was dusk outside, as we could see the burnt-orange hue of the setting sun outside of her window. There was something special about the view from Madea's room. It looked out over the playground, where she could keep an eye on Chris and me as we played. It also faced the western side of the apartment complex, a stretch of the highway that ran parallel to our complex and a beautiful condominium complex across the street. This might not seem like much, but there was something about the view of the open sky from her room that seemed to speak of promise and hope. For all the pain our family had experienced, her room brought such hope and comfort. Because of Madea's deep love for the Lord, it could easily be said that the presence of the Holy Spirit could be felt in her room.

We all knelt down on the floor, clasped hands and Madea offered up a prayer of thanksgiving to God. She thanked the Lord for His marvelous provision of an apartment, for each other and for keeping us safe and sound over the past few years. She spoke hopefully of His future provisions, and asked for strength to remain faithful and obedient to His will.

Shortly after we settled in to our new apartment, it was time to start school. It was now fall, 1976. Madeleine would be starting tenth grade at Trezevant High School, and Chris and I would enroll at Spring Hill Elementary School. I was starting the third grade at my fourth school in as many years. Chris was now in second grade.

I'm sure that amount of change has to affect a person, but children can be amazingly resilient. Although my elementary school transcript reflects that I was an "above average" student (my only "A" came in spelling) during the third grade, I felt like I struggled tremendously. You would think that, for a kid who loved playing school as a preschooler, things would be different. Despite my academic struggles I managed to keep my head above water, making new friends, growing accustomed to my new surroundings and accepting the fact that the home our original family grew up in would now become simply a place of visitation.

Madeleine, Chris and I were bussed to school, and Madea was often at home to greet us when we returned. Although I cannot recall many details from this period, everything seemed pretty normal. We had plenty of interaction with Daddy, although he was twenty-five miles away on the south side of town. Daddy was not one for taking us to ballgames and things like that as kids, but he was always available when we needed him. From time to time he would take us to the amusement parks and fairs, take us shopping or out to dinner, and he even provided some financial assistance to help us furnish our new apartment. By 1977, he and Madea were officially divorced and he remarried shortly thereafter. Although he was now taking up life as a new husband and stepfather, he never left us completely out of his life. I don't remember Madea being restrictive of his visitation with us. As a matter of fact, they never had a formal visitation arrangement. I never saw or heard the two of them argue over visitation. Daddy called from time to time, and although he may not have lived under the same roof with us, there was never a time when Madeleine, Chris and I didn't know where he was.

> *What you leave behind is not what is engraved in stone monuments but what is woven into the lives of others.*
> – Pericles (495 B.C.-429 B.C.)

Doing the Best She Could

Although we lived on welfare, Madea did a little babysitting from time to time to help make ends meet. By and large, however, our financial well-being was provided by Marsha. From the time we returned to Memphis until I would enter college, she sent money to Madea on a monthly basis. Eventually, Madea would find steady work as a housekeeper (as she had done during her teen years) for well-to-do White families. With no marketable skills, she did the best she could. She avoided debt like the plague, consistently returned tithe and offerings to our church, and always managed to have a little "stash" of cash tucked away in one of her clothes drawers. I was amazed at this, because I knew that Madea didn't make a lot of money. However, she lived with a quiet dignity that would not allow her low-income status to make her overly dependent on anyone else. This, coupled with her strong, implicit faith in God, allowed her to pass on to the rest of us an attitude of dependence upon God in all things and—as much as possible—self-help in practical matters. Her integrity carried her (and us) a long way.

In addition to Daddy's infidelity, my parents had some of the same common marital challenges that confront couples who have healthy relationships, such as communication, expectations of one another, etc. Conflict is inevitable in any relationship. How couples handle the conflict determines the fate of their relationship, and ultimately their family.

Picking Up the Pieces

At this point, however, a bigger question can be asked: "How does a person begin again after such a traumatic experience," or "How does a person begin to move forward?" Although I cannot answer that question for my parents or even my older brothers and sisters, I can say that for Madeleine, Chris and me, the emotional tone for moving forward was set by the attitude of Madea. She *knew* Jesus,

> *You must do the thing you think you cannot do.*
> – Eleanor Roosevelt

and because of that relationship, she allowed Him to pour His boundless love and grace into her heart, to sooth the intense pangs of her heart, to work through her own anger, disappointments, fears, and regrets.

As you are reading this, perhaps you are also reflecting on experiences in your life that were traumatic for you. Whether it has been your own family breakup, the death of a parent or other loved one, physical abuse, or another event, perhaps you may feel "stuck" in life, or at the very least as if that experience is tied to your emotions like a ball and chain. You want to move forward but don't know *how*. As I reflect back over the life of Madea, there are some things that I have observed about her that may be of some help to you. As you read these suggestions, please keep in mind that Madea was not a perfect person. She simply sought to find a way forward like any other human being, experiencing her fair share of triumphs as well as defeats. If these observations prove helpful to you, it is because they are traces of the Hand of God in her life, traces that may also be found in your life as well.

1. *Make God Your Primary Counselor.* To my knowledge, Madea never had professional counseling nor went through a formal divorce recovery program. In fact, I think it's safe to say that grief recovery ministries were not prevalent in the churches we attended then as they are today. I am not suggesting that these services are not needed for divorce or any other type of grief recovery, because they certainly serve a vital function in the healing process. I would urge you to seek quality Christian ministries in this area to minister to your unique needs.

   Yet, I strongly believe that, in addition to these services, you *must* decide that Jesus will be your chief counselor, and that He is *sufficient* to meet your specific emotional needs. How do you do this? By developing a plan of regular prayer and study of the Bible (especially passages that affirm your worth and purpose in the eyes of God) and other Christian literature. Three books I highly recommend in this area are *Steps to Christ*, by Ellen G. White, *Healing for Damaged Emotions*, by David Seamands, and *The Lies We Believe*, by Dr. Chris Thurman. These are excellent Bible-based resources that will kick-start your study life.

   Madea was an avid reader, especially of the Bible and other Christian literature. She did not waste time reading romance novels or horoscopes that predicted a "new love" for her life. I still have memories of her laying in her bed reading, whether early in the morning or at night before bed. Remember: she only had an eighth-grade education, but she would often correct my English grammar.

"The fear of the LORD is the beginning of wisdom: and the knowledge of the holy is understanding." (Proverbs 9:10).

2. *Ask God to Help You Forgive Others Who Have Hurt You, Or to Accept the Circumstances That Have Brought About Your Hurt.* I think one must make a *decision* to move beyond events that one cannot change. This one may not be easy—but it's possible. Therein lies the key: *it's possible.* I've heard it said before that forgiveness is a gift from God. That it is. Don't waste your time trying to develop and flex the muscle of forgiveness on your own because you'll go limp every time. Ask God to *give* you forgiveness in your heart, even though you may not feel it right away. Jesus said in John 16:24, *"Ask, and ye shall receive, that your joy may be full."*

Madea struggled with forgiveness at times. How do I know? Because in the early years after their divorce, whenever Daddy was single (he would go on to marry several times after their divorce), she would

> *Those who bring sunshine to the lives of others cannot keep it from themselves.*
>
> – James Barrie

invite him to our home for dinner on special occasions, such as Thanksgiving or Christmas. All would be well, and during the course of their conversation there might be some flashback to experiences when they were together that would evoke negative feelings from one or the other. Their voices might rise a little, and one might then begin accusing the other. Just as quickly as their voices would rise, however, they would collect themselves, remembering that they were in the presence of their children, and return to a more calm state. Though this did not occur often, I do remember it happening on more than one occasion. I also remember Madea's eyes watering a little, revealing some of the hurt that evidently was still there. To be fair to Daddy, he too still had his hurts.

My point is this: the fact that Madea invited Daddy to our home (and he occasionally returned the favor) for dinners indicates that she was *intentional* about trying to forgive. As a born-again believer in God, she knew how much God values forgiveness, and by His grace, tried to practice this in her life.

3. *As Far As Possible, Take Responsibility For Any Actions You May Have Taken That Have Added to the Pain of Your Situation.* As I have shared before, despite her limited formal education, Madea developed a good use and understanding of the English language. One word that she came to understand clearly was the word *codependence.* In an article entitled "Codependency and Codependent Relationships," author R. Skip Johnson states that "codependent relationships are where one person supports or enables another person's addiction, poor mental health, immaturity, irresponsibility, or under-achievement. Among the core characteristics of codependency, the most common theme is an excessive reliance on other people for approval and identity."[7] Although there are many facets of codependence, in short, codependency in relationships is destructive because it does not allow either person in the relationship to take adequate responsibility for the impact that their words or actions have on the relationship. Nor does it allow people to fully develop their potential as individuals.

> *That you may walk worthy of the Lord, fully pleasing Him, being fruitful in every good work and increasing in the knowledge of God…*
> – Colossians 1:10, NKJV

Taking responsibility for your actions in a relationship is just as important as *not* taking responsibility for the actions of your partner. Any relationship absent of this vital boundary is doomed for frustration, insecurity, and ultimately failure. Part of the forgiveness process is forgiving *yourself,* and to forgive yourself means that you acknowledge that you may have made decisions or taken actions or even fostered an attitude that has added to the pain of your experience. Sometimes people are not able to heal from a painful experience simply because they refuse to forgive themselves or others. This refusal to forgive can become a form of codependence. It is a barrier to moving forward. *"Anyone you forgive, I also forgive. And what I have forgiven—if there was anything to forgive—I have forgiven in the sight of Christ for your sake, in order that Satan might not outwit us. For we are not unaware of his schemes"* (II Corinthians 2:10-11, *NIV*).[8]

Sometimes we face very painful experiences in our lives. Oftentimes these experiences come early in life, through abuse, neglect, abandonment, death of a parent or other loved one, poverty and countless other unspeakable tragedies. Worse yet, they can occur when we're most vulnerable. God knows this, and in His infinite love and mercy He oftentimes shields the delicate fabric of our emotions from much of the severity of these hardships. God knows what we are feeling. He is *"touched with the feeling of our infirmities"* (Hebrews 4:15).

Shattered, But Not Broken

Believe it or not, behind each of these hardships—especially during the most painful episodes—is Satan himself. He, the "prince of this world," (John 12:31) instigates events and circumstances so as to wreak destruction in our lives. He hates us! He is fully aware of the glory of God's benevolent purposes and will stop at nothing to derail them. He knows full well the

> *You can do something in an instant that will give you heartache for life.*
> – Author unknown

healing power of Christ's words in Luke 4:18: *"the Spirit of the Lord is upon me, because He hath anointed me to preach the gospel to the poor; he hath sent me to heal the brokenhearted, to preach deliverance to the captives, and recovering of sight to the blind, to set at liberty them that are bruised."*

"To set at liberty them that are *bruised*..." Does this not include a great mass of humanity—perhaps even you? Many of us are weighed down by experiences, some of which were self-inflicted and some of which were not. We have been "bruised" by these experiences. The original Greek term for the English word "bruised" meant "shattered." In words calculated to arouse the most complex of our emotions while simultaneously igniting our deepest aspirations, Jesus declares that His mission in life is to bind up the shattered fragments of our lives. *"For this **purpose** the Son of God was manifested, that he might destroy the works of the devil"* (I John 3:8).

This chapter and Chapter Two were by far the most difficult to write. I'm convinced that their difficulty probably set me back several years in completing the overall book. I thank God for using my good friend and editorial assistant, Leanne Ebsen, who came in during the "eleventh hour" to help me bring clarity and cohesion to what was a mass of dangling and aimless sentences. I struggled terribly with how to portray the difficulty of this period in our family's life without overly characterizing Daddy as a heartless philanderer. The title of this chapter, after all, is "The Way Forward."

In essence, I struggled with how to bring Daddy forward into the present, to show the positive developments and transformation in his own life, as well as those in all of his children. He certainly made his share of mistakes, which he openly admitted many times to his children, sometimes amid tears of deep remorse and sorrow. Even after his divorce from Madea, he had several failed marriages. It was hard for me and my siblings and step-siblings to go through so many breakups, to form connections with his wives and their families, only to see those connections severed after a few short years.

In this moment, writing this makes it seem as if all his subsequent marriages were just a blur, momentary blips on the screen of my life. In reality, these are *real* people with *real* lives. I don't hold any grudges nor harbor any ill feelings toward Daddy's former wives, my former stepmothers. And, interestingly, I don't think that they (nor their children) still harbor any ill feelings toward Daddy and his children. This in itself is a miracle, especially when you consider how contentious and adversarial marital breakups can be, even for years afterwards, and how destructive the effects on the children of these unions can be.

> *Blessed is the man who finds wisdom, the man who gains understanding, for she is more profitable than silver and yields better returns than gold.*
> – Proverbs 3:13,14 NIV

New Man

If, perchance, I could categorize Daddy's adult life into distinct periods, there would be four of them, at least from my viewpoint. First, there would be the period of him as a young, married "rebel," indicated by his extramarital relationships. This would be followed, secondly, by a period of fervent devotion to God, marked by his spiritual leadership in our home as well as our church, the "tranquil" period, as I mentioned earlier. Thirdly, there would be the period of him as a fallen leader and, arguably, the initiator of our family breakup. This period would last for more than two decades, almost as long as his and Madea's marriage. But it would be marked by several failed marriages and temporary relationships, all in the pursuit to recapture the stable family life Daddy once enjoyed and for which he had always longed. Then, the last period, the one which in which he lived prior to his death in March 2018, is the period of the repentant man. What changed him? *The transforming power of God's grace!* In his later years, Daddy was able to look back on his life from a spiritual point of view and take responsibility for his actions. He truly embraced God's (and his children's) grace and forgiveness for his past deeds. At the time of his death at age 90, he enjoyed the longest period of marriage, with one woman, since he and Madea divorced…almost fifteen years with his wife Josephine. And he enjoyed the warmth and fellowship of his children. He was still *Daddy*!

This gives you another perspective of Ousley Perkins, Jr., the man. He was a man of his word, and he always took responsibility for his children. He always believed in providing for the material needs of his family and, as much as he could, their emotional

> *When you're through changing, you're through!*
> – Bruce Barton

and spiritual needs as well. He was a gentleman, courteous, respectful—and generous. Yes, Daddy *did* have a heart, and it was this trait above all else that allowed his former wives and their children to move forward "with malice toward none."

I enjoyed a wonderful relationship with Daddy and I can confidently say that he was one of my best friends in life. The deep bond we shared as father and son—a bond indescribable in its depth, mutual respect, affection, and trust, transcending mere paternal ties—didn't happen overnight. As you can imagine, we had to talk through a *lot* of things over the years, but I always tried to maintain a respectful attitude toward him even while discussing deep, painful experiences within our family and personal disappointments I had with him. I believe that all of Daddy's children, in our own ways, had to follow the same steps I suggested earlier as a process for moving forward after a painful ordeal in life:

1. *Make God Your Primary Counselor (and seek professional counseling, when necessary).*
2. *Ask God to Help You Forgive Others Who Have Hurt You, Or to Accept the Circumstances That Have Brought About Your Hurt.*
3. *As Far As Possible, Take Responsibility For Any Actions You May Have Taken That Have Added to the Pain of Your Situation.*

After their divorce, Daddy and Madea maintained a friendly relationship. Despite occasional setbacks, their willingness to move forward helped to set the tone for their children.

"Nothing Can Separate Us"

In spite of Daddy and Madea's divorce, I knew that they loved me deeply. As we three children continued on with Madea after the separation, I'm sure Chris and Madeleine felt the same way. My mother provided us with a comfortable home. I never went to bed hungry, we wore nice clothing, and there were toys under the tree at Christmas—*every* year. All of my older brothers and sisters who lived outside our home called from time to time, and they all made me feel loved. Through all the pain, confusion, disappointment, anger, and sadness they undoubtedly experienced, whenever I spoke with them I remember them vividly telling Chris and me to "take care of Madea" and that they loved us. To this day, there is hardly a phone call that I end with a brother or sister of mine without saying "I love you."

The deep, passionate bond that each of us share can be detected in a letter my sister Marsha wrote to Daddy in April 1977, while she was still stationed at Fort Knox. Almost a year had passed since Madea, Madeleine, Chris and I had moved back to Memphis. This letter profoundly captures the range of emotions experienced during this "reconstruction" period in our lives. With her permission, I share it with you in its entirety:

Dear Daddy,

Thanks for loaning the car to me. I hope that you got it back as it was given to me. I have your other set of keys. I will probably bring them back in July or September. How does it all go with you? I am doing fine. I got a letter from Maurice and he is doing fine. I saw Gloria's car and it is pretty. I saw Michael and he appeared to be doing fine. I did not notice anything seriously wrong with him. I do believe that he needs a little rest and a lot of guidance because he appears to be confused about life. I don't have the time to provide for him as I should. Once he gets out of the Army, I may let him stay with me for a while.

You know, I worry about my family and what will become of it. I have decided that all that is happening is happening for the best. Daddy, I really believe that one day we will all be together, all of us alive and well. We are too close to break apart. What has happened to separate us was not a separation. You see, you can never separate yourself from someone you love. I feel that we will be even closer once we do get together. All is not as bad as it seems. Time and patience will tell the tale. We need each other and I feel that we can accomplish more together than separate.

Daddy, I don't want us to ever be separated. I know that while I was at home on leave, I wanted to reach out and tell you how much I loved you, but I seemed to be restrained. I don't know why but I had a weird feeling. I saw you as my daddy but something was missing. Daddy, what's wrong? Something isn't right. I'm telling you this because I love you. I would never do anything intentionally to hurt you. But I feel that something is not right. You are here physically, but mentally you seemed to be miles away, as though you had something on your mind.

I can remember once you asked if would we kiss you when you were gone. Daddy, if I can love you while you're alive then I will have no regrets when you're gone. I love you and so do all of us. I guess you can say that we find it hard to adjust to the fact that we all aren't a family anymore. I will never believe that. I believe that we are still a family and will always remain as one.

Daddy, please try to understand what I am saying, because I love you very much. No matter what happens (I am sorry for the way I acted while on leave), I will never give up on you. I know that one day you will come back to us. I loved you and I will always love you. Maybe it's normal since I was the first girl. I understand you because I love you and because I feel so much for you. I can understand that you may have been very disappointed in all of us because you worked so hard to supply us with what you felt that we needed.

Daddy, when I was growing up, you supplied us with love, pride and self-respect. We need you still for those same factors.

I {cannot} find the words to express myself verbally, [so] I find it easier to express myself with written words. Daddy, [I was disappointed] in you [because I felt] that you were giving [to us] materially, and not physically. We need you for love only and nothing more. Madeleine loves you very much, [but] she resents the fact that she cannot reach you physically. When I saw Marcellus, he told me that all he had left [were] memories of the love we once had for each other. He told me that he was very happy then, and so was I.

Daddy, the difference is, now, I can't feel the closeness that we once had. Your children are still your children. No matter how old we may get in age, you are still our daddy. You see, you weren't just a father to us, you were our daddy. You can never deny that fact in life. Your children are very close to each other…Whether you knew it or not, we were admired as a family by so many people because we had a great deal of love and respect for each other. A friend of mine once told me that she really admired our family because we were all so different in personality but one in soul. That is true. Though we may have had different concepts of life, we did have one true clause in all [of our] personalities that kept us together and that was love.

Please don't feel as though I'm trying to confuse you or say things that aren't true because all that I've said is true. I realize that you may love M****. Personally, I like her also. She is a beautiful person. I must admit, I did not have any intentions of liking her at all. Because she did not pressure me, I found myself having a great deal of respect for her.

Daddy, I am going to say to you what you said to me. "You can't stop something halfway in life, you have to finish it." I thought about this: why did you tell me that? I also evaluated the reason as to how this statement applied to me as a person. Thank you, for those were great words of wisdom and I shall never forget them.

Daddy, when I was growing up (I'm not saying that I'm grown now, because I realize that I have a long way to go) I remember how you used to tell me to take care of your family if anything ever happened to you. Daddy, I'm trying to do that now. All that I try to do is in remembrance of you. You see, that's how I know that you've changed mentally. I went to see Michael for you. I know for a fact that if something was wrong, you would have been there the first time you heard that something was wrong. Daddy, you can't find fault with the rest of your children because we as the older children disappointed you. The reason for your separation of the mind from us is because you were disappointed with us.

Everyone has a stage of life wherein they become confused. You probably did also when you were 18 or 19 years old. But remember this: a child can never depart from the way in which he was taught. You took so much time to teach us the importance of a good life, how could you think that we could forget those important lessons we were taught with love? Whenever we needed you, you were right there.

Daddy, you taught us not to depend on other people because we had each other. I believed that. I know that you were right. Remember that you still have us; we would want you to come to us before anyone else. I am not as strong as you. I need guidance as much as anyone my age. The job bestowed on me is too much (I don't mean financially either). We need you so very much because we love you. I find it hard to say that you are dead and no longer exist, because I know that you aren't. I cannot separate my soul from yours because you are my father and will always be just that. Nothing can separate us. Daddy, take care and I hope that you understand that I wrote this letter in love.

Binding Up the Wounds

Unbeknownst to me then, God was already present, protecting, guiding, and slowly binding up the wounds of our family, helping us all to find the way forward. As for me, I was blessed. I was simply a child, whose childish concerns with life did not afford him the dubious responsibility of trying to make sense out of the emotional chaos surrounding our family breakup. No, that was left up to God. Only He is sufficient for such things.

4

Mr. Sheely

"A hundred years from now it will not matter what my bank account was, the sort of house I lived in, or the kind of car I drove...but the world may be different because I was important in the life of a child." —*Author Unknown*

Mr. Sheely stood about five feet, nine inches tall, and weighed about an hundred and seventy pounds. Although not completely bald, he was definitely thinning on top of his head. He wore his hair in a crew cut style, with his graying sides tapered close to his skin. Mr. Sheely was an ex-military man, having served in the Army. He had hairy arms and chest. He was of average build, always seemed to walk as if he were in military formation, and had an outrageously winsome smile that made nearly every feature of his face crinkle with bulldog-like appeal. His face was basically pale (he was Caucasian), but when he got angry it turned beet red, and his lips...to this day I still have vivid memories of those thin lips turning deathly white when he tightened them in anger. *Nobody* in my sixth grade classroom wanted to get on Mr. Sheely's bad side!

> *Character is power.*
> – Booker T. Washington

Though not a veteran of World War II, it seemed as if he relished in its lore more than in any other aspect of American history. Besides his hairstyle, Mr. Sheely occasionally wore army boots, camouflage pants, and military "dog tags" draped around his neck, complete with name, rank and serial number! He liked to roll up his long-sleeved shirts and sweaters, forming a nice creased cuff just above his elbows, like you would see regular military personnel do when the weather is warm. We rarely saw him in a shirt and tie, even for official school assemblies. At recess, he wore dark shades and patrolled the playground as if he were an MP—military policeman.

"6-03!"

Our classroom number was "6-03", pronounced "six-o-three". Wherever we went as a class, we were collectively addressed by him as "6-03". When it was time to go to lunch (Mr. Sheely nostalgically referred to the cafeteria as the "chow hall"), he would bellow out "line up 6-03. Chow time!" Like little military cadets, we would all line up at the door and wait for him to order, "Ready...march!" And off we would trot to the cafeteria. When it was time to return to our classroom, we would all hear that familiar voice rising high above the din of lunchroom noise, yelling "line up 6-03!" Mr. Sheely also had an uncanny way of getting us to quiet down in the hallways. If we got too raucous, all of sudden we would hear a thunderous "6-0-3!" That voice could

> *Personality has the power to open doors, but character keeps them open.*
> – Author unknown

scare the daylights *into* you. Needless to say, he promptly got our attention.

It would be easy to conclude, thus far, that Mr. Sheely was merely a hard-nosed, commando-style teacher. Indeed, he could be, but there was more. Beneath this robust, intense exterior was a deeply sensitive and caring man. He would often digress in the middle of his lectures and launch into either a World War II or personal story. If the story struck an emotional nerve with him, it was not unusual for us to hear his voice crack and see his eyes begin to water with tears. Mr. Sheely was completely unabashed by such displays of emotion. He would simply wipe his eyes, pull out a well-worn handkerchief from his back pants pocket, blow his nose as if he were tooting the horn of a Model T Ford, and pick up where he left off.

Comfortable In His Own Skin

Mr. Sheely was fiercely loyal to virtues such as honesty, decency, discipline, respect, and fairness. I especially appreciated the fact that he simply made no distinction among his students based on race, color, creed, nationality, *or* aptitude. I truly believe that he measured a person based on the content of their character. This says a lot for a man who lived in a suburban, predominately white middle-class neighborhood and taught in an elementary school similarly located (though racially mixed) in the late 1970s. He took a keen interest in his students—academically and personally. He could sometimes give lots of homework, for he was an avid reader and generally a knowledgeable person himself. In this regard he really challenged us.

Then, there were what I call "Fun Fridays." Almost every Friday afternoon was reserved for a favorite past-time of Mr. Sheely's: building model airplanes. On Fridays we could bring a plastic model of anything we wanted to build—cars, boats, airplanes, ships—and build it! Since Mr. Sheely specialized in World War II airplanes, most of us purchased the same. This was such a big hobby of his that he had a special workshop built in his backyard to house all of his model airplanes, which by his own admission numbered over five hundred—at that time.

Occasionally he would bring some of his models to class to show off. His models were always meticulously put together, with the finest and most accurate detailing in paint and insignias. He *never* had lumps of dried glue or smeared paint on any of his planes, like many of us had. Right down to the flesh color used for the pilot's face, all was perfectly done. I really admired (envied is more like it) his craft. Although I would visit his home from time to time, as he lived in the same neighborhood as some of my school friends, I never got a chance to go inside his workshop. All I had were my dreams of how it must have looked inside, with his B-29 Superfortress hanging by a thin thread from the ceiling, positioned as if it were about to open its bomb bay. And I'm sure he must have had a B-25 Mitchell lying around somewhere.

My favorite airplane was the F-4 Phantom. This aircraft was used during the Korean and Vietnamese Wars, but it just goes to show how broad Mr. Sheely's knowledge of twentieth century warplanes was in general.

An Unforgettable Experience

> *We make a living by what we get,*
> *but we make a life by what we give.*
> – Winston Churchill

Occasionally, Mr. Sheely would surprise one of us by purchasing a model and giving it to a fortunate student on Fun Friday. I will never forget the Friday afternoon he took me model shopping. It was just the two of us. Having gotten prior permission from Madea for the outing, we jumped into his little white Volkswagen bug and took off. Cruising down the streets of Memphis, we talked endlessly about airplanes. His knowledge of World War II stories was so vast that he held me spellbound.

We pulled into the parking lot of one of his favorite specialty shops. This was no Kmart or J.B. Hunters, places to which I was accustomed to going. Those stores carried a limited stock of models and paints. As we walked into this shop, I immediately sensed that I was in a place where I could probably find a model of any airplane I wanted, with all the necessary accessories of paint and decals to go with it. "Marlon," Mr. Sheely started, "you can pick out any airplane you want. And if you need some glue and paint, go ahead and get those too."

I couldn't believe my ears. He was being so nice—to *me*! I felt overwhelmed. Every airplane I knew of began to flash through my mind. I was at once indecisive, not wanting to pick a model which cost too much, nor did I want to pick a cheap one that I really didn't like either. After what seemed like hours of wandering around that store, I finally settled on a B-26 Marauder, a bomber used during World War II. I don't remember how much it cost, but I do remember it wasn't cheap because it was of a sizeable scale. Mr. Sheely didn't flinch. He whipped out his wallet, paid the attendant, and we walked out of the store—"floated" out of the store is more like the way I felt. I was virtually imploding with joy and excitement! I thanked him profusely.

It was getting dark and the Sabbath was drawing near. It was time to go home, so we jumped into his car. Driving home as the evening shadows fell outside, Mr. Sheely opened up to me. "Marlon, you've got a good head on your shoulders. You will go far in life if you keep using this (pointing to my head) the right way." His lips tightened and turned white but this time it wasn't because he was angry. Occasionally he would tighten them like that when he simply wanted to emphasize an important point.

> *Higher than the highest human thought is God's ideal for man.*
> – Ellen G. White

He went on to say how smart he thought I was. I did do well in his class. My official transcript for that 1979-80 school year reflects that out of 180 school days I was present for 175 of them, and I had an "A" average in every subject. I had gained a great deal of confidence in my academic work; what's more, the tremendous amount of respect I had for Mr. Sheely only propelled me more to excel in his class. I guess a part of me *wanted* him to think I was smarter than I actually was. Being an overachiever and a people-pleaser was something that would characterize me more and more as I entered junior high. I will talk more about that later.

The Power of INFLUENCE

Mr. Sheely broadened the perspectives of all his students. It didn't matter if you thought his teaching methods were unorthodox or "weird"; he simply got you to look at things differently. In other words, he got you to *think*. He appealed to things inside of me I didn't even know were there. If it hadn't been for Mr. Sheely, I doubt very seriously if I would have ever taken up building models as a hobby, nor, say, watching public television for anything other than Sesame Street.

Quite simply, I admired Mr. Sheely – a lot! When I think back on it, he was the first male teacher I ever had. No, I haven't taken the time to do a psychoanalysis of the effects a male teacher versus a female teacher has on students. But he did have an impact on me, the kind of impact that I hope I can have on my own son.

> *You cannot always build the future for our youth; but we can build our youth for the future.*
> – Franklin D. Roosevelt

Young boys need positive male role models. Ideally, I know that this is true across the ethnic spectrum; but since I am African-American, I know it to be especially true for African-American men, who, for instance, are disproportionately represented in the American correctional system in relation to the overall African-American percentage of the U.S. population. It was the cultural revolutionary Ghandi who once wrote, "It is easier to build a boy than to mend a man." As the divorce rate increases—even among Christian couples—more and more homes are headed by a single parent, and more often than not that parent is the mother.

Confronting A Most Urgent Social Problem

David Blankenhorn, in his book *Fatherless America: Confronting Our Most Urgent Social Problem*, gives a startling analysis of the outcomes of fatherless homes and the impact that the absence of this most important of role models has upon American society:

> Fatherlessness is the most harmful demographic trend of this generation. It is the *leading cause* of declining child well-being in our society. It is also the engine driving our most urgent social problems, from crime to adolescent pregnancy to child sexual abuse to domestic violence against women. Yet, despite its scale and social consequences, fatherlessness is a problem that is frequently ignored or denied…It remains largely a problem with no name.
>
> If this trend continues, fatherlessness is likely to change the shape of our society. Consider this prediction. After the year 2000, as people born after 1970 emerge as a large proportion of our working-age adult population, the United States will be a nation divided into two groups, separate and unequal. The two groups will work in the same economy, speak a common language, and remember the same national history. But they will live fundamentally divergent lives. One group will receive basic benefits—psychological, social, economic, educational, and moral—that are denied to the other group.
>
> The primary fault line dividing the two groups will not be race, religion, class, education, or gender. It will be *patrimony*. One group will consist of those adults who grew up with the daily presence and provision of fathers. The other group will consist of those who did not. By the early years of the next century, these two groups will be roughly the same size.[9]

It is important to note that just because a father may be absent from the *home* of his children does not mean that he need be absent from the *lives* of his children. I think this is a larger point of Blankenhorn's analysis. This was the case with Daddy. During this period of my life, he wasn't in my home on a daily basis, although I knew that I could reach out to him (and him to me) whenever I wanted. I felt that he was always in my life.

Today, I sometimes marvel at my two children. Though young adults now, I reflect back on their teenage years, because when I was a teenager, I didn't have my father in my home as they did. I have often thought about how I might have developed differently had I had my father in our home on a daily basis. In my opinion, no matter how emotionally strong a mother may be, an emotionally strong and balanced fatherly presence in the home cannot be equaled. Effective fathering is essential to healthy child development–socially, physically, academically, and spiritually.

The reality is that we all need positive role models in our lives, both men and women, boys and girls. They help to inspire us to achieve more in life, to hitch our proverbial wagons to a star, and to persevere.

"Just Throw Your Heart Over the Bar" – Challenging You to Go Beyond

Effective role models are important because, if nothing else, they *encourage* you. For sure, a good role model will not lie to you, making you think that your behavior is okay when it's actually wrong, or not correcting mistakes you make in other areas. This encouragement is vital to a person's development, especially a young person.

> *Whether you think you can or whether you think you can't— you are right."*
> – Henry Ford

Consider this story from the book, *Living With Your Dreams*, by David Seamands. It illustrates so powerfully how encouraging words can have a life-changing impact on a person:

> A high school student was practicing the high jump in preparation for the state contest. Each time his coach would raise the bar up a little higher. Finally, he put it up to the record height for that event. The teenager protested, "Aw come on, Coach, how do you think I can ever jump *that high*?" The coach replied, "Just throw your heart over the bar and the rest of you will follow."[10]

Has anyone ever encouraged you to become more than you thought you could be, to stretch your dreams further than you thought possible? If so, how did that encouragement make you feel? Did you just brush them off as being "too nice" or painting too rosy a picture of what your life could be? If you did, then perhaps you need to revisit those words (if you can remember them) and see if there was more truth to them than what you originally thought.

Although only a sixth grader at the time, I had my share of fears. I was a young, chubby Black kid from a broken home whose parents had limited resources. The following year I would be entering junior high school, where I would no longer spend the entire school day in just one class. Furthermore, I had heard that I would be responsible for making sure I made it to all of my classes on time—with only five minutes between classes. There would be many more students in junior high school than there were at Spring Hill elementary. There would be more temptations, greater in intensity. And the work, I also heard, would be harder. In short, I would be a lot more responsible for myself than I had to be in elementary school.

Mr. Sheely helped to instill confidence in me. The flame of that confidence would ignite a series of achievements as I entered the next stage of my life, as well as a conviction that is still with me today.

PART II

Middle Passage

5

First Light

"We know what we are, but know not what we may be."
—William Shakespeare

On February 15, 2000, millions of people across the U.S. witnessed a couple get married on a nationally televised reality show called "Who Wants to Marry a Multi-Millionaire?" They had never before met. The bride, a woman named Darva Conger, had competed with fifty other women on the two-hour show for the affections of multi-millionaire Rick Rockwell. Ms. Conger was a former emergency room nurse and had served in the U.S. Air Force. She, along with the other women, was willing to marry a man whom she had not seen and knew very few details about. All during the show Mr. Rockwell was able to view the women but they could only view a silhouette of him.

> *Seeing yourself as you want to be is the key to personal growth.*
> – Anonymous

Finally, at the end of the show, Mr. Rockwell chose Ms. Conger and the two wed right there on the show. As the winner, Ms. Conger was awarded a 3-carat diamond ring and more than $100,000 in prizes. The marriage, however, didn't last. It was annulled in April 2000.

The question is asked, *"Why* did they get married in the first place?" The answer is simple: they both craved a few moments of worldwide fame, no matter how short-lived or embarrassing it may have been.

What would you do to get recognized? How important is it for you to *feel* important? The answer to this question differs from person to person, but the reality is that all of us have an instinctive—perhaps unshakeable—need to feel important, to feel *valued*.

As I entered the seventh grade at Trezevant Junior High School in the fall of 1980, little did I know that my "instinctive need" was about to be fulfilled in ways I could not have imagined at the time. Although my school transcript says differently, I really didn't view myself as a "smart" kid. I knew that I had done fairly well in Mr. Sheely's class but I didn't view myself as a successful student. That would all change by the end of my seventh-grade year.

> *Most people are very close to becoming the person God wants them to be.*
>
> – Dr. John Maxwell

Positive Reinforcement

Trezevant Junior High and Trezevant High School were both located in the same building in what was at that time a quiet residential neighborhood in a northerly suburb of Memphis called Frayser. The overall building had two stories and the two schools were separated only by main doorways on both levels. Although it was easy to pass between the junior high and high schools, the classes were structured in such a way that students from each school remained primarily in their own portion of the building for much of the day.

It seemed like whenever I ventured onto the high school side of the building, I felt like I had crossed into another world. The high school students were much bigger than my junior high classmates, so it seemed to me. The high school students also appeared to have much more freedom than I had. After all, some of them were permitted to leave campus during lunch time, a privilege that at least to my thirteen-year old mind was as big as having your own car—which some of them had as well. I simply marveled at the adult-like ways in which some of the high schoolers carried themselves. Needless to say, I seized every opportunity I had to "cross-over" onto that side whenever I could, and I couldn't wait until the day when I too would "belong" there.

In junior high, I was assigned to Mrs. "L" as my homeroom teacher. Every day we spent the first fifteen minutes of our school day in her class, where she would take roll, make announcements, and then allow us to talk among ourselves before going on to our next class. She was a middle-aged, medium-sized African-American woman with a smooth light-brown skin complexion and a warm smile. Her hair always looked like she had pressed it the night before. She had a mild disposition but would occasionally raise her voice to get our attention. Though not very old at the time, Mrs. "L", nonetheless, had the look of a favorite grandmother. To me, she was more than just my homeroom teacher. Like Mr. Sheely, she was also an encourager to me.

Then, there was Mr. H., my history teacher. "Coach" H. as we all called him, was a middle-aged White man with sandy-colored hair, a graying beard, glasses, and a warm smile. He had a small potbelly and wore overalls which made him look like a mild-mannered lumberjack. Coach H. coached the girls' basketball team. He was a fun-loving, gentle man who had the affection of all the students, Black or White.

Coach H. was more than funny to me; he encouraged me greatly. As the semester wore on, I found myself doing well in all of my classes. While some of my male classmates tried valiantly to establish themselves as either class clowns or "cool dudes" who had the nerve to talk back to their teachers, I was very self-conscious of my reputation and worked very hard at being "liked" by all of my teachers. Frankly, I was a people pleaser; besides, I knew that Madea would not put up with any disrespect from Chris or me to any of our teachers. Plus, I knew that as nice as Coach H. was, he would not put up with any foolishness either. For some reason Coach H. saw something in me that won his kindest compliments. I grew to not only like him but respect him, and I valued his favor.

> *The only person that can stop you from becoming what God intends for your life is YOU!*
> – Author unknown

Last, but not least, there was Ms. Carpenter (now deceased), a forty-something single Black female with a short afro, ultra smooth dark skin, and shiny white teeth. She was always immaculately dressed and had an absolutely regal disposition. In short, Ms. Carpenter commanded respect! Very few students ventured to cross the line and speak disrespectfully to Ms. Carpenter. When she was displeased with a student, she had a look that made you want to climb into a hole and not come out for a while. I grew to love—and fear—Ms. Carpenter. She taught math and did so exceptionally. She was very effective at explaining concepts and would patiently work with you one-on-one to help you understand them. Ms. Carpenter was very careful in issuing her compliments. But as I consistently earned A's in her class she, too, showed me favor. She had a way of showing me this favor while simultaneously maintaining a posture that said "If you get out of line I know how to put you back into your place." I understood her and always respected "the line." I would eventually grow to consider her a great confidant of mine, long into my adult years.

I excelled in Ms. Carpenter's class as I did in all of my other classes. By the end of my seventh-grade year I was a straight-A student. At the annual year-end junior high awards assembly, I walked away with the most academic awards of any seventh-grader. That awards ceremony was memorable for more than just the awards I received. Here's why…

"Mackie" and the "Crooner"

I met two of my best friends my seventh-grade year. One of them is named Anthony Macklin. I liked Anthony from the start, as we had a couple of classes together. Coach H. nicknamed him "Mackie", a title that stuck with him throughout our junior high and high school years.

One day as I was leaning out of my bedroom window at our apartment complex I was surprised to see Anthony walking along the driveway with some of

> *Friendship…is not something you learn in school. But if you haven't learned the meaning of friendship, you really haven't learned anything.*
> – Muhammad Ali

his cousins. Up until that point, we had had little interaction with each other and I'm sure he had no idea that I thought well of him.

I yelled out to him, "Mackie!" Startled, he looked up and recognized that it was one of his classmates. "Hey, what's up?" he responded. We talked briefly but that simple little encounter started a friendship. Little did I know, but in the beginning Anthony didn't like me as much. He thought I was stuck up and arrogant because I was a straight-A student—and he never thought we would become friends!

My second best friend is named Montego Jackson. We simply call him Tyrone. He began attending Trezevant during the second semester of my seventh-grade year. We had a couple of classes together, but I was not drawn to him initially. For one, he had good looks—I was chubby and beginning to experience acne; he was athletic—I wasn't; he was a girl-magnet—I could only wish to be; and he was an A-student. He seemed to have it all. My jealousy of him was overshadowed only by my contempt for one more trait that he seemed to relish in himself: he fancied himself a crooner of old-school rhythm-and blues songs. Tyrone has *never* been a polished singer, but that didn't matter to him then—or now. In class, before the teacher called things to order, he would bellow out tunes—especially to the girls—from groups like The Temptations; The Jackson Five; Earth, Wind, and Fire; or New Edition, as if he were onstage at a nightclub. And this would continue as he went from class to class!

My idea of him, however, changed in one afternoon. It was at the year-end junior high awards assembly. He, too, received several academic awards as we were both inducted into the Honor Society. Honor Society recipients were especially recognized and were seated onstage in front of all their classmates. Tyrone and I happened to be seated next to each other and exchanged congratulations. From there, conversations between us continued and a friendship blossomed.

> *Lots of people want to ride with you in the limo, but what you want is someone who will take the bus with you when the limo breaks down.*
> – Oprah Winfrey

Early into my eighth-grade year Anthony, Tyrone, and I would form a trio. One of the first things we learned about each other is that we each have the same middle name: Anthony *Tyrone* Macklin, Montego *Tyrone* Jackson, Marlon *Tyrone* Perkins. We've always relished in this "coincidence" and felt like it was divine evidence that our friendship was meant to be.

I am truly humbled by the reality that we have been best friends for over thirty years now and have *never* had a period of separation between us. We would later add Orlandus "Lan" Young to our trio, a guy with whom Anthony and my brother Chris were familiar. Lan can have a fiendish smile when he wants to and, like Chris, has a penchant for the comical. The gift of friendship is truly one of life's greatest compensations!

Awakening

I chose to entitle this chapter "First Light" because the words themselves evoke images of an awakening. That's exactly what had happened to me by the end of my seventh-grade year. I had had an *awakening*. The consistent, positive encouragement that I received from my teachers had a profound impact upon me. This encouragement did more than just make me feel good about myself. No, it was much, much more than that. A conviction was born in my heart and mind at age thirteen—a conviction that I was destined for something special.

I believe it was more than just my fanciful imagination. There was a different look in the eyes of my teachers when they would encourage me. They weren't just looking *at* me, they were looking *beyond* me, as if somehow through divine inspiration they could "see" down the timeline of my life a realization of the potential that lay within me. The Psalmist David expresses it best: "*O LORD, you have searched me and known me! You know when I sit down and when I rise up; you discern my thoughts from afar. You search out my path and my lying down and are acquainted with all my ways*" (Psalm 139:1-3, ESV).

> *The purposes of a person's heart are deep waters, but one who has insight draws them out.*
> – Proverbs 20:5, NIV

This newborn conviction about my destiny did something else for me: it made me keenly aware that bad choices on my part could derail my life's course, could make me forfeit my future, and I didn't want this to happen. Why not? Because my thoughts about my future produced such powerfully positive feelings inside of me—feelings of distinction, importance, and value—that, although I didn't know exactly what I would eventually do or become, it didn't matter. I felt that whatever my ultimate destiny would be, it was going to be so beautiful and so worthwhile that I was fearful of allowing *anyone* or *anything* to mess it up!

Who Turned Out the Lights?

I have often felt that the Devil fights especially hard to derail a person's life during their *early teen years* or often into young adulthood. As I like to put it, he tries to cut your knees out from under you before you can even begin to walk in life!

The Devil doesn't want us to experience true joy in life, to know that our deepest aspirations in life can also be the same things that God wants for us, so that we don't necessarily have to feel that there is a perpetual conflict between what *we* want out of life and what *God* desires for us. No, the Devil doesn't want you to experience the inner peace and emotional stability that comes with living in complete surrender to the Will of God for your life. The ancient Jewish king Solomon puts forward this insightful counsel:

> *The greatness of the man's power is the measure of his surrender.*
> – William Booth

*"**Remember** also your Creator in the days of your **youth**, before the evil days come and the years draw near of which you will say, 'I have no pleasure in them'* (Ecclesiastes 12:1, ESV).

Dr. James Dobson, a well-known Christian psychologist and founder of the worldwide Christian radio program *Focus on the Family*, wrote a very encouraging book for youth entering what he calls the "critical decade" of a person's life, those years between ages 16-26 when the most critical decisions that will govern the rest of one's life are made. Here is an excerpt from his book, *Life on the Edge: A Young Adult's Guide to A Meaningful Future*:

> If you are between sixteen and twenty-six years of age, this book is written specifically for you. Others are welcome to read along with us, of course, but the ideas are aimed directly at those moving through what we call the 'critical decade.
>
> Some of the most dramatic and permanent changes in life usually occur during those ten short years. A person is transformed from a kid who's still living at home and eating at the parents' table, to a full-fledged adult who should be earning a living and taking complete charge of his or her life. Most of the decisions that will shape the next fifty [years] will be made in this era, including the choice of an occupation, perhaps the decision to marry, and the establishment of values and principles by which life will be governed.
>
> What makes this period even more significant is the *impact of early mistakes and errors in judgment. They can undermine all that is to follow.* A bricklayer knows he must be very careful to get his foundation absolutely straight; any

wobble in the bricks at the bottom will create an even greater tilt as the wall goes up. So it is in life…

Your next ten years will pose hundreds of important questions for which secure answers may be slow in coming. I struggled with many of them when I was in college, such as, What will I do with my life? What kind of woman should I marry? Where will I find her? Will our love last a lifetime? What are my strengths and weaknesses? Should I plan to attend graduate school? Can I qualify for admission? Am I talented enough to make it professionally? And what about God? Where does he fit into my plans, and how can I know His will? I recall pondering these questions and thinking how helpful it would be to talk with someone who had a few answers—someone who understood what I was facing. But like most of my friends, I never asked for help. The years rolled on, and I gradually bobbed and weaved my way through…"[11]

Whether you are in the 'critical decade' that Dr. Dobson refers to or not, just know that the Devil doesn't want you to catch a glimpse—a "first light" experience—of what your life can be. He knows all-too-well how beautiful and profoundly inspirational such experiences can be, igniting within you an unquenchable desire to discover *and* fulfill your life's calling or purpose. You should know this too!

————————————

————

Stepping Out of the Shadows

The first day of classes of my eighth-grade year is notable, interestingly, because of a lunchroom experience that Chris had. He was beginning Trezevant Junior High after coming from Spring Hill Elementary School. Like all other seventh-graders, his first day of school was filled with getting accustomed to a new schedule, going to multiple classrooms, and adjusting to the height and size difference with the high school students. For me, I now had a year under my belt and felt as if I were a seasoned veteran. Then came a chance encounter over lunch in the school cafeteria, an experience that Chris would recount for many years afterward.

"You must be Marlon Perkins' brother," came the polite inquiry. According to Chris, this came from the most beautiful girl he had seen in a while. She had long black hair, beauty queen looks, and a friendly smile. Her name was Sonya, a petite, attractive eighth-grader with whom I had become acquainted the year before.

"Yes," replied Chris nervously. "How did you know?" "You look just like him. Your brother is really smart. Everybody in junior high knows who he is. What's your name," she asked. "Chris," he replied. "Well, hi Chris, my name is Sonya. I'm in the same grade as your brother. Would you like some of my ice cream sandwich," she asked as she flashed a friendly smile, a smile that Chris said made him melt like butter. "Yes, thanks," he said.

He was in disbelief that on his very first day in junior high school a girl as beautiful as Sonya would even take an interest in him. The two would go on to talk more and laugh, which wouldn't be hard to do because Chris always had a friendly personality. He said the only downer during their encounter was that he was quickly identified, not as Chris Perkins, but as "Marlon Perkins' brother."

> *Purpose is the God-given desire of the heart to make a difference somewhere.*
> – Author unknown

Chris would get a lot of that his first year at Trezevant, and would have to face the same question at various times throughout his junior high and high school career. Until he could establish his own identity among our peers, for a while he felt as if he were standing in my shadow, especially with the teachers. He felt that early on they expected the same from him academically as they had seen from me. As it turns out, he made more B's and C's than he did A's, but he would go on to establish his own identity in time. The differences in our personality types were obvious: I was the more serious bookworm; Chris was the free-spirited, comical one. Sure, Madea would get on him a little bit when we brought home our report cards, and Chris would hunker down for a while and dive into his studies, but he never gave up being who he was. Looking back, I admire him for that...a lot.

The Woman Next Door

The summer of 1982 was a defining one for Chris and me. It all began when a single lady named Cynthia moved into an apartment across the hall from us earlier that year. A twenty-four year-old divorcee with two small boys, Cynthia was an upbeat, friendly person who instantly clicked with Madea. As she often did with other acquaintances, Madea shared her faith with Cynthia and invited her to attend church services with us. Madea became a mother-like figure to Cynthia, and Chris and I became like older brothers to Cynthia's two boys.

She and the boys would come over to our apartment in the evenings when Madea returned home from work and the two would talk and laugh. Cynthia also loved to cook, and one of her masterpieces was fried chicken. Now, without a doubt, Madea could hold her own in the kitchen. Today, when most parents work long hours and either don't have or take the time to cook nightly meals for their children and therefore feed them fast food several times a week, Madea, on the contrary, believed in cooking every day, except Sabbaths (Saturdays). She would often begin cooking her evening meal before she left for work in the morning, and finish it up when she returned home in the afternoon.

We had four-course meals every day. Unfortunately, as a teenager I hadn't yet acquired the appreciation for good home cooking that I now have. I still shake my head in amazement at myself because I didn't appreciate Madea's fine southern cuisine consisting of mustard and collard greens, skillet and hot-watered cornbread, lima beans, green beans, pinto beans, squash, chicken—baked, smothered, and fried—macaroni and cheese, pot roast, salisbury steak, sweet potatoes, mashed potatoes, spaghetti and meatballs, and occasionally fried fish. Because Madea observed biblical restrictions on eating certain foods, pork products and certain sea foods like lobster, clams, catfish, or shellfish were never served in our home; neither were any alcoholic drinks. Still, there were plenty of other foods that did not meet with such restrictions, and Madea worked her magic with them. Chris and I may have preferred hamburgers and French fries and chicken nuggets far above these other foods, but I can honestly say that we *never* went to bed hungry.

> *And in the end it's not the years in your life that count. It's the life in your years.*
> – Abraham Lincoln

Yet there was something different about Cynthia's Southern fried chicken. For one, her chicken pieces looked bigger than Madea's. Secondly, they were seasoned differently. She told us her magic secret: she would first dip her chicken parts in milk and stirred egg yolks before covering them in her specially-seasoned batter mix. The consistency of the milk-and-egg mix coupled with the batter mix gave the chicken parts a thicker covering when fried, therefore making them look bigger. Chris and I always looked forward to eating Cynthia's fried chicken.

"C'mon, Move It Piggies!"

Cynthia became like a big sister to Chris and me. She was always down to earth and real in her conversations with us. By the summer of 1982 Cynthia had built up enough rapport with our family that she felt comfortable giving Chris and me a directive: we needed to lose some weight along with her. Cynthia had resolved that the time had come for her to lose the weight she had picked up but had never shed since having her two boys. She also thought that Chris and I would make good workout partners with her.

> *The only person who likes change is a wet baby.*
> – Mark Twain

So, several times per week, Chris and I would trek across the hall to Cynthia's apartment and join her in an aerobic workout routine. We huffed and puffed as she shouted above the rock music blaring through her stereo, "Up, down! Side to side! Faster, faster! C'mon, move it piggies!" We also began jogging in the early mornings, and although we didn't completely give up our junk food addiction, we were a little more "observant" of what we ate, meaning that instead of having *two* hamburgers when Madea cooked them we only ate one. To celebrate our summer of hard work and commitment, Cynthia took Chris and me to dinner and a movie. We feasted at Godfather's Pizza (Chris and I devoured the pizza like food-starved kids!) and then saw the premiere of the movie *Rocky III*. Cynthia remained close to our family until she moved to California almost a year later.

When we returned to school in the fall, I was entering the ninth grade and Chris was in the eighth grade. Due to our summer exercise program, we were noticeably slimmer, which drew raves from both our peers and teachers alike. My 29-inch waist was the smallest it had been since I was a boy. Gone were our chubby cheeks and bulging waistlines. Gone, too, was some of the anxiety and inferiority complex that I had had with my weight.

What I lost in weight, however, I picked up in acne. My youthful hormones were changing, and the smooth, baby-like texture of my facial skin would soon begin to resemble the crater-marked surface of the moon. This created another inferiority complex within me, one that I tried to compensate for with superior academic performance and recognition. Once again, at the year-end awards ceremony of my freshman year I walked away with some of the highest academic awards for any freshman.

Pride & Prejudice

As I entered my sophomore year, my academic confidence continued to soar. My first crack at public speaking came through a statewide oratorical contest that was opened to all high schoolers. I was strongly encouraged to enter the contest by some of my teachers. Each contestant was challenged with writing and delivering a speech on the topic "My Responsibility: Involvement." Our delivery could be no shorter than three minutes and no longer than five minutes in length. Each speech would be judged on a variety of points such as content, delivery style, persuasiveness, articulation, and overall appearance. Contestants would be matched against one another on a city-wide basis, with city-wide winners moving on to face other students from around the state on a regional basis, and regional winners would face off for the final rounds of statewide competition in Knoxville, TN. The grand prize was a $1,000 scholarship to the school of your choice, as well as a little media publicity.

> *Within our dreams and aspirations we find our opportunities.*
>
> – Sue Ebaugh

Eager to test my skills against equally-talented students from across the city of Memphis and hopefully the state as well, I entered the contest. Trezevant High School was not a private, well-heeled college preparatory school located in one of the priciest zip codes in Memphis. It was an average public school with its fair share of talented students, academically and athletically. I had fared well against my peers at my school; now was my chance to really test my abilities. I won the citywide competitions fairly easily, even going up against talent from prestigious private schools in both the city and the county. My confidence was really boosted because this was my first real exposure to public speaking in front of large audiences. I advanced on to regional competitions which were held in the capital city of Nashville, TN. Madea and Chris accompanied me on the trip.

There I met a young girl who, like me, had won her citywide competitions and had advanced to the Regionals. Although I can't recall her name, I do remember that she was petite, confident, and had a nice smile. We took notice of each other because during the regional competitions, we had each won our respective rounds but never had to compete against each other. After each round, we would give each other congratulatory greetings. Madea and her mother warmed up to each other fairly quickly as well. After the regional competitions were completed, we both advanced on to the final rounds of the statewide competition to be held in Knoxville, TN. It was inevitable that, with continued success, we would eventually square off against each other.

If you're familiar with the shape of the state of Tennessee, then you know that it resembles that of a handsaw. Memphis is located in the extreme lower left corner of the state; Knoxville is located diagonally across from Memphis in the extreme upper right corner of the state. The drive time from Memphis to Knoxville is about eight hours. When Madea, Chris, and I left for Knoxville, I was nervous but confident at the same time. Sensing that I needed to work off

> *It's fine to believe in ourselves, but we mustn't be too easily convinced.*
> – Better Homes and Gardens

some of the nerves, Madea let me do some of the driving. By now, I had gotten my speech delivery down to a science. I practiced it over and over during the drive, having Chris time me on each practice. I was ready for the final rounds of competition.

To my surprise, I easily won the semi-final round and advanced to the final round. So did my friendly female counterpart whom I'd met in Nashville. I was confident—overly confident to be exact—a fact that Madea eerily warned me of the morning of the final round of competition. "Marlon, you need to humble yourself son. You're getting a little arrogant. *Pride goes before destruction, and a haughty spirit before a fall*" she said, quoting Proverbs 16:18. "Ok Madea," I replied, "I'll be ok." The truth is, the helium of self-confidence had swollen my head so big that I *couldn't* hear what Madea was really trying to tell me.

A Lesson In Humility

There were three of us left for the final round of competition. I was the second speaker, just ahead of my friendly counterpart from the Nashville round. My delivery flowed so smoothly and rhythmically that I knew instinctively that I had come in well under the five-minute maximum length. I believed that I had in fact set a new time record for delivery. A couple of the judges smiled politely at me as I sat down. I knew that I was going to win, no matter what my counterpart did. True to form, she gave an outstanding delivery, but not as good as mine, so I thought.

Then came the announcement for the statewide winner. "In third place," began one of the judges, "we have Marlon Perkins from Trezevant High School in Memphis." "*Third place?*" I thought to myself. "What do you mean, '*third place*'"! I was in disbelief and couldn't wait until the announcement was over so that I could approach the judges. "How did I come in third place?" I asked forthrightly. "Marlon," began the judge, "you gave an outstanding speech, perhaps the best of the three contestants. You would have won the competition today except for one thing: your speech was timed at just under three minutes. And as you know, there is a three-minute minimum on delivery. I'm sorry, but you lost the competition on time, not on a lack of talent."

> *It is good to follow one's own bent, so long as it leads upward.*
> – Andre Gide

I fought hard to keep back the tears and sore disappointment I was feeling as I congratulated the other two contestants, especially my friendly counterpart. She and her mother both congratulated me and wished us well. Alone with Chris and Madea back in our hotel room, the tears and sobs flowed down my face like a steady stream from a broken water faucet. Chris understood me and didn't try to give me a pep talk at that time. I couldn't stop thinking about the withering words of warning Madea had given to me earlier that morning: "*Pride goes before destruction, and a haughty spirit before a fall.*" Often your greatest strength can also be your greatest weakness. In my case, *confidence* was both a strength and a weakness. We need help to keep things like our gifts and talents in perspective: "*In all your ways acknowledge **him**, and **he** will direct your paths.*" (Proverbs 3:6, *ESV*)

True Confidence

As I see it, much of American culture and idealism is steeped in the humanistic quicksand of rugged individualism, self-determination, and the "power of the person." Although these traits—within their proper sphere—play an important role in one's success in life, all-too-often they are mistakenly revered as existential gods (aided, sadly, by popular self-help gurus), as if there were some mystical power in the traits themselves rather than in a Higher Power.

Sadly, many become entrapped in a seemingly endless search for purpose and meaning in life. Even when they do experience success in life, they find that in the effort to boost their own confidence they do so, invariably, at the expense of demeaning or belittling others. As gifted as I believe that I am in some areas of my life, I thank God that He constantly reminds me that *He* is the source of all power in my life, that success comes *only* when my will is linked to His Will. He who looks within *himself* to find the confidence necessary for personal achievement looks with eyes beclouded by the cataracts of

> *It is what you learn after you know it all that counts.*
> – Coach John Wooden

pride and arrogance. Instead, says Proverbs 3:26, "...*the Lord will be your confidence...*" (*ESV*).

Despite the obvious pain behind my loss in the oratorical contest, there would be a silver lining to it all. Little did I know that this would be a "first light" experience, awakening within me the gift of speaking that would prove to be so instrumental in discovering and fulfilling my life's destiny.

I once watched a made-for-television movie on the life of the great golfer, Tiger Woods. A dinner scene between the boy wonder and his parents made a deep impression on my mind. Earl Woods, Tiger's father, was attempting to persuade Mrs. Woods of the benefits of gaining media exposure for their gifted son, who at this stage of his young life was already making golf history as an amateur. Mrs. Woods wasn't having any of this media nonsense. She shook her head in opposition. Exasperated, Mr. Woods thundered, "We have a diamond-in-the-rough, and it is our job to nurture, polish, and refine that diamond!" "First Light" experiences reveal the diamond-in-the-rough-like potential that lies within you, and if you will allow Him to, God will use a variety of means—people, places, or even predicaments—to nurture, polish, and refine that diamond. As things turned out, two years later I would be given two more opportunities to deliver life-defining speeches. Both opportunities would occur during my senior year in high school.

Defining Moments

I really enjoyed the activities that were planned for our senior class over the last month leading up to our graduation. There was the senior luncheon, Class Day, and the prom. I relished these activities because for the first time during my high school tenure, I was able to finally relax and enjoy my classmates. I had been entirely too focused on grades and getting accepted into college during my junior and senior years that I had neglected to take time to get to know more of my classmates—outside of Anthony, Tyrone, and few other friends—on a more personal basis.

One of the more memorable experiences I had during my senior year involved getting our prom and graduation dates changed to accommodate my belief in the Sabbath. Originally, both events had been scheduled for a Friday night. I spoke with our principal, Mr. Robert Sadowski, about it. As for the prom, he suggested that I speak to our senior class about this at one of our class meetings, and that essentially it would take a class vote to change it. Changing our graduation date, however, would be more difficult. Number one, all graduation dates were set by the Memphis City Public Schools district. Number two, any change in the graduation dates would set into motion a domino effect on the other graduations, therefore making it extremely difficult if not impossible to change. Nevertheless, Mr. Sadowski promised to petition the school district about it.

> *Courage is the first of human qualities because it is the quality which guarantees all others.*
> – Winston Churchill

In my senior class, there were two other students who were Seventh-day Adventists and for whom the Friday night schedules would present a conflict as well. I spoke with them about it. They, too, badly wanted to attend our senior prom and graduation, and hoped that somehow our senior class would agree. They encouraged me to use my "influence" as senior class president to persuade a vote in our favor. I was a little nervous about getting up in front of almost two hundred students, many of whom I did not even know on a personal basis, and ask them to change their prom date because of some "religious beliefs" that less than two percent of our senior class held!

The date finally came. It was one of our general senior class meetings that we held during the year to discuss the activities that we would get involved in. On this day, the meeting went well, and I intentionally saved the part about our prom and graduation date changes for last. As we got ready to conclude, I mentioned to the class that I had one more thing to share. I was surprised that a lot of the chattering and bantering about came to a respectful hush, as if everyone was genuinely interested in what I had to say.

I put forth my best oratorical skills. I stood erect and forthright, as if I didn't have a nervous bone in my body. Never mind that I *actually* felt as if my insides were going to completely disintegrate. "What I have to say to you today," I began, "involves our prom and graduation dates. Both of them have been scheduled on a Friday night. There are three of us in our class (I named the two other students and included myself) whose religious beliefs prohibit us from engaging in any secular activities from sundown on Friday night until sundown on Saturday night." "Why is that?" someone asked. "Because we are Seventh-day Adventists," I replied, "and we keep the Bible Sabbath, which begins at sundown on Friday night and continues until sundown on Saturday night."

> The courage we desire and prize is not the courage to die decently but to live manfully.
> – Thomas Carlyle

I really didn't have the knowledge to give them a full theological understanding of the Sabbath, but on that day I didn't need to. I was just amazed at the receptivity to our request that everyone seemed to have. I think there was one more question that was asked, then the two other Adventist students said a few things, and it was voted unanimously to change our prom night from a Friday to a Saturday night.

Thinking back, that was a very proud moment for me. It was one of the few times during my teen years when I really had to stand up for my faith and risk being ridiculed and insulted. When it was all said and done, we passed the test, and this speech, unlike the one in Knoxville two years earlier, would *not* fall short!

I don't know how much time passed after that meeting, but one day as I was walking from one class to another, Mr. Sadowski stopped me in the hallway. "Marlon, I have great news for you! The school district has decided to change our graduation from a Friday night to a Thursday night. It will be held on Thursday night, May 29, at the Cook Convention Center. It worked after all!" I was in disbelief. It had really happened. The school district had *really* changed the date. I couldn't thank Mr. Sadowski enough, and quickly went off to class, as happy as I had ever been since I could remember.

The second defining speech came on graduation night. For much of the time during my senior year, there was a three-way race for class valedictorian between Tyrone, me, and another classmate of ours, a girl named Stephanie Taylor. Stephanie and I had known each other since elementary school and we both began an almost meteoric rise, academically, when we entered Trezevant Junior High School. Honestly, I think that Stephanie edged both Tyrone and me in overall smarts, but somehow we had managed to gain a slight edge over her grade-wise. This friendly (but feverish) competition continued throughout our senior year, until class ranks were finally revealed. Tyrone was valedictorian and finished with a 4.2 GPA. I finished second in class rank, graduating as salutatorian with a GPA of 4.19. Stephanie had finished third, with a GPA a little over 4.1. (Don't worry – she would go on to have a very successful career in bioengineering and I'm sure her pay grade has surpassed Tyrone's and mine!)

> *It is good to have an end to journey toward; but it is the journey that matters, in the end.*
> – Ernest Hemingway

A Glimpse Into the Future

As class valedictorian and salutatorian, Tyrone and I were asked to give speeches to our class on graduation night. The Cook Convention Center in Memphis was electric on Thursday night, May 29, 1986. As our classmates mingled with each other for the last time as a group, Tyrone and I helped each other put on our robes, making sure that everything was in place. We both were nervous, as we had never before had to publicly address a crowd as large as the one gathered that night, over a thousand people.

With the preliminaries of the evening's program out of the way, the time had come for us to deliver our speeches. As salutatorian, I had to go first. Although I had prepared written remarks (which had been carefully screened by both school principals), something came over me during my delivery. As I uttered a phrase in the speech I found myself taking flight, meaning that

I diverted from the prepared script. I began to speak off-the-cuff, from my heart.

What was meant to be nothing more than a commencement address turned into something of a Martin Luther King, Jr.-like sermon. In fact, I made reference to King's leadership during the Civil Rights Movement and how he, along with countless other ordinary Americans, had managed to non-violently bring staunch defenders of racial segregation to their knees. I made reference to the efforts of these Civil Rights workers as the backdrop from which to admonish my fellow classmates to allow God to direct their talents for greater ends as well. On several occasions during the remainder of the speech, the auditorium erupted in applause. School principals, classmates, parents, and visitors alike were all on their feet cheering and clapping, some shouting "Amen."

I was shaking from head to toe as I returned to my seat. Tyrone draped his arms around me in congratulations, and both principals beamed from ear to ear. There was a distinct feeling that, on that evening, I had stepped out of the stereotype of being merely a "smart" student to being something more. Looking back, perhaps you could say that this was the first "sermon" I ever preached. Little did I know that the spectacle of it all—the cheering crowd standing on its feet in applause, the church-like feel that swept over the auditorium, and me, draped in a robe, standing at a podium with a microphone—was but a preview of what was to come.

> *It's not what I have in my hand, but what God has in His hand that matters.*
>
> – Author unknown

6

School Daze

"The only thing worse than being blind is having sight but no vision."

–Helen Keller

Since my earliest days of junior high school I knew that I wanted to go to college. It's amazing how deeply ingrained that conviction was, considering how many young people today consider college so far beyond their reach that they don't invest a lot time–academically–to prepare themselves for it or, worse yet, they don't think about it at all, regardless of the obstacles. I did, however, think about it—a lot. Every academic goal I had in junior high and high school had its beginning in this conviction. Every academic award achieved, every leadership position held, whether it be on the student council, Honor Society, Senior Class President or otherwise, every major community activity engaged in—it was done with a view toward enhancing my overall profile for college.

Preparing for the Next Step

I applied to four schools: Dartmouth University, Princeton University, Christian Brothers College (now University), and Rhodes College. Both Christian Brothers and Rhodes were in Memphis, but Princeton and Rhodes were my top two choices. I was accepted by Rhodes and Christian Brothers, but was turned down by Dartmouth.

Interestingly, Princeton offered me the opportunity to go back to Northfield Mt. Hermon, a college preparatory school located in western Massachusetts that I had attended during the summer of 1985, between my junior and senior high school years. At that time, Northfield had a "thirteenth year" program, which was an additional year of learning beyond twelfth grade for students who had demonstrated academic promise for Ivy League schools like Princeton, but were not quite yet ready for the actual academic rigors of such schools. For such students, Princeton offered scholarships to attend the thirteenth year at Northfield, with the hope that this year would help to hone their skills to the point where they would be competitive with other applicants.

I decided not to go that route and instead opted to go straight to Rhodes. After all, Rhodes enjoyed a very strong academic reputation for a school its size, boasted a low student-teacher ratio, and had the "look" of an Ivy League school that I coveted, complete with its medieval gothic architecture, bell tower, and sublime landscaping.

> *Desire is the starting point of all achievement, not a hope, not a wish, but a keen pulsating desire which transcends everything.*
> – Napoleon Hill

My last year of high school was spent feverishly applying to colleges. I was so excited about it. At the beginning of my final semester in high school, I already knew what my ranking was, and so I just sort of "let loose" that last semester, gaining my only two "D's" in my entire middle and high school years. Ever since junior high school, I felt that I had pushed myself so hard to get accepted into college. I had been so focused on this one goal even to the neglect of fostering stronger relationships with more of my high school peers along the way. Now that I had been accepted into college, I "celebrated" by relaxing my study habits. "After all," I reasoned, "I wasn't going to lose my academic rank, so why not *relax* a little bit?" Unfortunately, I underestimated the extent to which this relaxation would take me and the consequences that would come with it…consequences that wouldn't be fully realized until the end of my first semester at Rhodes but would have a devastating effect nonetheless. I'll explain that further a little later in this chapter.

Sidetracked

But for now, I think it's important to note that "relaxing" one's efforts to achieve certain goals can not only be counterproductive but can also be dangerous to one's success in life. The wise king Solomon explains why in this little parable taken from Proverbs 6:9-11, ESV: *"How long will you lie there, O sluggard? When will you arise from your sleep? A little sleep, a little slumber, a little folding of the hands to rest, and poverty will come upon you like a robber, and want like an armed man."* The word "sleep" in this parable can be interpreted to mean a variety of things, like laziness, slackness, or even a lack of focus.

Focus is key to your success in life, to realizing not only your God-given potential but more importantly I think, your God-given *purpose*. If you are to properly steward your God-

> *Many intelligent people never move beyond the boundaries of their self-imposed limitations.*
> – Dr. John Maxwell

given talents in fulfilling your God-given purpose, then you *must* maintain focus in life. This focus is so key that Solomon goes so far to say that just a "little sleep," a "little slumber," a "little folding of the hands to rest"—this slight lack of attention can have devastating consequences, so that *"poverty will come upon you like a robber, and want like an armed man."* When you think about it, the "sleep" of inactivity can sometimes lead to the death of one's dreams.

The whole college admissions process, though, was very exciting to me. I filled out my own admission and financial aid forms. Since we lived below the federal poverty line, I qualified for the maximum amount of grant aid from the Federal and State governments. As a result, I would not need much financial help from Madea. The whole process was quite an educational experience for me.

During my junior year in high school I began thinking about the ACT and SAT college entrance exams. I decided it would be worthwhile to take both—although not necessary—because I would be applying to several colleges and all of them would require one or both of the standardized tests. I was a little concerned because although I had done well academically in high school, I seemed to have a phobia when it came to taking certain standardized tests, especially those where the stakes were so high. Deep down inside I had a fear that somehow I would be "exposed" by the ACT and SAT exams, meaning that I would score so poorly that it would be shown that I was only a small-school wonder whose studies had not sufficiently prepared him for college. It certainly looked that way after my first semester in college. More on that later.

Staring Down the Competition

I began doing research about the exams and found out that I could take preparatory classes for them, which I did. I would take one of the exams, the ACT, in the fall semester of my senior year and I would take the other during the early winter semester. I was fortunate in that both examinations offered alternative Sunday testing for those whose religious beliefs conflicted with the regular Saturday testing. Both tests were really challenging for me. I took one of them at the University of Memphis (formerly Memphis State University) and the other at the Memphis Board of Education building. I remember feeling the pressure of each test when I first walked into the testing room.

Although I had routinely faced my academic responsibilities with an immense amount of confidence, a lot of that "swagger" waned when confronted with these standardized tests. As I looked around the room at my peers, a wave of thoughts rushed over my almost-feverish mind. Naturally, I thought, there was probably a mixture of public and private-school kids, some not-so-smart, some as smart and those smarter than me. And then there were the "county" kids—students who attended public schools outside of the city limits where more tax dollars (per school) afforded them better-looking schools, higher-paid teachers, and oftentimes more modern equipment, all of which translated into only one thing in my mind: they were invariably smarter than me. Immediately, I knew that I was facing some stiff competition. The fact that these kids were even taking these tests indicated that they were serious about going to college and must have put in the hard work to get to this point *just like I did*. And no doubt they were high achievers at their respective schools *just like I was*.

> *In the world to come, I shall not be asked, 'Why were you not Moses?' I shall be asked, 'Why were you not Zusya?'*
> – Rabbi Reb Zusya of Anipoli
> (1718-1800)

I tried to shake off these morbid thoughts and boost my confidence. After all, there was a lot riding on these tests, and all of those academic achievements and awards I had would only have meaning insofar as I fared well on these exams. I told myself that I *was* smart, just like those other kids, and I would do well as I had always done.

All in all, each test took me about four hours to complete, as I worked my way through the oftentimes complicated maze of multiple-choice questions, testing my grammar, reading comprehension, history, science and math skills. There were some questions that I had left unanswered, and although I didn't have the greatest feelings of achievement when I left both tests, I still hoped that somehow I had fared better on them than I thought I had. Within a few weeks of each test, the results came in: my scores were within well-accepted levels and I was greatly relieved.

Armed with these scores, I set about applying to four schools: Princeton University, Dartmouth College, Rhodes College and Christian Brothers College (now Christian Brothers University). Both Rhodes and Christian Brothers were located in Memphis, which presented attractive possibilities to me because of my strong desire to remain home near Madea. I was accepted by Rhodes and Christian Brothers, but chose Rhodes.

I was so excited the day I received my acceptance letter in March 1986. My elation over being accepted, however, was quickly tempered when I received a letter from the financial aid office several weeks later. Tuition, room and board for my freshman year would top $10,990.00. At first, this seemed like an insurmountable number. Neither my ACT nor SAT scores were strong enough to qualify me for any merit scholarships offered by Rhodes, so I immediately began seeking out other scholarships. With a combination of federal, state, school grants and other scholarships awarded locally, I managed to raise every penny of my school fees without borrowing a dime. I was very proud of myself! Never mind that the scholarships were only awarded for one year and I would be back at the fundraising efforts a year later. I was entering the school of my choice debt-free.

> *Purpose is the master of motivation and the mother of commitment. It is the source of enthusiasm and the womb of perseverance.*
> – Dr. Myles Munroe

Is This Really the One?

With my admissions and financial aid responsibilities behind me, I began investigating every aspect of college life at Rhodes. It was quickly evident that out of a student population of 1400, over 96% were Caucasian. Although my high school had a much closer ratio of Black-White students, with Blacks being in the majority, I was not bothered by the fact that I would be stepping into an environment where I was in the minority. After all, my confidence level at that point was at its highest. After graduating salutatorian of my graduating class, I felt I would be on par—academically—with any of my peers entering Rhodes.

In late spring 1986, Rhodes hosted an informal gathering for area students who had been accepted. There we met with current students at the school ranging from freshmen to seniors and listened to their experiences at Rhodes. Each story only heightened my excitement about the school. I was convinced that I was going to the Harvard or Princeton of the Mid-South, and it was in my own backyard.

Three Black male students—all sophomores— interested me in particular: Johnny Moore, Steve Becton and Russell Wigginton. All three were athletes at Rhodes, with Johnny and Steve starring on the football team and Russell with the basketball team. Johnny and Steve were former standouts with their respective high schools in Memphis, and Russell was from the Nashville area. They took an interest in me that evening,

> *It is one of the most beautiful compensations of this life that no man can sincerely try to help another without helping himself.*
> – Ralph Waldo Emerson

as if they really wanted me to come to Rhodes. This made me feel all the more comfortable, as the four of us huddled together around a table to talk more personally. In retrospect, they were probably as eager to get another Black male at Rhodes as I was about going there.

Their genuine interest in me only helped to solidify in my mind that I was making a good decision to enter Rhodes. As I would later find out, Johnny was the biggest prankster of them all, and he believed in using every inch of his 6'4" 265-lb frame to "throw his weight around"—on and off the field. As big and burly as he was as a starting defensive end with the Rhodes Lynx, he stood just as tall in his academic studies though, and was in actuality a teddy bear at heart. He would later go on to establish a very successful career in the banking and finance industry in Memphis.

Steve was a little more reserved than Johnny, but had a fiery determination underneath his soft-spoken, Southern demeanor that fueled his success as the starting tailback for the Lynx. His calm persona and winsome smile would later serve him well as a counselor.

Russell, perhaps, was the mildest of the three. He would sometimes serve as a go-between between Johnny and some of the other underclassmen whenever Johnny felt like, well, you know, "throwing his weight around." Like Johnny and Steve, Russell had handsome features, with a lighter skin tone, wide grin, deep tenor voice and hearty laugh. His winsome demeanor, too, helped make him an instant hit with everyone, Black or White. I felt like I could talk to Russell about anything, and it seemed like his door was never closed to me. He was an avid fan of history whose unique people skills would eventually land him a career as a college administrator, even serving as an assistant to the President at Rhodes for a period of time. I deeply appreciate the impact all three of these men had on my experience at Rhodes.

Needless to say, I left the gathering that evening as if floating on a cloud. My dreams of going to college were becoming a reality with each passing day. I tried to take it all in as I drove home. I was both excited and fearful. I was excited that I was going to such a prestigious college, but fearful of the still unknown rigors of collegiate studies. "Would I fare as well academically as I had in high school?" "What if I flunked out?" "Would I be able to make it?" "If not, how would this impact my sense of destiny?" Despite the doubts, I still felt assured that this next step in my life was only propelling me closer to my destiny, whatever it would be. Oh, that elusive destiny!

> *Choose a job you love, and you will never have to work a day in your life.*
> – Author Unknown

Moving On Up

One day in July 1986, Daddy called Chris and me and asked us, "How would you like a new car?" Excited, we told him that we'd love a new car. He said he would come and pick us up later that afternoon and take us to get our new car. Chris and I were out of our minds with excitement. We were going to have our *own*, brand new car!

Daddy had purchased us a 1986 Pontiac 1000, a small four-door, four-cylinder gas saver that was perfect for us. It was meant to be a graduation present for me, but we had to share it because we both needed a car. Chris and I took great joy in fixing it up, complete with a customized banner across the tinted portion of the front window, stylish hubcaps, a pair of furry dice hanging from the rearview mirror, and a customized license plate.

I got my first job that summer, as my friend Tyrone helped to get me a job at McDonalds. As stated earlier, I interviewed with Della, the store manager, and it went well. She was very nice, and actually took an interest in me, showing me the ropes of the job, making sure that I was well-trained.

Later that summer, the Rhodes admissions department submitted dorm room assignments for incoming freshmen. I was assigned to a room with a guy named Mark West from Nashville. Since our room assignments included the home address and phone numbers of our roommates, Mark and I were able to contact each other. His Southern accent seemed friendly enough over the phone, which I felt was a good indication of things to come. We moved into our dorm room one weekend in late August, as freshmen had to arrive a few days earlier than upperclassmen for freshman orientation. Mark seemed "older" than a typical eighteen-year-old. He was a few inches taller than me, and wore a beard and horn-rimmed glasses which already made him look like a distinguished professor. He had a winsome smile, and his parents seemed nice too. It wasn't long after we moved in that I discovered just how disciplined he was.

Mark declared (early) International Studies as his major, although freshmen had until the end of the first semester of their sophomore year before they were obligated to do so. Mark already knew what he wanted to major in and, better yet, what he wanted to do with his life. He was just that focused.

> *The few who do are the envy of the many who only watch.*
>
> – Jim Rohn

Unlike me, he had very disciplined study habits. Often, upon returning to our room after classes, I would find him sitting at his desk in the middle of the afternoon studying. He loved the David Letterman show, which he watched religiously Monday through Friday nights just before going to bed. Normally, bedtime for him was around 11:00 p.m. When I awoke in the morning, it was not unusual to find him—again—sitting at his desk, fully dressed, and studying, with just his desk light on as a courtesy to me. It seemed as if he was always on time for class.

All in all, Mark just seemed to have his life organized, focused, which (as it appeared to me) made it easier for him to negotiate the ups and downs of college life effortlessly and painlessly. I never heard him complain about money, whether it be for school fees (he had a full merit scholarship) or personal reasons. The same was true for his social life. Mark was the quintessential Southern gentleman, affable in his demeanor, polite in his gestures, and gentle with the belle of his choice. He was careful in his use of certain "words," making sure that when he did use them around girls that they were sure to elicit a hearty laugh rather than a judgmental frown. Nonetheless, he maintained some sense of religious piety (his father was an ordained minister and author) and moral virtue.

> *There is no substitute for hard work.*
> – Thomas Edison

Learning to Adjust

As for me, I was now working two jobs, one on campus and one at McDonald's, and taking about twelve credit hours of courses. In my freshman year at Rhodes we were on trimesters instead of a normal two-semester year. That first trimester I took a psychology course, a micro-economics course, an English course, and one other course. My studies were very difficult at first and didn't come as easily as they had when I was in high school.

I remember my psychology class in particular. I had heard from other students that the professor had once breast-fed her baby as she lectured. At first glance, you would think that she were a poster child for the liberal craze that raged across college campuses in the U.S. during the 1960s and early 70s. Although I generally enjoyed her lectures, I was annoyed at the way she graded my research papers and found it puzzling. The red ink that streaked across my papers reflected more of an emphasis on her part, so I thought, to correct grammatical errors rather than to indicate lapses in content, which seemed more important in my opinion at the time.

Another thing which I found puzzling was the way that I felt certain of my papers were graded. For instance, I would put my heart and soul into writing a paper, thinking that it truly reflected the best of my thoughts and research, only to be disappointed when I received a C or C- for it. Then one day it occurred to me to try something a little different. I didn't have much time left in the semester, so I thought I would go for broke and try something new. I decided that I would just let my thoughts go, in the sense that I wouldn't be so uptight and I would just write using a lot of big words but in essence saying very little, or so I thought. I got an A- on my next paper and was genuinely shocked. Personally, I didn't think the content of that article was worth the paper it was written on, but evidently the professor thought differently. Based on the success of this approach, I decided to try my new "method" again and again. I think I got an A-/B+ on the next paper. At the end of that semester, I felt like kicking myself for not having come up with my brilliant idea earlier, because it probably could have prevented me from getting that C- I got in the course.

I was having a great time that first semester, being able to stay up late, and do whatever I wanted to do, including being able to drive off campus and get late-night snacks. My favorite thing was to go out for a late-night snack at McDonald's with some of my friends, and come back and watch the sitcom *Three's Company* at 10:30 p.m. As a result, I picked up a lot of weight. We could eat as much food as we wanted in the school cafeteria, and this was a welcome departure from the a la carte meals in high school. So I ate all of the hamburgers, fries, chocolate chip cookies and ice cream I could get my greedy hands on.

> *The soul which has no fixed purpose in life is lost; to be everywhere, is to be nowhere.*
> –Michel Eyquem de Montaigne

Could It Really End So Soon?

I knew that my grades were suffering, and a lot of it had to do with undisciplined habits. I studied in high school, but there were some things that came easy to me. College was different. I needed to study more and be more focused and disciplined. Earlier, I mentioned that I had adopted a "relaxed" attitude toward my studies during my last semester in high school. I also talked about the dangers of losing focus on your personal goals. Now, my relaxed attitude and lack of focus showed at the end of my first semester at Rhodes, because I was placed on academic probation. My GPA at the end of my first semester was a whopping 1.5. I felt doomed. Within six months, I had gone from graduating salutatorian of my senior class with a 4.1 GPA to being placed on academic probation at my esteemed Rhodes College. To say that I was depressed is an understatement. I remember getting a letter from the academic dean, stating that if I did not bring my GPA up to 2.5 by the end of the next semester then I would be expelled from Rhodes. I was so depressed and so scared of being kicked out of college, *the* one goal I had been focused on throughout junior high and high school. And I, too, was afraid that everyone who knew me would soon know that Marlon Perkins, "Mr. Salutatorian" and Rhodes "scholar," had now been placed on academic probation and possibly faced being expelled from college. I had a severe bout of freshman "school daze."

Over the Christmas break of 1986, I prayed like I had never prayed before, begging God to help me bring my grades up. I went back to Rhodes with a sense of urgency. Praise God, I was able bring my grades up, earning over a 3.0 GPA for the second semester. It was such a feeling of relief when I received a letter from the academic dean, informing me that I had been taken off of academic probation.

> *If we survive danger it steels our courage more than anything else.*
> – B.G. Niebuhr

A New Opportunity – And Roomie

As I entered the third trimester, Mark decided to switch roommates. In the room next to ours, one of the roommates moved to another room and Mark, who had become friends with him, decided to move in with him. I was assigned a new roommate, a Black student named Reggie Burse. Reggie's father was an officer in the Air Force, and their family had recently moved back to the U.S. after being based in Okinawa, Japan. Reggie and I would remain roommates for the remainder of our collegiate careers.

I remember meeting him for the first time. He stood about five feet, eleven inches tall, with a short afro haircut, square jaw, baby smooth facial skin, a gentle smile, and a noticeable gap between his upper two front teeth. He wore a corduroy suit jacket, dress shirt, blue jeans and eyeglasses. He was a handsome, studious-looking fellow, who appeared a bit shy at first. The more liberated Reggie, I would later find out, would not dare wear a sport coat unless he were going to church or some formal event. His wardrobe of choice included Army fatigues, Army boots, and a T-shirt, which showed off his physique. Reggie was quite muscular and didn't mind showing it!

It didn't take long for Reggie and I to develop a comfort level with each other. Like Mark, Reggie was quite disciplined when it came to studying for his classes. Unlike Mark, he wasn't the most tidy person, and so I now took more responsibility for keeping our room clean than previously.

Our third trimester was a very relaxing one. I was no longer under the pressure to bring my grades up. I only had to take two classes that semester. My first one began at 11:40 a.m. That last semester was literally spent getting up late in the morning, going to classes until mid-afternoon, "cooling out" the rest of the afternoon, eating dinner, studying two or three hours in the early evening, sometimes hanging out with friends, driving for a late-night snack at McDonald's, watching late-night sitcoms until one or two o'clock in the morning, going to sleep, and then getting up the next morning and starting the routine all over again. This time, however, I didn't lose complete focus as I had previously.

That time was also a turning point for me with respect to the focus I needed to apply to my studies. I would have to declare a major no later than the end of the first semester of my sophomore year. I was still unsure what that major would be. One thing I did know for sure, however, was that after taking micro and macro economics, a business degree wasn't for me. At that point, I was

> *Efforts and courage are not enough without purpose and direction.*
> – John F. Kennedy

still taking electives, trying to figure out what direction, course-wise, I wanted to take. One of the two classes I took that third trimester was a political science course called Black Politics, taught by Dr. Mark Pohlmann, who was Chair of the political science department. He would eventually become my faculty advisor.

A Small, Big Step Forward

Dr. Pohlmann was a tall, slim guy. He stood about six feet four inches tall, had light brown hair, blue eyes, and wore a beard that made him resemble more of a lumberjack than a college professor. He was an athletic guy who had played basketball during his collegiate years, and had spent some time teaching in Russia. While the typical male professor wore a shirt, tie and dress slacks, Dr. Pohlmann wore a shirt, tie, and corduroy pants.

It didn't take me long to warm up to him. I thought he was really down-to-earth. From what I recall, I might have been the only Black student in a predominately white class studying the subject of Black Politics. Dr.

Pohlmann didn't show any uneasiness with this scenario as he taught the course. I came to appreciate that he was a White professor who truly sympathized with the historical plight of African-Americans to achieve full political liberation.

I loved his teaching technique. He utilized what is called in teaching circles the "Socratic method." In a typical fifty-minute course, he would lecture for about fifteen or twenty minutes, and then we would spend the balance of time in discussion. Sometimes, he would ask a question on a particular topic and seek feedback from anyone. At other times he would pick a student to whom he would pose a question, similar to what the ancient Greek philosopher Socrates did. He would then ask a series of follow-up questions to the same student or students, all with the purpose of driving home the general theme of his lecture for that day. What I didn't know at the time was that he was teaching us *how* to think.

> *The purpose of life is a life of purpose.*
> – Robert Byrne

In his course, I became acquainted for the first time with such African-American greats as Booker T. Washington, W.E.B. Dubois, Marcus Garvey, Frederick Douglass, Malcolm X, Martin Luther King, Jr., Sojourner Truth, and others. I was totally immersed in Dr. Pohlmann's lectures and in the course material. Not only did I receive an A-minus for the course, but I had found my academic major—Political Science. At the end of the course, I thanked Dr. Pohlmann fervently for teaching the course and helping a floundering young student find his academic compass. Needless to say, I received a 3.7 GPA for my two courses that third trimester, which helped to further boost my overall GPA. Life was looking up.

At the end of each school year, there was a tradition at Rhodes which allowed students, through a lottery system, to choose which dorm room they wanted for the next school year. Reggie and I went to register for the lottery. There was a guy standing in line next to us named Andrew Wiggs. Andrew was a nice, quiet, slim guy who had been in both of my economics classes. I introduced Reggie to him and the three of us struck up a light conversation. As it turned out, Andrew's roommate had moved on as well. Reggie and I looked at each other with a wry grin, as if we knew what each other were thinking. I then turned to Andrew and asked if he'd like to room with us. He wrinkled his brow as if suspicious and asked us if we were serious. "Yeah," we replied. He shrugged his shoulders, smiled, and accepted. It was a good–no, perfect– match from that moment on.

I had gained a little confidence after having done so well toward the end of my freshman year. I didn't know much about politics, but I really enjoyed my classes with Dr. Pohlmann. I enjoyed being able to grapple with tough intellectual ideas. So, at the beginning of my sophomore year, I took another fifteen credit hours of study, declared Political Science as my major, and I was assigned Dr. Pohlmann as my faculty advisor. I met with him and we set about charting the next three years of my academic career. After finishing this, I was able to settle down and just focus on my studies.

Another interesting thing happened my sophomore year. Dr. Pohlmann introduced to his Political Science students the idea of forming a mock trial team because Rhodes was going to be competing in mock trial competitions among NCAA Division III schools. This was especially intriguing to those poli-sci students who were on a pre-law track, as I was. Out of all of those who tried out for the team, only a few were selected, and of those who were selected, it was expected that they would begin practicing for the competitions immediately.

> *Success is where preparation and opportunity meet.*
> – Bobby Unser

We were trained to argue cases from both the prosecution and defendant positions. This was totally new to me. At that time, I was a strong believer that, in most cases, there was only *one* right and *one* wrong position. My personal code of ethics at that time taught me to find that right position and stand on it. It was completely foreign to me to *not* believe in a position but have to argue in its favor nonetheless.

Who, Me?

Of those who were selected to be on the team, they were truly the best and brightest Poli-Sci majors. That's why I was surprised when Dr. Pohlmann invited me to be on the team. I couldn't believe it. I knew that I liked poli-sci, and that I was eager to show my colleagues that I was just as good as they were, I just wasn't sure that I was in fact just as good as they were.

Take, for instance, Eric. Eric stood about 6'2", had a slender frame, a great smile, and a cockiness about him. At that time, I couldn't think very quickly on my feet. Eric had the makings of a great trial lawyer. If he were playing the role of an attorney—prosecutor or defense—and he were cross-examining you as a witness, you were in trouble. He was quick to find holes in your testimony and knew how to back you into a corner argumentatively, leaving you no way of escape. I watched him in action with intense interest, trying to gauge his mannerisms and the methods he used to go about his craft.

Once, while I was practicing cross-examining him, I was careful to use a series of questions that, I thought, were gently leading my prey into my trap—a method that he used with great success. As he answered my questions, he had this sly smirk on his face, as if he knew exactly where I was going and was only waiting for the appropriate time to spring the trap, which he did with all the smug pomposity he

> *Strong lives are motivated by dynamic purposes; lesser ones exist on wishes and inclinations.*
> – Kenneth Hildebrand

could muster. Not only did he spring the trap, but he exposed my line of questioning in such a way that I was left at odds with how to even proceed next.

It was embarrassing. It is expected of the cross-examining attorney to *always* be in control of the witness. Needless to say, no "competent" attorney would ever allow himself to be put in that position. Eric was indeed a hard nut to crack. At the end of the day, however, it was done in fun and good-natured humor, as members of the mock trial team were only trying to make each other better for the real competition. In all truthfulness, I wished I could have beat him at cross-examination just one time!

With more practice, I finally began to hone my skills. I was becoming quicker at thinking on my feet—the trait of a good attorney. I so badly wanted to impress Dr. Pohlmann and my classmates, some of whom I secretly harbored a deep respect for their intellectual prowess.

Finally, the time came for us to go off to competitions. It was announced that each round of competition would take place over a weekend, from Friday through Sunday. My heart sank. I remember having to tell Dr. Pohlmann that I couldn't go with the team, that he would have to find a replacement for me. He asked why. I told him that the competitions would be held on a Saturday and that this would conflict with my religious beliefs.

I explained to him that I was a Seventh-day Adventist and that Seventh-day Adventist Christians keep the Biblical Sabbath, which begins at sunset on Friday and ends at sunset on Saturday. Although I was not a committed Christian at the time, I still knew factually that Saturday was the Sabbath and that I would be breaking the Sabbath to go to the competitions. He said that he understood and that he would find another replacement. Still, it was an honor for me to be thought of so highly among my colleagues to be asked to be a part of such a team. That year, our team went on to place third in Division III competition.

From that point forward, I would be asked to be a part of the mock trial team each of my remaining years at Rhodes. And each year I would practice with the team, only to stay home when they went off to competitions. In spite of not competing, I found that this was an extremely beneficial experience.

A Providential Invitation

Toward the end of my sophomore year, Dr. Pohlmann approached me about applying for a summer internship in the Washington, D.C., office of U.S. Representative Harold E. Ford, Sr., a Democrat from Memphis. He was the first African-American to represent the state of Tennessee in the U.S. Congress. Congressman Ford was offering a series of internships called "The Lyndon B. Johnson Congressional Internship" to select students from colleges across Tennessee. Dr. Pohlmann asked me if I would be interested in applying, to which I eagerly said "yes." The internship would begin in mid-June and run through early August, and would pay one thousand dollars per month. That was it. Each student had to secure his/her own lodging, food, and transportation throughout the internship.

> *The man who follows the crowd will never be followed by a crowd.*
> – R.S. Donnell

I went ahead and applied and met with one of his administrative assistants who had flown to Memphis to interview me. I was excited to receive the letter from Congressman Ford stating that I had been accepted for the internship. So, in June 1988 I flew off to Washington, D.C.

This experience coincided with certain spiritual interests I was having as well. Those spiritual interests happened in a very strange context. In the spring of 1988, I underwent an emotionally challenging time. Perhaps much of it had to do with Madea's health condition at the time. She had contracted Bell's Palsy that spring, and her face was disfigured for several weeks. She also had these dismal forebodings that somehow her death would be imminent. It was a very trying time for her. I was the oldest at home, and she often talked about how she was having a hard time keeping up with paying the bills. I felt like she needed more of me emotionally than I could give. I was not emotionally mature at that time, not enough to be the head of our household. Thankfully with time, her condition improved and with Chris maintaining watchfulness over her, I was able to proceed with my plans to go to Washington, D.C.

I will never forget the day I flew into D.C. It was so hot and humid outside, and I wore a 100% cotton white button-down shirt, underneath a brown-colored plaid sports jacket. As there was no one to meet me at the airport, I had to take the subway to the bus station, carrying four pieces of luggage. The bus dropped me off in front of Columbia Union College (now Washington Adventist University), a Seventh-day Adventist university in Takoma Park, MD. It was the cheapest place I could find. I was drenched in sweat as I carried my

> *A musician must make music, an artist must paint, a poet must write, if he is to be ultimately at peace with himself. What a man can be, he must be.*
>
> – Abraham Maslow

luggage into the men's dormitory. I checked in, only to discover that there was no record of my room reservation at the front desk. Someone had to search for the Dean, and they finally got me registered. I arrived on a Sunday afternoon, unpacked, and got ready to go to work the next day.

Each morning I had to catch the bus at 7:00 a.m. in order to make it the train station in time to get to Capitol Hill before 8:30 a.m. Congressman Ford's office was in the Rayburn House Office Building, named after the former House of Representatives Speaker Sam Rayburn.

Washington, D.C., is a lovely city. It was so much fun being an intern that summer. On Capitol Hill, there is an underground network of shops for the Congressmen and their staff which is connected by railway between both houses of Congress as well as the office buildings for the representatives and senators. Capitol Hill is a very nostalgic place. In the Capitol Rotunda, there are several murals painted on the ceiling depicting various scenes and statesmen throughout American history: the signing of the Declaration of

Independence, George Washington, James Madison, Thomas Jefferson, and others. Of course, 1988 was also an election year in the U.S., so I saw Vice President and Presidential candidate George H.W. Bush and various Reagan Cabinet members such as Secretary of Defense Frank Carlucci. I even posed for pictures with Senators Al Gore and John Glenn, among others.

Looking the Part and Ready to Work

My first day on the job I made sure I was sharply dressed…I looked my professional best. I went down to the office and met the different people who worked in Congressman Ford's office. He wasn't in the office my first day, but I met his various Legislative Assistants (L.A.'s), the receptionist, two personal secretaries, and two other interns. I remember getting there and getting accustomed to the work we had to do. The interns were each given different responsibilities. Although each of us had to answer some of the constituent mail which came to the office, I was also given a special research project on gang violence in the city of Memphis. I had to report to Congressman Ford personally on my project before the summer was up.

> *The quality of a man's life is in direct proportion to his commitment to excellence, regardless of his chosen field of endeavor.*
>
> – Vince Lombardi

One of the best research tools available on the planet is called "CRS" – the Congressional Research Service. The service is available exclusively to U.S. Congressmen and their aides. As a legislative branch agency within the Library of Congress, it employs research assistants to conduct policy and legal analysis on any topic in a non-partisan fashion. As I was conducting my research on gang violence, all I needed to do was to provide them with a topic or issue and a few key words and they would prepare entire reports based on the number of pages that I wanted. They would be as detailed as I needed, and most often the research would be available within twenty-four hours, or two to three days maximum. I could only dream about having access to such a research agency to help me with term papers back at Rhodes!

Black, or African-American?

It was a lot of fun hanging out on the Hill, going to different functions and receptions and meeting all of the other interns from around the country. All of the African-American interns organized into a group. That summer was the first time I was introduced to the term "African-American."

On one occasion, all the African-American interns held a forum on the steps in front of the House of Representatives to discuss the pros and cons of accepting the title "African-American." Nationally, this was a hotly debated issue at the time, and my fellow African-American interns, who certainly were among the brightest students at their respective schools, reflected this heat within their own conversations/debates on the Hill that summer.

Personally, I didn't think much of the issue, but I was careful not to voice my neutrality for fear that it might further agitate the already strained nerves of some of my more vocal colleagues. At one point, there arose a general consensus among the African-American interns that we should make a public statement about the issue and give "one" voice in favor of the title "African-American." So, one hot afternoon we all gathered on the steps in front of the House of Representatives and held a public hearing.

> *Blessed is the man who finds wisdom, the man who gains understanding; for she is more profitable than silver and yields better returns than gold.*
> – Proverbs 3:13-14, NIV

I wish I could say that we managed to make the evening news of every major television station across the country, but that wasn't so. We did have a few Congressmen and their staffers stop by to see what all of the fuss was about. Of course, we had the full support of the Congressional Black Caucus. Former U.S. Representative Mike Espy, a Democrat from Mississippi, was on hand to lend the vocal support of the Caucus. He posed for a photograph with our entire group, with some standing on the steps and others seated casually along a stone railing.

All of us, nonetheless, were dressed in formal business attire and tried our best to look as professional as we could. To look at the photograph today would recall to mind the ideas of the late African-American intellectual and co-founder of the National Association for the Advancement of Colored People (NAACP), W.E.B. Dubois, concerning the "talented tenth," a group comprising roughly ten percent of the African-American population that he believed would represent the best and the brightest among African-Americans in every generation. I even wore fake but scholarly-like horn-rimmed glasses to go along with my lawyer-like suit. Oddly, for all my neutrality on the subject, I still managed to be positioned in the foreground of the picture.

State and Church

But then, again, there were my spiritual interests. During my first week in D.C., I was able to make contact with a couple named Spencer and Peaches, who were related to a family in my home church in Memphis. They were young at the time, in their mid-twenties, without any kids. I went to church with them on Sabbaths. They attended the Capitol Hill Seventh-day Adventist Church, located in a historic district of downtown D.C.

Although one could appreciate the church's old hardwood floors, Puritan-like church pews, its pipe organ situated on a platform high above the main sanctuary, and stained-glass windows, it was a different story when it came to the air conditioning...there wasn't any! And boy was it hot on Sabbaths! The sauna-like humidity, however, wasn't nearly as warm as the warmth of the congregation. It would take fifteen or twenty minutes just to greet the number of visitors who attended on a *weekly* basis, many of whom were from other countries.

> *Let the youth be impressed with thought...that life's true aim is not to secure the greatest possible gain for themselves, but to honor their Maker in doing their part of the world's work...*
> – Ellen G. White, Education

Their pastor, Wintley Phipps, was also a well-known soloist. No doubt many of the visitors came just to hear him sing. What I (and I'm sure many others) did not know was that Pastor Phipps could also preach! In fact, his sermons and worship services were so Spirit-filled that, when I left church, I couldn't *wait* for the next Sabbath to arrive. I really enjoyed going to church there, hanging out with Spencer and Peaches and their friends on a Sabbath afternoon, enjoying a good fellowship dinner, and then hanging out again on Saturday nights. On Friday nights at Columbia Union College (now Washington Adventist University), a lot of the students who were still on campus for summer school would get together in the basement of the campus church, Sligo Seventh-day Adventist Church, for a vespers service. We called it "sing-spiration." We'd sing songs and give testimonies. It was fun being around other young people my age who [unlike me at the time] were confident in expressing their faith.

For the first time, I realized how diverse the Seventh-day Adventist Church was. Coming from the Mid-South and from a local church whose leadership was exclusively African-American, it was quite an awakening for me to discover that the predominant leadership of my denomination was Caucasian, not African-American. Silver Spring, MD, which is located near Takoma Park, is the world headquarters for the Seventh-day Adventist Church. Given that Washington, D.C., is a cosmopolitan city itself, it only made sense that our denomination's headquarters and its surrounding churches and institutions would attract members from all over the world. There, I met students from all over the world, which helped to broaden my cultural perspective.

There was something about being around all of the young people at CUC, going to church on Sabbaths with Spencer and Peaches, and the sing-spirations on Friday night. It just began to awaken spiritual sensibilities in me that beforehand had laid dormant. There was something taking place inside of me that was different, and I really enjoyed it.

> *As modern people we are all on a search for significance. We desire to make a difference. We long to leave a legacy.*
> – Os Guinness, The Call

Pages and Politics

While working on Capitol Hill, I learned that there is a difference between a congressional *intern* and a congressional *page*. Mostly, pages are teenagers still in high school and are required to wear uniforms, whereas the interns were college-age students who, although not required to wear uniforms (which I thought made the pages look quite nerdish), still were required to dress in professional attire.

Working on the Hill definitely acquainted me with legislation, the terminology used in legislation, how to follow up on constituent inquiries, and how to research public policy issues. In addition, just the glory and splendor of being in Washington, D.C., especially during an election year when so many public personalities were in and out of Capitol Hill, made it an exciting time for me. Many of the dignitaries held public forums and talks with the interns. Unfortunately, at that time, Congressman Ford was embroiled in his own legal battles back in Tennessee and therefore did not spend much time in his office. It was pleasant meeting his three sons, the eldest of whom followed in the footsteps of their father and eventually succeeded him in his congressional district. That would be Harold Ford, Jr. When I met him, Harold Jr. was still in high school, debating over where he would go to college and law school.

While I worked for Congressman Ford I met several people, one of which was a lady named Mavis (not her real name). She was a Legislative Assistant for Congressman Ford, and later left his office to start her own business. Mavis had a law degree from the University of Virginia and was very smart – *very* smart. She really helped to shape my thinking about a career in law and introduced me to several lawyers and others who had worked in and around the legal field. I must admit, the money was very tempting. One day I had breakfast with a guy who was interning for a large law firm in D.C. Still in college himself, his internship period was for only three months, but during those three months he would earn over $14,000. To me, that was a lot of money for a college student to earn, let alone for only three months' work. Maybe Daddy's vision for me to become a wealthy college graduate was a possibility after all! Time would tell.

> *The poorest person in the world is a person without a dream...The most frustrated person in the world is someone who has a dream but doesn't know how to bring it to pass.*
>
> – Dr. Myles Munroe

My last day in D.C. was August 5, 1988. As the day drew nearer, I began to count down the days until I could go home. This had been the second time in three years that I had spent the summer away from home. The first time was back in 1985 when I was at Northfield Mt. Hermon. I was so excited to be returning home to Memphis. I was able to go back home, see all my family and friends, and enter my junior year with a renewed sense of purpose. And I had matured in many ways. I just felt that I was getting back on track and was now shaping myself for a career in law. So, when I went back to Rhodes, I went back with a renewed dedication to seeking a career in law.

Yet, there was still this lingering thought in the back of mind, since my junior high days, that I was destined to be something very special in life. Was this destiny to be in law? In spite of this nagging sense of indecision, I still felt convicted that I needed to stay the course in my Law studies, and hope that ultimately my drive would lead me to my destiny. At times, it was frustrating to me, to not have that true conviction of *knowing* that I had indeed found my destiny. As I have stated before, although I didn't know exactly what my future standing would be, *I did know* that it would be something so utterly beautiful and majestic that I dared not let anyone or anything derail me from the path to achieving it. No, my internal compass would not allow me to veer too far away from my "course."

Gaining A Clearer Grasp

In this chapter, I chose to share details of my college life, primarily to illustrate the intense personal struggles I faced at times. For the first two-and-half years of my college career, I was truly in a school "daze." You could see the triumphs as well as tragedies, the contradictions in feelings I had about my life's ultimate purpose.

If there were one thought I wish to get across to you in this chapter it is the fact that I was *emerging*. That is, I was gaining a clearer grasp of who I was and what I would be about in life. Little did

> *Our background and circumstances may have influenced who we are, but we are responsible for who we become.*
> – Author Unknown

I know at the time, but the various experiences I had throughout much of my college career were but a preparation for the life-changing experience I was about to have going into my junior year at Rhodes.

Oftentimes, before God reveals the true nature of one's calling, a person may feel as if they are in an emotional or spiritual daze. They may feel as if the everyday events of their lives have little to no *real* meaning. As I wrote in the preface to this book, "Great masses of people awaken every day to a purpose no more inspiring than paying the bills, saving for a bigger house or boat, or desperately hoping that their retirement years won't be filled with the drudgery of survival-based employment."

Time Is Not Nearly As Important As TIMING

Have you ever felt as if you were on a merry-go-round, career-wise, in life? You're constantly moving, except your motion is not really moving you *forward*, just keeping you in orbit, so to speak. Your job or career may make you feel as if you are active, but deep inside you question whether you are truly *productive*. In the apt words of a friend who once wrote to me, "Life tends to lead us about as if by an unseen nose ring tugging hither and yon. And like a beast of burden we follow in mindless obeisance."

Then, there are those times in life when you feel as if you are at a complete standstill, as if you are somehow frozen in time. Not only do you question the appropriateness of your current job (or lack of a job), in relation to your own internal feelings about where you should be or what you should be doing in life at the present time, but you may even question if your life itself has any real value or meaningful impact on the larger society around you.

I have come to believe that these "dry" periods in a person's life—the times when you feel that your productivity on your job, church, or other areas of life is not moving you forward in any meaningful way, or the periods in your life when you feel as if you are at a complete standstill—are times that God uses to teach us patience,

> *To have no set purpose in one's life is the harlotry of the will.*
> – Stephen Mackenna

and trust. Sometimes, time is not nearly as important as *timing*. God knows *what* He wants to accomplish through our lives and *when* He wants to get it accomplished. "Dry" periods help to develop within us the patience of spirit that is so necessary to navigate the various trials that confront us in life. Patience of spirit also helps to keep us from making rash decisions that could significantly alter our life's course, and ultimately our destiny. Patience is so important that Jesus said in Luke 21:19, ESV, *"By your endurance* [patience] *you will gain your lives."*

In her book, *Sacred Contracts: Awakening Your Divine Potential*, author Caroline Myss shares an experience in her own life that I think speaks so profoundly to the idea of developing patience as we await the development of God's plans for our lives. I wish to share it with you here:

> Over the past eighteen years I have had a series of related dreams that all revolved around one consistent image: an airplane taking flight. The first dream featuring this airplane occurred in 1982 when I was at a tremendously low point in my life. Just a few years before, I had been getting increasingly disillusioned with my work as a journalist.

Then one day I was given an assignment to cover a workshop on death and dying by Elisabeth Kübler-Ross. The level of suffering in that workshop, and the astounding way in which Kübler-Ross was able to help people devastated by the death of a loved one, inspired me to return to school to study religion and mythology. But the post-graduate degree in theology that I earned didn't help me find my niche any more than my B.A. in journalism had. Two years after leaving graduate school, I was struggling to find a clear direction for my life. Working as a secretary in the Department of Pharmacology at Northwestern University, I could not figure out where I was going.

I felt as if I were living on a pendulum that was oscillating between worlds. My spiritual studies lifted me up, but then I was swung back to earth and the panics and fears of ordinary life, and I became stuck in a deep depression. After months of this dark time, I reached the point at which I said to a friend, 'I've got to do something. A part of me is dying, and if I don't do something soon, I will die.' I meant it.

Then I had a very unusual dream. I was the only passenger in a small but high-powered jet plane. My plane was still on the ground, idling in what looked like a stall in a barn that held a number of other planes in similar stalls. Each of the other planes took off in succession, as they were meant to, but my plane continued to wait for permission from the control tower. I grew angrier by the minute. Finally, I relayed a message to whoever was sitting in the control tower. 'Hey! What about me?'

'Turn your motor off,' came the reply. 'We're holding you until the skies are safe for your journey.'

My plane was in a stall just as I was stalled physically, emotionally and professionally. Yet, the control tower, which to me, even in the dream represented God, sent the message that I was cared for and watched over. Still asleep, I became saturated in the feeling that God was in His Heaven and all was right with my world.

When I awoke from the dream, I was content to *wait for my appropriate time of departure.* I lost my desperation to find a concrete direction for myself. Every part of my life looked different from that moment onward. I was being watched over; there was a plan for me that was already in motion behind the stillness and frozenness of my external life.[12]

In the next stage of my life, the hazy picture I had about my own life's purpose would come into clearer focus, and I too would come face to face with experiencing my own release from an eight-year holding pattern.

Early Family Photo, ca. 1958 Back row: Daddy and Madea, with Michael in Daddy's arms. Front row, L-R:, Marsha, Marcellus, Maurice, and Gloria

Southern belle: Madea (ca. 1950)

My favorite family photo - the last one we ever took together, in 1971. Back row, L-R: Michael, Marsha, Marcellus, Maurice, Gloria, Madeleine (far right). Front row, L-R: Chris (in Daddy's arms), Daddy, Madea, me (in front of Madea).

Madea enjoying a beautiful afternoon on the lawn with her baby boy (me) in September 1968. She is flanked by Gloria (left) and Marcellus (right).

Happy baby: Enjoying some sunshine in my baby carriage in September 1968.

Celebrating my 5th birthday with Chris on March 24, 1973. See one of Madea's famous homemade cakes front and center: double-layered chocolate cake.

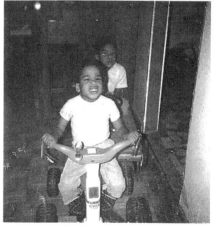

Chris and I enjoying our new Christmas toys in December 1973. I'm sitting in my red fire truck behind Chris, the one that Madea accidentally ran over (see chapter 1).

At the top of his game: Daddy (second from right) recognized as one of the top salesmen at his car dealership. (ca. 1973)

Brother and sister: Gloria and Maurice enjoying a happy moment together in the hallway of our apartment (ca. mid 1980's).

Billie's Boys: Madea, with Chris (left) and me. (ca. 1974)

Billie's Boys II: Madea and me at Chris's college graduation, May 1992.

High School graduation night, May 29, 1986: L-R): Best friend Montego Tyrone Jackson (valedictorian), Me (salutatorian), my high school friend, academic competitor, and ranked 3rd in our class, Stephanie Taylor, and Mr. Sam Chambers, Vice Principal.

Together: Chris and me after my high school graduation.

My boys: 37-plus years of non-stop friendship. L-R: Orlandus "Lan" Young, Tyrone, and Anthony "Big Mac" Macklin.

College roomies: Reggie Burse (left), me, and Andrew Wiggs (right) hanging out on the Rhodes College campus sign, fall 1989.

Lawyer tales: Me posing with another student for the cover of the Rhodes College Political Science department's pre-law brochure, summer 1989. (Photo: courtesy Rhodes College)

Billie's Boys III: The last pic that all 5 of the boys took together, at Michael's home in Oakland, CA, September 1993. Back row, L-R: Chris, Me, Michael, Maurice, Marcellus, and Marcellus's daughter Malinda. Front row, L-R: Melissa (Chris's wife), my wife Shurla, Lorraine (Michael's wife), Michael & Lorraine's daughter Clarissa "Muff" (in Lorraine's arms), and Michael and Lorraine's daughter Tamara.

Band of Brothers: My eldest brother Marcellus (middle) with Chris (left) and me enjoying a happy moment together at Maurice's funeral in Oakland, CA, September 1998.

Arizona "Law Dawg": My sister Madeleine, during her days as a Deputy Warden in the Arizona Department of Corrections.

Marsha's brood (L-R): Marsha's son John, daughter Brittany, Brittany's husband Fred, Freddie Jr. (in his dad's arms), Marsha's husband Gregory, Marsha

Pastor speaks: Addressing my congregation at Living Waters in 2012.

Brothers and sisters from another mother: Daddy (standing) enjoying dinner with David (far left), Harold, Sandra Jean, and Carla Denise (far right).

Classy lady: my beautiful sister Brenda, at Daddy's 90th birthday dinner.

Father and son: Daddy and I enjoying a happy moment together, at our home church in Memphis, TN, ca. 2010. Daddy was always well-dressed in public.

Gloria and family: Gloria with her husband Sam (left of her), and sons Sam III (far left), Jason (middle back row), and Mark (right of Gloria).

Grand Finale: Daddy enjoying his 90th (and last) birthday with Josie and a host of family and friends at their home in May 2017.

The later years: Daddy and Josie enjoying a moment together at their wedding reception, December 2003.

Father and Mother in the Ministry: Shurla and me with Drs. Roland (far left) and Susie Hill.

Young love: Shurla and me, attending the Andrews University spring banquet together, April 1991.

Mid-century mark: Enjoying my 50th birthday, March 24, 2018 with Shurla (left), son Marlon Jr., and daughter Reba. It was bittersweet, for I had just eulogized Daddy the day before.

Caught napping: With Marlon Jr. & Reba on a plane trip to Michigan in August 2015. Marlon Jr. would be enrolling as a freshman at my graduate school alma mater, Andrews University.

Daddy's girl: Reba

Daddy's boy: Marlon Jr.

Together: Shurla and I enjoying her birthday in Las Vegas, June 2017. (Photo: ©Cashman Photo.)

PART III

Decisions Determine Destiny

7

Answering Destiny's Call

"There are two great days in a person's life –
the day we are born and the day we discover why."
–Author Unknown

With my internship finished, I went back to Memphis and picked up my work at McDonald's and the continuing education department at Rhodes. The fall semester was still a few weeks away.

One day I was in the copier room at the Meeman Center, making some copies. One of the professors from the Philosophy department, Dr. Larry Lacy, walked in and waited to make some copies of his own. Since the Philosophy department was located in the Meeman Center as well, I had seen Dr. Lacy on many occasions. He was somewhat taller than my 5'10" frame, and was slender with a kind, gentle bearing. He wore black glasses—which gave him a sort of 1960s studious look—and had a rather wry smile.

By nature he was a soft-spoken person, and in general looked the part of a philosophical sage. Although I thought that Dr. Lacy was a nice person, in reality I had a very low opinion of his department. To me, most of the Philosophy majors looked like liberal hippies who only chose that major because they had no real aspirations in life (other than a life of "thoughtful" contemplation) and thought that a Philosophy major was the easiest way to a college degree. All of that said, it was simply my opinion at the time, and in actuality I knew nothing of the Philosophy department. My opinion would soon be changed.

Politics Meets Philosophy

As Dr. Lacy waited, he and I struck up a polite conversation about our summer experiences. I told him about my internship in D.C. and how I was studying to be a lawyer. He asked me if I had ever considered taking a Philosophy course. I told him that I thought it was interesting that he should ask me that question, because I had had a similar discussion with one of Congressman Ford's attorneys one day in his office as he waited to see Ford. He too had suggested that I take a Philosophy course. Now that Dr. Lacy had asked me the same question, I begin to think that perhaps there was something to this Philosophy thing...it might actually help to sharpen my critical thinking skills and expand my range of thinking in general.

Dr. Lacy told me about a new course in the Philosophy department that would be offered in the fall called "Philosophy of Law." It would be taught by a twenty-eight-year old doctoral candidate at the University of Chicago named Doug Corbitt. Dr. Lacy went on to say that the course's aim would be to analyze some of the writings of both classical and modern philosophers so as to show the relationship between philosophy and legal reasoning. After some thought, I decided to enroll in the course when school started.

> *Successful people make a habit of doing what unsuccessful people don't want to do.*
> – Thomas Edison

When the Student Is Ready the Teacher Will Appear

My first impressions of Professor Corbitt were positive. Little did I know that I would soon forge a friendship with him. Corbitt stood about my height, with brownish-blond hair, a clean-shaven face, an athletic build and a boyish smile. His mannerisms were open and friendly. He took his work seriously, and if you didn't (which was the case with a couple of students), he would let you know about it—sometimes in front of everyone else!

The required reading for the course was some of the hardest reading I had ever had in my life. We read the works of philosophers such as Bentham, Locke, Mill, and Immanuel Kant. Philosophy was a totally new intellectual endeavor for me. Studying the reasoning patterns of these classical philosophers was sometimes akin to trying to figure your way out of a maze—even with a bird's eye view! It seemed as if every word was pregnant with meaning, and I would often get stuck trying to figure out the meaning of a single sentence when I should have been able to understand the entire page, or so I felt. I quickly got behind in my reading. I tried my best to sound prepared in class, and even gave it my best shot when called upon to answer a question or two, but deep down inside I knew I wasn't doing my best in his class.

Somehow Corbitt and I began to develop a friendly relationship. I really liked his intellectual style. His class was held every Tuesday evening for three hours. He lived in Conway, Arkansas, about two hours from Memphis. Our relationship grew to the point where one night he offered to take me out to dinner after class. This quickly grew into a regular event. Corbitt *loved* the buffet at Ryan's Steakhouse in east Memphis, so much so that it became our restaurant of choice.

> *Relationship is where God meets with us. It is the only pathway leading to that ultimate discovery called purpose we so zealously desire to know and so ignorantly forsake in the process.*
>
> – Marty Shirey

We had a great time just hanging out. I had the chance to unburden my heart to him. At that time, I was so serious as a student and was always concerned about my future. It is one thing to be called a "son of destiny," but here I was, a twenty-year-old college student with a deep conviction that his life was meant for something, and meant for something definite, but not yet sure exactly *what*. I felt comfortable unburdening the issues of my heart to Corbitt, whether they were issues over dating, my courses at Rhodes, my career and future, or even my family life. Corbitt was so accepting, and it was strange to think that I could ever relate to any professor of mine on such a personal level, let alone share deep, personal issues with him. Our relationship would remain strong for several years after my graduation.

The Power of Bible Reading

Another thing that his course did for me, as part of my spiritual pilgrimage, was that the required reading in Philosophy inspired me to begin reading the Bible more intently. So even though I struggled with that course, I find it interesting today that I took my first philosophy course at the same time that I began to take an interest in reading the Bible. I had also taken a course in religion that same semester. Between the research that I had done on the Bible for that religion course and the readings for my Philosophy class, I now decided to try reading the Bible for devotional purposes. Although I had had a nice spiritual experience in D.C., I wouldn't say at this point that my Christian experience had begun to fully take shape. That would take place in the spring of 1989.

I began to read the Bible just to see if I could get into it. So I started reading in the gospels: Matthew, Mark, Luke and John. In between classes, I would often retreat to my dorm room and pick up my reading in the Bible. Interestingly, the more I read in the Bible, the better I understood philosophy. I couldn't understand why.

There is something about reading the Bible that really expands one's mind. Madea, for instance, went no further than the eighth grade, but the depth of her intellect on certain things went far beyond her academic pedigree. I sometimes marvel at the fact that although I had a college degree, she would often correct my grammar in conversations; she could also, from time to time, quote a great line from classical literature. The fervent, poetic tone with which she would quote Bible texts would sound as fluid as if she were reading from a Shakespearean sonnet. And her wit was equally as sharp as her knowledge of the Bible. "Boy," she would sometimes say to Chris or me if we did something that she thought was overly silly, "if I were to put your brain in a bird it would fly backwards!" She was a woman of the Word, and she would often encourage me to read the Bible for myself.

> *As wax takes the impression of the seal, so the soul is to take the impression of the Spirit of God and retain the image of Christ.*
> – Ellen G. White

Though simplistic, it is no less true that for the human mind to attempt to fully comprehend God would be the same as trying to fit an ocean into a teacup. It is also true, however, that the mind expands like a balloon when the Word of God enters it. How? Because God enlarges your mental capacity to understand Him...and *receive* Him. "*I will give them a heart to know that I am the LORD, and they shall be my people and I will be their God, for they shall return to me with their whole heart*" (Jeremiah 24:7, *ESV*). As one Christian author explains,

"Looking unto Jesus we obtain brighter and more distinct views of God, and by beholding we become changed. Goodness, love for our fellow men, becomes our natural instinct. We develop a character which is the counterpart of the divine character. Growing into His likeness, *we enlarge our capacity for knowing God.* More and more we enter into fellowship with the heavenly world, and we have *continually increasing power* to receive the riches of the knowledge and wisdom of eternity."[13]

I came to realize that in order to understand philosophy, you have to be able to understand the reasoning patterns of the philosopher. This intellectual exercise helps a person to think critically, categorically, and analytically. It really expands your mental horizons. To this day, I credit my abilities in critical thinking to the combination of reading my Bible and reading philosophy. It was very rigorous reading, but it was reading nonetheless which challenged my mind and made me concentrate so that I could understand the concepts and analogies of the writer. Philosophers and lawyers are especially adept at choosing words that are not easily understandable to express themselves. It's called "legalese." Lawyers sometimes try to hide the meat of their meaning behind words. As I look back at my liberal arts education at Rhodes, it caused me to feel confident that I could "think" for myself.

I'm Going Somewhere

In the spring of my junior year, 1989, a new course on the Civil Rights Movement was being offered in the Political Science department. Little did I know at the time, but taking this class would set me on a direct course toward discovering my life's purpose.

A new Black professor had come to Rhodes named Dr. G. (a pseudonym). His arrival was actually a result of some of the work that the Black Students Association (BSA) at Rhodes had been doing with the administration to increase efforts to attract qualified Black professors to the campus. His arrival was also a novelty insofar that there weren't any other Black professors on campus at that time. So Dr. G. came in to teach the course on the Civil Rights Movement. I was so excited about this course. There was a lot of reading, however. At the same time, I took another Black studies course, that focused somewhat on the Civil Rights Movement, but from the perspective of the late 1960s entitled "1968: The Way We Were."

The Book That Started It All

One of the books that Dr. G. required for his course was a biography on the life of Dr. Martin Luther King, Jr., entitled *Let the Trumpet Sound: A Life of Martin Luther King, Jr.* Dr. King clearly was a key leader during the Civil Rights Movement of the mid-1950s to late 1960s. I have often said that of all the books I was required to read during my college years this was one that I actually *read* from cover to cover.

> *Your purpose is the key to your life. It tells you what you are supposed to be and why.*
> – Dr. Myles Munroe

This book, more so than the course itself, was the beginning point to awakening within me my life's purpose. It is not enough to say that I simply read the book—no, I *devoured* it! I so enjoyed reading that book that I literally could not wait to return to my dorm room in the evening, crawl up into a chair, and just read for two or three hours at a time. Under the amber glow of light from a floor lamp, I found Stephen B. Oates' book on King to be more than just a historical recounting of the life events of King – his book was truly literary drama.

Oates allowed me, the reader, to enter the world of Martin Luther King, Jr., to become (as if) personally acquainted with the family he was born into (both his father and paternal grandfather were ministers), and to understand the crucial role that religion and church life played in his own life and early academic interests. I noticed that King's upbringing and mine had similarities. Like me, he was extremely inquisitive and introspective as a kid. Although many images of King portrayed today are that of a stoic, reserved, and highly intellectual man, as a child he too had some mischievous ways. Like me, he was also an overachiever in that he entered college at age 15, and after graduating four years later he went on to enter graduate school at age 19. By today's standards, that's almost unheard of.

Oates wrote that although King had decided to enter the ministry like his father and grandfather, he had also rejected some of the more conservative theological viewpoints they had, so much so that he chose to enter what was considered to be a liberal seminary at that time, Crozier Theological Seminary in Chester, PA. It was an eye-opener to me to see that Martin Luther King, Jr., this historical icon of deep religious faith and idealism, had himself as a youth struggled at times to make Christian ideals and faith *his own*, not merely the offspring of his parental upbringing.

Then there was Oates' recounting of King's dating life while at Crozier and at Boston University where King took up his doctoral studies at age 23. I was especially drawn to Oates' recounting of how King met his wife-to-be, Coretta Scott. As it turned out, a mutual friend of Martin's and Coretta's arranged for the two of them to meet over lunch one afternoon. She knew that Martin was one of the most eligible African-American doctoral bachelors at Boston University, and believed that her friend Coretta, a "Southern belle" from Alabama who was attending the famed New England Conservatory of Music on a scholarship, needed to meet him. For Martin, it was love at first sight. In his own calm, confident, and laid-back way, he was able to win the heart of this beautiful woman who, though attracted to him, was cautious of his motives at first and wasn't too sure that she wanted to date a minister.

> *What lies behind us and what lies before us are small matters compared to what lies within us.*
> – Ralph Waldo Emerson

The two, nonetheless, would go on to wed in 1953. In 1954 they moved to Montgomery, Alabama, where Martin would take up his first pastorate at the historic Dexter Avenue Baptist Church. A year later, in December 1955, the Kings' lives would be forever changed as they were thrust onto the regional and national spotlight through their involvement in one the most defining events of the modern day Civil Rights Movement—the Montgomery Bus Boycott of 1955-56.

Oates' portrayal of Dr. King during this event made a distinct impression on me. Most notably, I was deeply impressed with how I thought that King was seemingly "pulled" into the Montgomery Bus Boycott and, ultimately, the Civil Rights Movement.

By "pulled," I do not mean to suggest that King didn't have a choice in the matter, because he certainly did. Both Martin and Coretta fully understood the plight of African-Americans across the segregated Deep South, having grown up there themselves, and were both convicted that they should use their God-given talents and means to help fight against the racial injustices there. Yet, as I read the events leading up to their involvement in the boycott, I couldn't help but believe that King felt as if a Divine summons had been issued upon him to take the leadership of the boycott movement.

Internally, he was reserved, even timid at times, and questioned the ultimate impact his involvement with the boycott would have on his own professional development. After all, he had his own aspirations of someday taking up a teaching position at a university. Would his involvement in the boycott derail him from this? Would he be getting himself involved in something that he couldn't easily remove himself from?

These were questions that he grappled with, and yet he still gave over to the "pull" he felt upon his life to get involved. I could relate to King's feelings during this period because at this point in my own life I too was being "pulled" in a direction that was completely foreign to me up until now. By the time I finished reading Oates' book, I knew that my life had been directly impacted for a specific reason. A whole new feeling of expectancy swept over me. My life, I knew, was changing.

> *All men should strive to learn before they die, what they are running from, and to, and why.*
> – James Thurber

Revival

My spiritual interests that summer were also growing. At my home church, our pastor, Dr. Roland Hill, ran a revival. My thirst for the spiritual things of God led me to attend the three-week series. Considering the amount of responsibility I had at the time, school and work-wise, this was a considerable commitment of my time. But it signaled a significant directional change for me, one that was turning from the material things of life to the spiritual.

Ever since I had finished reading the book on Martin Luther King, Jr., for some strange reason I had begun to think more and more about becoming a minister. Attending the revival was more than just a time commitment – it was a *heart* commitment. I guess, too, a part of this sudden interest in theology came about because I had also begun to question the beliefs of my denomination, the Seventh-day Adventist Church.

Seventh-day Adventists uphold the Biblical Sabbath, the seventh day of the week, as a holy period of "rest" from certain secular activities, including most forms of employment. "How could the majority of Christians," I thought, "be wrong about which day of the week is the correct day of worship?" This was just one of several questions I had about our denominational beliefs.

This questioning really underscored a deeper transition of thought that was taking place in my mind. I was beginning to realize that I wasn't settled on the prospect of going to law school and becoming an attorney. Although I really enjoyed my political science courses, the mock trial team, and the whole enterprise of arguing and counter-arguing a point, I knew deep down that I was not truly enthralled with becoming an attorney.

The truth is, the only reason I was pursuing law was because I was good at it and I thought that it could be my ticket to riches and fame. That was it! This had more to do with the approval of my family and friends as well as my desire to create a name for myself. And I justified all of these selfish thoughts with the core conviction that this was a part of my destiny.

But as I contemplated what I thought a minister's life would be, my first thought was: "How can I live on a minister's salary?" The lifestyle looked too simple, too poor, too ordinary. It was difficult for me to accept the thought of my becoming a minister, when I contrasted my vision of Marlon Perkins,

> *There is no other truth that compares in importance for successful living with the truth that there is a benevolent God who is working out His plans in the affairs of men.*
> – Carlyle B. Haynes, *God Sent A Man*

the powerful attorney receiving world-wide acclaim against the more lackluster Marlon Perkins, the minister who would labor tirelessly in an obscure ministry, in an obscure church, in some obscure town—all at a pitiful fraction of the pay I could earn as a lawyer. No, my destiny was much brighter than that, so I thought at the time.

In reality, I still didn't know who I was or what I wanted to do with my life, and yet I had sense enough to know that law school just wasn't the place to find myself. Yes, I still had the conviction that my destiny was going to be something beautiful, but I didn't even recognize it yet or know how I was going to arrive at it. Now my interests were turning, but in still subtle and almost imperceptible ways. The book on the life of Dr. King had sparked something profound in me and for the first time in my life I became interested with the ministry and life of a pastor.

I had seen how God had used Dr. King to bring about meaningful change in society. Up until that point, I really didn't believe that Christianity nor Christians had the power to make substantive changes on society in general. Although I participated in various church activities, like singing in the choir, and youth activities in my local church, my interests were more about the social activities happening within the four walls of the church every Saturday morning. I had never taken Christianity seriously enough to think that I, like the Bible states, could be the "salt of the earth," and that my influence as a Christian could have a *real* and meaningful impact on others around me.

As I've said, the way that author Stephen Oates portrayed Dr. King's life in *Let the Trumpet Sound* did more than just chronicle historical events. His portrayal of King was literary drama at its best, because the portrayal of King from boyhood… to young adult…to world icon and then finally as a martyr made King come alive in a way that I had never seen or heard before. That portrayal made me think

> *Recognizing who we <u>aren't</u> is only the first step toward knowing who we are. Escape from a false sense of life purpose is only liberating if it leads to a true one.*
>
> – Os Guinness

differently about the power of Christianity in general and how that power could impact my own life specifically. Now I, like Dr. King, found myself in that same struggle… to make Christian ideals and faith *my own*, not merely the offspring of my parental upbringing.

Summoned by the Zeitgeist

The Germans have a term for the word destiny; it's called *zeitgeist*, referring to the spirit of an age or time period. It has been well said that few things are more powerful than an idea whose time has come. I would add that few things are more powerful than the emergence of individuals whose lives have been summoned by the zeitgeist. In reading Oates' book on King, I knew that my own life was being profoundly impacted. All of those years where the thoughts of my own destiny or purpose in life had laid dormant in the recesses of my mind were now being brought to the forefront.

My soul was deeply stirred within me, but yet without a destination. At this point, I was still unclear as to what my *exact* purpose was, but I knew that Oates' book had brought me closer to its realization. So, for a time I still toyed around with the idea that perhaps I would become a powerful attorney or do something in the field of law where I would be recognized. Looking back, a lot of that thinking was because I wanted my family to be proud of me and see me as a success. Daddy had wanted me to go into the field of law because my grandfather, his father, had a love for the law and owned several law books, although he had very little formal education. This had made quite an impression on Daddy and he had been telling all of his friends that I was going to law school, so I think that idea brought a lot of pride and joy to him.

Though, at that same time I said to myself, "maybe I ought to go and study theology." I wanted to go to a seminary, not necessarily because I wanted to be a minister, but because I reasoned that a seminary was the appropriate place to learn about "religion" while maintaining the academic respectability I so yearned for. I was enamored

> *Do not go where the path may lead, go instead where there is no path and leave a trail.*
>
> – Ralph Waldo Emerson

with the fact that King had gone into the ministry and that the ministry had helped to shape his life as a person…a person who was fit to be a leader of the massive movement known as the Civil Rights Movement, and a man who undoubtedly spoke with passion to the spirit, the *zeitgeist*, of the times in which he lived.

Even though I understood the impact that a life of ministry had had on Dr. King's influence on society, I had yet to comprehend the source of his power and ability to do so. So, I thought to myself that maybe I would go to seminary to study theology and then I would go to law school. I had an intense interest in both. And I also wanted to know more about the beliefs of my church, the Seventh-day Adventist Church, and why we believe what we believe.

I felt that, if nothing else, I needed to study these beliefs in an environment where I could learn from some of the most educated men and women in my denomination. This meant that I would need to go to the Seventh-day Adventist Theological Seminary located on the campus of Andrews University in Berrien Springs, MI, a small rural township nestled in the southwest corner of Michigan, approximately ninety miles east of Chicago. Since my next academic goal was to obtain a Master's degree, this was the premier graduate training institution for Adventist pastors and church ministry leaders in North America.

Time to Act

With that thought in mind, at the end of the revival I felt impressed to go to Pastor Hill and talk to him about what I had been thinking. I felt that a visit to the seminary could perhaps be the determining factor in helping me to resolve the indecisiveness I had been feeling between law and ministry. The truth is, ever since I had graduated from high school, Pastor Hill had been trying to influence me to go to Oakwood College (now known as Oakwood University) in Huntsville, AL. Oakwood University is the only predominately African-American Adventist University in North America and is also listed among the Historic Black Colleges and Universities in the U.S. He and his wife Susie were graduates of Oakwood University and they petitioned hard for the college-bound youth in our church to attend Oakwood.

> The world has the habit of making room for the man whose actions show that he knows where he is going.
> – Napoleon Hill

Understandably, they felt that an Adventist college or university would be the prime place for Adventist youth to not only get a quality Christian education—one that would prepare them for the present time as well as eternity—but would also be a place where these youth could meet their life's mate, a person with whom their Christian values could be shared. I, on the other hand, had always felt that I needed to stay close to home, close to Madea, and go to college in Memphis. Whether true or not, I felt that she needed me close to home, which is why I had decided to go to Rhodes.

Pastor Hill readily agreed to take me to Andrews University. We made arrangements to leave a couple of weeks after the revival. Earlier that spring, I had quit my job at McDonald's to take up a better-paying part-time position at Federal Express. I was now working in the overnight document sorting department Monday-Thursday evenings from 10:30 p.m.-4:00 a.m. I also worked Sundays from 6 a.m.-2 p.m. This was the best part-time job I'd ever had. Not only was the pay great for part-time workers, but my work schedule didn't interfere with my day classes and I also received a variety of benefits, including flying privileges and profit-sharing bonuses. Most importantly,

I didn't have to compromise my Sabbath convictions and work on Friday nights or Saturdays.

So, one Sunday afternoon after I had finished at Federal Express, I went over to Daddy's house, showered and changed clothes, borrowed his car, and went to pick up Pastor Hill and one of our church elders, Tom Armour (now deceased), who would be accompanying us on the trip. Pastor Hill and I had agreed that he would make arrangements for our on-campus lodging, but I would have to pick up the tab for gas and meals. And…I would do most of the driving. This agreement worked fine until about twenty minutes into the trip. The exhaustion from having worked most of the day caught up to me and I became too sleepy to drive. I promised Dr. Hill that I would only get a "little" sleep and then I would resume the driving duties. Needless to say, I didn't keep that promise— I slept for most of the overnight drive!

This Is It!

I remember when I awoke the next morning. Dawn has just broken and we were driving into the main campus entrance, where a sign read "Andrews University." The crispness of early fall air quickly reminded me that I was farther north than where I had started out the day before. Driving along the winding entryway, there were a few people taking a morning walk or jog. Squirrels hopped happily on the lush green lawns, going from tree to tree. The sun was burning a dark orange hue

> *The person born with a talent they are meant to use will find their greatest happiness in using it.*
>
> – Goethe

across the horizon as the birds chirped along with their morning song. I was immediately impressed with the serenity of the campus.

A feeling of peace swept over me. I knew this was where I needed to be. Although our two-day visit included touring the campus, meeting with professors (some of whom still remembered Pastor Hill) and visiting with some of Pastor Hill's friends who still lived near the campus, my decision— so I thought—had been made the moment we drove onto the campus. I left Andrews feeling that much of the anxiety I had been experiencing over the tug of war between law and theology was resolved. I was being called, I felt, into the ministry, and seminary was where I needed to be.

Still Conflicted

It was with this general feeling of relief that I entered my senior year at Rhodes in the fall of 1989. As a senior now, it felt good to know what I was going to be doing with my life after graduation. Many of my peers, however, hadn't yet experienced such relief. It can be a daunting feeling to be a senior in college and *not* know what you want to do with your life—especially knowing that you've already spent tens of thousands of dollars just to get you to that point! Reggie, Andrew, and I moved back in to our room in Voorhies Hall for the last time. Of course, we got caught up on our summer activities, talked about all of the things we just *had* to do before the year was up, and what our plans were going to be after graduation. Andrew would be applying to graduate school to pursue an MBA, Reggie was going to follow in the footsteps of his father and enter the Air Force (he was in the ROTC program at Rhodes and would be entering the Air Force as an

> *Purpose serves as a principle around which to organize our lives.*
> – Author unknown

officer), and I…I still hadn't yet told them that I was thinking about my decision to study to become a minister.

Although I had been undergoing a spiritual conversion myself and now had these intense feelings about becoming a minister, I still was somewhat conflicted as to whether or not I was actually making the right decision. I certainly wasn't yet prepared to open up my heart to them and explain the confusion and uncertainty I was really feeling inside. And I wasn't prepared, either, to talk to them about my spiritual convictions. Reggie and Andrew both knew my personal flaws, and although I was being drawn to Jesus, my life wasn't perfect. I didn't want to open up to them too soon and let them know what I was really feeling inside for fear that my shortcomings would quickly resurface and I would look like a hypocrite.

This was my pride at work. I didn't want to look "soft" to my roommates. After all, the three of us took great pride in the reputation we had managed to build up among our peers, a reputation that exuded supreme confidence in ourselves and one that, on occasion, sent the not-so-subtle message to everyone else that we didn't even care if you liked us or not. And lastly, I was so self-conscious about the idea that law and ministry seemed like polar opposites career-wise that I thought that I would come across as indecisive and unsure about myself if I admitted that I was going into the ministry. The safest and most reasonable course, I decided, was simply to keep up the front that I was going to law school. After all, who wanted to look uncertain about their life at this late stage in their college career? Not me! As far as they were concerned, I was still going to apply to law school.

My Ticket to Happiness…So I Thought?

Back on campus, back in my political science classes, the allure of law once again began to occupy much of my thinking. The allure was heightened by two things. One, Dr. Pohlmann, for the third consecutive year, invited me to be on the school's mock trial team. Our team had gotten better each year it competed in the national competitions, going from third place my sophomore year to first place my junior year. Expectations for a repeat national championship were high again my senior year. Once again, I accepted Dr. Pohlmann's invitation to join the team and practiced with them right up until it was time to go to the national competitions, which I declined to attend, once again,

> *Men, like nails, lose their usefulness when they lose direction and begin to bend.*
> – Walter Savage Landor

for religious reasons. Nevertheless, I reasoned that since I had been asked to be on the mock trial team—for the third consecutive year— that evidently Dr. Pohlmann saw tremendous potential in me for law.

I further reasoned that this "potential" must have been a clue to my ultimate destiny, which would involve becoming a high-powered lawyer who had a wide circle of influence…and who made a lot of money, of course. Power, money, influence: this was my ticket to happiness in life, so I thought.

A second contributing factor to my indecisiveness was a college bulletin I came across from Emory University in Atlanta, GA. Emory was launching a new graduate program seeking to bridge the interest gap between law and theology, offering a five-year course in which one could get both a Master of Divinity and a Doctor of Jurisprudence. This was extremely appealing to me because, as I reasoned, I could get both degrees in 5 years rather than the traditional 6 years…and I wouldn't have to choose between the two vocations. The only problem I faced now was the fact that the only way I would be able to study, academically, Seventh-day Adventist beliefs was at a Seventh-day Adventist school. I certainly couldn't do that at Emory.

The battle between law and theology raged on in my heart until one Sabbath afternoon. I remember a conversation I had with Pastor Hill about this dilemma, and I will never forget his remarks to me after having listened patiently to my concerns. "Marlon," he began, "I really don't think the Lord is calling you to go to Andrews to *merely* get knowledge. He is calling you into the ministry, and the [Adventist] seminary is where you need to be." That settled it for me…at least for now.

Dealing With Doubt

In reality, the battle would continue to rage on in my mind. I felt like a clock pendulum, swinging back and forth between two worlds—one law, the other ministry. Depending on the circumstances at the time, I could easily find myself completely immersed in either world, rationalizing to myself why I should commit to that vocation. What I didn't know, however, is that my indecisiveness would soon come to a head and I would be led to choose one above

> *Fixedness of purpose is the root of all successful efforts.*
> – James Allen

the other. But it would now be God who orchestrated a series of events that would ultimately lead me to the "great decision." The Bible is so true when it states, *"a double minded man is unstable in all his ways"* (James 1:8, KJV).

It started with a chance encounter with a fellow church member one Sabbath morning in the church foyer right before the worship service began. I had arrived at church late that morning, late for my Sabbath School class… but just in time for the worship service. One of the Sabbath School teachers, who shall remain anonymous, approached me as she saw me entering the church. "Marlon," she began, "I'd like to talk to you." We stepped off to the side of the main entrance, out of the way of traffic coming in and out of the church.

She said, "Marlon, I hear that you're thinking about going into the ministry. Is that true?" "Yeah, it's true," I responded.

In my mind, I wondered how she knew that I was thinking about this. After all, I had taken painstaking efforts not to reveal the true nature of my feelings about this. It was bad enough that I was struggling between law and ministry, with giving up the prospect of money, power, and influence that I thought I could have with a career in law, only to enter into a vocation that on the other hand was pulling heavily on my heart strings. But I just didn't see how I could possibly make the kind of money I felt was a measure of success, by being a minister, and therefore that alone made it much less appealing to me. This struggle was causing me great mental anguish. Plus, the prospect of being a high-powered lawyer "appeared" to be much more appealing also to everyone who knew me—my classmates, my friends, my fellow church members, and my family…especially Daddy. And, at that time, I was still very protective of my "image" and my reputation as a smart young man who had his head on straight.

Now, here was this church lady asking me a personal question about this matter. It caught me off guard. How could she have known about this? I would later reason that perhaps it had gotten out to the congregation that Pastor Hill had taken me to visit the seminary. To my dismay, she continued. "You know, Marlon, you've started a good career path in law at Rhodes, which is a good school. You really should be careful about jumping career tracks at this point in your life. If you do that, you might find it more difficult to switch again further down the road should you change your mind. I'm not telling you that you shouldn't go into the ministry, but I do think you should think twice about leaving law at this time. Pray about it, Ok?" she said with a serious look on her face. Having spoken her mind, she turned and walked away…leaving me stunned and speechless.

> *A person is never what he ought to be until he is doing what he ought to be doing.*
> – Author unknown

So I contemplated what I'd just heard. I thought, "*So… you're not telling me that I shouldn't go into the ministry, but you're also telling me that I shouldn't change career paths either, right?*" To me, this was double-speak for "Marlon, don't go into the ministry!" As if I had not already been secretive enough about my feelings, now I really became like a turtle and withdrew deeper into myself. The inner turmoil and self-doubt which I felt worsened after this experience.

You see, the only personal reference I had for the ministry, outside of Dr. King, was my own pastor, Pastor Hill. Whenever I thought about the life of a pastor on a personal level, I always thought about Pastor and Mrs. Hill.

I really held them and their two young children, Mian and Sonia, in high regard. Pastor Hill was a humble man, a good preacher, and a good pastor. His wife Susie was very clearly supportive of his ministry in the church. They were really kind to their parishioners, and although we hadn't developed a close relationship at that time, I was becoming increasingly comfortable with talking to Pastor Hill about becoming a minister.

Outside of these qualities, however, there was nothing materially-speaking that I found enviable about them. They were simple people. Their mode of dress was always neat and orderly, but not flashy. They lived in a nice but simple home, in a nice but simple neighborhood, and had nice, but simple lifestyles. There was nothing about their lifestyles that shouted "Hey, look at me. I'm important and I've got money and I AM SOMEBODY TO BE RECKONED WITH!" Although I wasn't the type that would talk about my smarts or wealth, I certainly wanted a *lifestyle* that would do the talking for me! Two problems persisted with me about ministry: I couldn't *see* where a career in ministry would take me, and I felt pretty sure that I couldn't make the kind of money I wanted to make if I became a minister. The two problems, however, definitely had a common denominator: *fear*.

> *The only failure a man ought to fear is the failure in cleaving to the purpose he sees to be best.*
> – George Elliott

Facing Fear

For the next several weeks, this fear intensified as I felt myself thinking more about ministry and less about the law. Oh, I tried to keep up the front about law school, but that's all it was—a mask. I found myself reading my Bible more, paying attention in church more (rather than wishing that the worship service would hurry up and end so that I could go out to eat with my friends), and wanting to attend other worship services, like the mid-week prayer meeting service. My spiritual life was growing, and were it not for fear, my spiritual growth would have completely crowded out my long-cherished hope for a career in law. But fear put up a valiant fight—until it confronted Madea one Saturday night.

This second event orchestrated by God started off rather mildly. That Saturday evening I was driving Madea home from church. As I listened to her talk about the day, my mind wandered off to my inner turmoil. The feelings were welling up inside me as if a volcano was getting ready to erupt. Finally, I interrupted Madea, telling her that I needed to talk to her about something.

By now, she already knew that I had been thinking about the ministry. She knew that Pastor Hill had taken me to visit the seminary and I had shared my happiness about this visit with her when I returned. But beyond that, I really hadn't opened up to her much about what I was really feeling inside. I didn't know if she had noticed that I was taking more and more of an interest in spiritual things, like wanting to get more involved in activities in the church or crawling up in bed on Saturday nights and reading devotional books. Before this time, Saturday nights had been the only night of the week that I could hang out with my friends because I was in school the rest of the week. We would either go out to eat or go to a movie or some other social event.

Now, I just wasn't as anxious to do those things on a Saturday night. A peace I had never known was coming over my life. I felt that I was becoming more "settled" in my ways. Although I had to wake up at 5 or 5:30 a.m. every Sunday morning to go to work at Federal Express, I was now looking forward to the 25-minute drive

> *Trust in the Lord with all your heart and lean not on your own understanding; in all your ways acknowledge him, and he will make your paths straight.*
> – Proverbs 3:5-6, NIV

from our apartment in north Memphis to the Federal Express hub in south Memphis. I still have warm memories of driving down Interstate 240 those Sunday mornings, watching the sunrise burn a crisp burnt-orange color across the horizon as the soft, melodious hum of Christian music played gently through the radio. Yes, these were moments that I felt that God spoke into my spirit, and I learned that God's ways "*...are ways of pleasantness, and all [His] paths are peace*" (Proverbs 3:17).

"Madea," I began, "I'm really struggling with something..." "What's that son?" she replied. My mood was subdued as I stared out at the dark road ahead of us, my right hand on the steering wheel and my left arm perched on the door with my left hand propping up my chin. The light chatter that had been taking place between us now came to an abrupt end. I struggled to find the words to begin. After a few moments of silence, Madea urged, "Go ahead son, tell me what's troubling you." Slowly, I responded, "Madea, I'm afraid...I'm afraid of going into the ministry." After a little more silence,

I continued: "I'm afraid of going into the ministry because I can't *see* where it is going to lead me. I'm so used to setting goals for myself and being able to *see* the path ahead of me. With ministry, I can't see it, and I feel I have no control over where it will take me. I'm also afraid that there's not much money in it. How am I going to pay off the student loans I already have *and* the money I would have to borrow to go to seminary? I'm afraid Madea. I'm really afraid." Tears began to well up in my eyes, revealing the mental anguish that had held me captive for so long.

Madea Weighs In

I had somehow hoped that at that moment she would have taken my hand gently, and spoken soft, reassuring words to me. That was not to be the case. The mention of the word "fear" triggered something fierce in her. She began by quoting scripture: *"God hath not given us the spirit of fear; but of power, and of love, and of a sound mind"* (II Timothy 1:7). *"There is no fear in love; but perfect love casteth out fear: **because fear hath torment**. He that feareth is not made perfect in love"* (I John 4:18). She rattled off these verses as she had so many times before when talking about fear.

She said, "Fear is a tool of the Devil, son. You *can't* let fear keep you from doing what God is telling you to do. When I l left your daddy, I was afraid. Sure I was. I had a teenage daughter and

> *The man without a purpose is like a ship without a rudder – a waif, a nothing, a no man.*
> – Thomas Carlyle

two small boys to take care of. I didn't have any education or a job and we were going to a place we had never lived before." She went on to recount her experience of when we arrived in Elizabethtown, KY, fourteen years earlier. She talked about how the Devil had tried to make her afraid enough to want to turn around and go back to Memphis, back to Daddy. She also talked about our move back to Memphis a year later, of how once again she didn't know how she was going to make a living for her herself and her children.

"God has been with me all the way, son. You have to trust Him!" Madea pointed her finger as if she were preaching to a congregation, thundering at me just as she had some sixteen years earlier when she had accidentally driven over my shiny red fire truck after I had parked it behind her car. Rather than be shocked by her strong words, I understood the true feelings beneath her rough exterior. In her own way, she was showing me love…tough love, which made me cry more. I needed that cry. Someone has well said that "tears are the detergent of the soul," and my soul desperately needed a deep cleansing at that moment.

Softening her tone, Madea continued. "Marlon, God loves you, and so do I. If He's calling you into the ministry, you have to trust Him. If anybody has to trust the Lord it has to be a minister. Fear not, son, God *will* take care of you." With that, she spoke a few more encouraging words, and at that moment, I felt as if a big weight had been lifted from my spirit.

Madea's "tough talk" and reassurance that evening carried me for several more months, until early spring of 1990. Although by then I was completely convinced that becoming a minister was where I needed to be, I still hadn't yet applied to the seminary. Oddly enough, I was still holding back, trying to convince myself that I was making the right choice. By now, I had pretty much given up the idea of going to law school. *But if I didn't commit to going to seminary, what was I going to do now? Graduation would take place in just a few months, and I really needed to have a definite idea of what I was going to do afterwards.* God would now orchestrate one more dramatic event that would finally settle all my indecisiveness.

> *There is no road to success but through a clear strong purpose. Nothing can take its place. A purpose underlies character, culture, position, attainment of every part.*
> – Thornton T. Munger

The Struggle Ends

This event, like the previous two, happened on a Sabbath. I arrived late to church and Sabbath School had already begun. Rather than go to my class, which was in the sanctuary, I decided to slip into the new member class taught by Pastor Hill in the church library, which was right off the foyer. The class, as usual, was packed, so I slipped into a seat on the back row. Pastor Hill was already teaching. Sitting on that back row, I watched him with intense interest. All of a sudden, the Holy Spirit came over me.

As I watched Pastor Hill standing before the class teaching, I envisioned myself doing the same thing. I saw myself standing before a group of people, teaching the Bible just as Pastor Hill was doing right now. Then, I heard the Holy Spirit begin speaking to me in soft, encouraging ways…as if to say, *"Don't worry, it's going to be alright. You don't have to be afraid to go into the ministry. Don't worry about how you're going to make it financially. I am leading in your life. Everything is going to be fine. I will be with you."*

These words kept playing in my mind over and over and over again. Inside, I was overcome with emotion. The presence of the Lord upon me was overwhelming. As I watched Pastor Hill, dressed in his nice but simple suit, I felt as if the Holy Spirit was washing away all of the materialistic stereotypes I had built up in my mind concerning the lifestyle I wanted to live. At that moment, I didn't care about making a name for myself. I didn't care about making a lot of money or having a lot of power. All I knew was that I was tired of fighting, tired of swinging back and forth between two worlds, one materialistic and the other spiritual…and I was tired of keeping up the perception that I was going to law school, as if somehow that was the more "respectable" career to choose over ministry. In those few moments, the Lord had completely worn me down, not by a relentless badgering of my conscience, but by a gentle wooing of the Holy Spirit, as if to say, *"Come Marlon, take me by the hand, and walk with Me."*

> *Blessed are the single-hearted, for they shall enjoy much peace. If you refuse to be hurried or pressed, if you stay your soul on God, nothing can keep you from that clearness of spirit which is life and peace. In that stillness you will know what His will is.*
>
> – Amy Carmichael

The battle inside of me was over! I was *ready* to give in and trust God; I now *wanted* to take the journey of faith with Him.

Daddy's Encouragement

As hard as I tried to fight them back, tears began to well up in my eyes. Finally, the class was over and I was the first one out of the room, standing just outside the library door as the others left the class. I kept my head down, trying not to let anyone see me cry. Amazingly, no one came up to me. At that moment, Daddy walked into the church. Immediately, we made eye contact. He smiled momentarily, until he saw the tears coming down my face. He quickly walked over to me. With a tense look on his face he asked, "Son, what's wrong?" Thoughts raced through my mind faster than I could find the words to express them. "Can we talk, Daddy?" "Sure we can, son," Daddy replied, his tense look signaling that his concern was growing by the second. "Let's go and sit in your car and talk," I said.

Together we walked, side by side, father and son, out of the church into the bright sunshine outside. Daddy has always had a tender spot in his heart for his children, especially when he sensed one of them was in danger. I knew that he was deeply concerned about what was wrong with me at this moment, and I knew that now was the time for me to finally open up to him about the turmoil that had been going on inside my heart.

We climbed into his car. Daddy could easily get high-strung, especially when he sensed danger or felt threatened. Now remember…Daddy had grown up on the streets of inner city Memphis. He understood better than most the importance of being "ready" when danger approached because it could mean the difference between life and death. Although he was obviously concerned, he was now calm. He looked at me and softly asked, "Son, what's wrong? Tell Daddy what's wrong." I was emotionally full to overflowing. At that moment, I so badly wanted to shout out "Daddy, I'm *not* going to law school! Please stop telling your friends and our family members

> *Your fulfillment in life is dependent on your becoming and doing what you were born to be and do.*
> – Dr. Myles Munroe

that I'm going to be a lawyer. I'm not! I've been fighting it a long time, but I feel like I'm being called into the ministry. I'm going to be a pastor!"

That's what I *wanted* to say, but that's not what I said. I felt that if I did say those things to him, they would come across as disrespectful, and as frustrated as I was at the time, the last thing I wanted to do was to disrespect Daddy. I couldn't find the words to say what I really wanted to say, so all I could say to him, over and over again, was "Daddy, I just want to do God's Will. I just want to do God's will!" This was all I could say to him: "*I just want to do God's Will*." After repeating this seemingly endless line, we both sat silently for a few moments. Then I felt more confident to try to explain my feelings further. "Daddy, I feel like I'm being called into the ministry. I'm so tired right now…so tired. I've been fighting it for a long time, and I'm tired of fighting it. I know you want me to go into law, but that's not what I'm being called to do. I'm being called to be a pastor."

As I said this, tears welled up in my eyes again. The atmosphere in

Daddy's car was solemn and subdued. I believe God was in that car! Then Daddy smiled, put his arms around my shoulder and pulled me closer to him. "Son, don't worry. I understand. I don't want you to feel any pressure from me. *Whatever* you decide to do I will support you. I love you, son." Daddy shed a tear as well, but for different reasons. Years later, when he and I recounted this experience, he told me what he had really been feeling. When he walked into church that morning and saw me crying, he immediately thought someone had spoken a cross word to me or had done something to hurt my feelings. Instantly, he was angry and ready to go to war. He was waiting for me to tell him who had done it, and he was ready to confront whoever had done it.

When he realized, however, that my tears were not over hurt feelings but over a worn-out and conflicted conscience, his entire demeanor changed. When he saw that the Hand of God was upon me, and the forces, the *spiritual* forces, that were drawing me into the ministry were much bigger than any idea he

> *Words have an awesome impact The impression made by a father's voice can set in motion an entire trend of life.*
> – Gordon MacDonald

had relished of me going into law, he too gave in. What's more, he was relieved to know that nothing bad had happened to his son, that my tears were not tears of pain but tears of joy. At that moment, I felt in my heart that Daddy had finally released me from his expectations. We hugged each other again, and Daddy kissed me on my forehead. It felt so good to have his acceptance of my choice. It was with lighter hearts that we both walked back into church that day.

Like Dr. King, I had a summons upon my life, and I answered Destiny's call. Through this experience, I was developing a "listening heart" to the voice of God as well as sharpening my spiritual eyesight. God sometimes communicates "audibly" by placing thoughts upon the mind, as if He were speaking in a *"still small voice"* (I Kings 19:12). At other times, he communicates through visions, flashes of thought, or even dreams. *"For God speaks in one way, and in two, though man does not perceive it. In a dream, in a vision of the night, when deep sleep falls on men, while they slumber on their beds, then he opens the ears of men…"* (Job 33:14-16, ESV).

God Speaks...Are You Listening?

As you reflect on this chapter, perhaps you have heard the "Voice" of God speaking to your heart about your life's purpose. God makes known to us His purposes for our lives. He *"opens the ears of men,"* and He will speak directly *to* you. He may speak through a book, a sermon, a conversation, or even through "a *vision of the night"*; whatever method He uses, His message will be clear: *"For I know the plans I have for you,"* declares the LORD, *"plans to prosper you and not to harm you, plans to give you hope and a future"* (Jeremiah 29:11, NIV). God is speaking your destiny into you. Are you listening...and answering?

Then, some may say, "I have developed a listener's heart; I know that God speaks to me. But how do I know that what I'm hearing is actually His Will and not my own. In other words, how do I *know* what God's Will is for my life?" For those with such questions, I'd like to offer three ways that I think one can *know* God's Will on almost anything.

> *Bring me men to match my mountains: Bring me men to match my plains: Men with empires in their purpose and new eras in their brains.*
>
> – Sam Walter Foss

1. Develop A General Knowledge of the Bible. I have often said that I take great delight in the fact that there is nothing—no experience or circumstance—that I will ever face in life for which there is not some counsel in the Bible that can speak directly to that experience or circumstance. *"Your word is a lamp to my feet and a light to my path."* (Psalm 119:105, ESV). *"The unfolding of your words gives light; it imparts understanding to the simple"* (Psalm 119:130). God's counsel *never* deviates from either the precept or principle of His Word—the Bible. The more you read and become familiar with various passages of the Bible, the sharper your "ear" will become to the Voice of God. The Bible, therefore, should be the chief reference book for your life!

2. Develop Your Discernment Skills. God, through the Holy Spirit, makes impressions upon our minds. These impressions become our *sixth sense.* Our sixth sense is not mere intuition—it is *discernment.* Discernment is to our ability to make sound judgments what 3D is to television viewing: it adds *depth.* Random House Dictionary defines discernment/insight as the ability to see into "inner character or comprehend underlying truth." Dr. John MacArthur, author/speaker for the television ministry *Grace to You*, offers this further observation: "In its simplest definition, discernment is nothing more than the ability to decide between truth and error, right and wrong. Discernment is the process of making careful distinctions in our thinking about truth. In other words, the ability to think with discernment is synonymous with an ability to think *biblically*." If you're wanting to know what God's Will is for your life, then develop your knowledge of the Bible, and in developing your knowledge of the Bible you will also develop your spiritual eyesight, which is discernment. Reading your Bible will help you "hear" God's Word: *"So faith comes from hearing, and hearing through the word of Christ"* (Romans 10:17, ESV). Discernment will help you to "see" God's Word as it is applied in various life situations. Let me explain further.

> *It is through faith that the impossible becomes a reality.*
> – Pastor Edward Harden

Can You 'See' It?

When God sent Moses to Pharoah to declare that Pharoah should release the children of Israel from bondage, Moses was reluctant. Simply put, he was afraid. He was going before a visible king—arguably the most powerful figure on the planet at that time—with a solemn command from an *invisible* King. Listen to God's counsel to Moses, as recorded in Exodus 7:1-2, ESV: *"And the LORD said to Moses, "See, I have made you like God to Pharoah, and your brother Aaron shall be your prophet. You shall speak all that I command you, and your brother Aaron shall tell Pharaoh to let the people of Israel go out of his land."* Notice, again, verse 1: *"See, I have made you like God to Pharoah…".* The original Hebrew word used for "God" in this phrase is the word "Elohim." Elohim refers to the Godhead—God the Father, God the Son, and God the Holy Spirit. In essence, God was telling Moses not to be afraid because He wanted Moses to "see" that when he went before Pharoah, Moses would be—if we are to read the Hebrew text literally—*as God (Elohim) Himself!* Moses would have all of God's power and authority at his disposal, so long as he remained on God's errand. How was Moses to "see" this? Would God literally transform him into a head of state, a king himself? No, not literally. Through the spiritual eye of discernment God wanted Moses to understand (*believe*) that as God's servant his power and authority would be far superior than that of Pharoah. This reality is what God impressed upon the mind of Moses. God is still seeking to make such impressions upon the minds of His servants today!

3. *Put God to the Test.* God responds to the heart cries of His people. *"Call to Me, and I will answer you, and show you great and mighty things, which you do not know"* (Jeremiah 33:3, NKJV).[14] One of the surest ways you can know God's Will is through His *providential acts.* God acts on our behalf, and sometimes exactly according to the way we request. This is not to suggest that God only gives us what we want or desire; this certainly is not true, no truer than the fact that a good parent doesn't always give his or her child exactly what they ask for. But, on occasion, a good parent *does* give his or her child *exactly* what they ask for simply because they *do* love them. And in doing so, that parent is helping to build confidence, security, appreciation, and *trust* in the heart of their child. Plus, as any good parent also knows, it always feels good to hear their child say with excitement, "Thanks Mom/ Dad. I love you!" I know that I do.

Passing the Test

One of the best stories found in the Bible about putting God to the test is the story of Gideon in Judges 6. In Gideon's day, God's people, the nation of Israel, had turned away from observing His commandments and statutes and had been turned to idol worship. Gideon's own father, Joash, had erected an altar of worship to the pagan god Baal. So steeped in rebellion had God's chosen people become that God withdrew His Hand of protection from them and gave them over to persecution by their enemies, the Midianites: *"The people of Israel did what was evil in the sight of the LORD, and the LORD gave them into the hand of Midian seven years. And the hand of Midian overpowered Israel, and because of Midian the people of Israel made for themselves the dens that are in the mountains and the caves and the strongholds"* (Judges 6:1-2, ESV). God had a plan, however, for the deliverance of His people, and Gideon would play a crucial role in that deliverance:

> *"[11] Now the angel of the LORD came and sat under the terebinth at Ophrah, which belonged to Joash the Abiezrite, while his son Gideon was beating out wheat in the winepress to hide it from the Midianites.*

*¹² And the angel of the L<small>ORD</small> appeared to him and said to
him, "The L<small>ORD</small> is with you, O mighty man of valor."*

*¹³ And Gideon said to him, "Please, sir, if the L<small>ORD</small> is with us, why then
has all this happened to us? And where are all his wonderful deeds that our
fathers recounted to us, saying, 'Did not the L<small>ORD</small> bring us up from Egypt?'
But now the L<small>ORD</small> has forsaken us and given us into the hand of Midian."*

*¹⁴ And the L<small>ORD</small> turned to him and said, "Go in this might of yours
and save Israel from the hand of Midian; do not I send you?"*

*¹⁵ And he said to him, "Please, Lord, how can I save Israel? Behold, my
clan is the weakest in Manasseh, and I am the least in my father's house."*

*¹⁶ And the L<small>ORD</small> said to him, "But I will be with you, and you shall
strike the Midianites as one man."* (Judges 6:11-16, ESV)

A divine summons had been placed on Gideon's life. Destiny was calling!
Gideon's response, one of fear and extreme caution, reflects what many
often do in the face of a seemingly overwhelming summons from God.
Perhaps you have been in Gideon's shoes, sensing a Divine call upon your
life to do something that goes beyond your wildest imagination. How have
you answered Destiny's call in your life? Or are you still reeling from the
magnitude of God's request?

Gideon, despite his father's backslidden ways, had been raised with a
knowledge of God and His commandments. Gideon had trained his ear
to be sensitive to the voice of God in his life. When the angel of the Lord
suddenly appeared before him, Gideon discerned that this was the voice of
God speaking to him and not some demonic apparition. But now, when
faced with a task that in his human comprehension seemed impossible,
Gideon wanted further assurance that God was indeed calling him to lead
His people out from under the oppression of the Midianites. Gideon wanted
to *know* that this was God's Will:

*"³⁶ Then Gideon said to God, 'If you will save
Israel by my hand, as you have said,*

³⁷ behold, I am laying a fleece of wool on the threshing floor. If there is dew on the fleece alone, and it is dry on all the ground, then I shall know that you will save Israel by my hand, as you have said.'

³⁸ And it was so. When he rose early next morning and squeezed the fleece, he wrung enough dew from the fleece to fill a bowl with water.

Reflecting on this experience, one commentator wrote: "But now a doubt arose, since wool naturally absorbs moisture when there is any in the air; the test might not be decisive. Hence he asked that the sign be reversed, pleading that his extreme caution might not displease the Lord."[15]

³⁹ Then Gideon said to God, 'Let not your anger burn against me; let me speak just once more. Please let me test just once more with the fleece. Please let it be dry on the fleece only, and on all the ground let there be dew.'

⁴⁰ And God did so that night; and it was dry on the fleece only, and on all the ground there was dew.

Gideon had put God to a specific test, a test that only God Himself could pass because the request that Gideon made was not humanly impossible. Yes, there are times when we can put God to such tests and have full confidence that God will, without a doubt, make His Will known. *"For the Lord loves justice; he will not forsake his saints"* (Psalm 37:28, ESV).

Destiny Called – I Answered

> *When you discover your mission, you will feel its demand. It will fill you with enthusiasm and a burning desire to get to work on it.*
> – W. Clement Stone

Driving home from church that evening, I reflected back over the day's events, over the past year and all the emotional turmoil I had experienced. Then, I went back further. I reflected back on all those years since junior high school when I first felt the tug of destiny upon my heart and mind, when I first felt convicted that my life had a great purpose. The realization came to me, at that moment, that I had finally come to understand what my life's purpose would be. I had found it! A deep and abiding peace swept over me.

For the first time in a long time I was completely at peace with who I was... and who I would become. It was the ending of one life-altering experience, and the beginning of another.

Years later, I asked my brother Chris to reflect back on this period in my life and share with me what he had observed taking place in me during this time. As I've said earlier, I was very private about the spiritual matters which were stirring in my heart, so private that I did not share them with my own brother whose bedroom in our apartment home was next door to mine. My senior year in college was Chris's junior year at Christian Brothers College. In the following moving and insightful letter, he shared his thoughts for me in a way that let me know that despite my lack of communication with him about my feelings at the time, he was still sensitive to the changes I was going through. His sensitivity is reflective of the deep emotional bond we shared as brothers.

> Going into the ministry did not seem out of character for you. While in college, even though you majored in political science, it did not seem as if you were as ambitious as I was in succeeding in the material world. As I saw you contemplating the ministry, I was curious; however, at that time my attention was primarily focused on me and problems I had...
>
> Overall, what stood out for me, the most, was that I remember seeing a change come over you. I saw Jesus prick [your] hardened heart and bring it into submission to Him. Again, you had a short temper at times and lacked a great deal of patience and tolerance. We all have our deficiencies, but when the Holy Spirit speaks to our heart and conversion takes place, the change becomes as distinct and clear as noonday from midnight. For you, the change was a much more forbearing attitude and a willingness to learn about spiritual matters. Also, you became a lot less easily provoked. I am glad that you are a pastor, because, *"Thus says the Lord: "Let not the wise man boast in his wisdom, let not the mighty man boast in his might, let not the rich man boast in his riches, 24 but let him who boasts boast in this, that he understands and knows me, that I am the Lord who practices steadfast love,*

justice, and righteousness in the earth. For in these things I delight, declares the Lord" (Jeremiah 9:23-24, ESV).

With all of the wisdom, prudence and exactness that you displayed during your formative years, it is no surprise to me that you responded to the Lord's call. As I have known all my life, true greatness begins with the fear of the Lord. I have learned *"that the way of man is not in himself, that it is not in man who walks to direct his steps"* (Jeremiah 10:23, ESV). Fortunately, you came to that realization also.

Yes, fortunately I did indeed.

8

From Acorn to Acorn: the Anatomy of Purpose

"Except the Lord build the house, they labor
in vain that build it..."
–Psalm 127:1

Coming to peace with my life's purpose proved to be a major turning point for me. I had been at a crossroads during my senior year in college. I was nearing the end of my collegiate career and although I thought I knew what I wanted to do after graduation, the reality was that I didn't have a clue. I was lost...career-wise, as well as spiritually.

Since that period in my life, I have said that God saved me in two ways my senior year...He saved me from myself, career-wise, and He saved me spiritually. Not only did I experience a calling into the ministry, but I felt the call of God to surrender my life to Him spiritually. I was re-baptized at my home church, and for the past twenty-five years it has been my unbridled joy to proclaim publically my salvation in Jesus Christ. I will forever be grateful to God for intervening at a pivotal point in my young life and giving me the firm conviction about the direction and purpose of my life. Praise His holy name!

Carlyle B. Haynes, in his book *God Sent A Man*, a narrative on the life of the biblical character Joseph, captures the importance of a young person having a clear sense of purpose in life. He writes,

"It is a good thing for any youth to discover *what he is fit for, what his life is to be, what he is in the world to accomplish,* and to acquire a sense of *mission*. If, in addition to his own groping impressions about it, he is fortunate enough to have come to him the realization that what he is to do with his life is what *God has appointed for him*, and is fitting him to do, he is doubly blessed. He can then settle down to his work with a comforting sense of solid assurance, and patiently carry on each day, awaiting God's time for the accomplishment of God's purposes and designs.

Such a discovery saves a man much fretting and disappointment and waste of time—to come early in life to an understanding of what he is to do, what it is he is fitted to accomplish, and exactly what work he is to be about. If he can so analyze his personal gifts and station in life—see with unclouded vision the circumstances, the conditions, and the complications that belong to and surround him in his associations and relations to others, or to the world—and learn to *discern the will of God as it teaches him what he is and for what he ought to live*, he will indeed have taken a great step forward."[16]

Taking "a great step forward" is exactly what I was doing when, on a bright Sunday morning in June 1990, three weeks after graduating from Rhodes College, Madea and I crammed into my little white Ford Festiva and headed for Andrews University Theological Seminary. All my earthly belongings were packed into that little car, and I would be leaving home for good. My journey into young adulthood was officially launched that day and I wanted Madea, my mother

> *Efforts and courage are not enough without purpose and direction.*
> – John F. Kennedy

as well as my spiritual guide, to be with me on the start of the journey. By now, all of my family and friends knew that I would be leaving home to take up ministerial studies. Much to my surprise, when I finally had opened up about my decision to all my friends, they weren't shocked at all…in fact they said they could really see me as a Pastor and gave me their complete support. Tyrone, Anthony, Orlandus and I, along with a few more friends of ours, had gone out for one last celebratory dinner before I left.

And then there was Chris. That Sunday proved to be bittersweet for him.

He and I hugged and said our good-byes, and of course he, Madea, and I had prayer in our living room before Madea and I left. My Aunt Betty, one of Madea's sisters, lived in an apartment downstairs from ours. Before leaving, I had gone down to kiss her good-bye. She had decided to stay in bed a little longer that morning and told me that she wasn't feeling well. Tragically, Madea and I would find out a day later that Aunt Betty had collapsed in the living room of her apartment on Sunday afternoon, and she would take her last breath as Chris held her head in his arms, desperately trying to revive her. Like Madea's mother and another one of Madea's sisters, Aunt Betty had died of a massive heart attack. Strangely, all of them died at age 57.

The 'Secret' of Success

I had saved enough money to purchase Madea a one-way plane ticket back to Memphis, and all I had left over was $150 cash. That was it! That would be enough money to pay for gas and food along the way. Andrews University had

> *The secret of success is constancy to purpose.*
> – Benjamin Disraeli

made it clear that I needed $2,000 to register for classes. But I didn't have $2,000, nor money for any other expenses after I arrived in Michigan. I had resolved in my mind, though, that God would simply have to provide for these needs. And He did – thanks to student loans! Madea and I arrived on the campus at 2 a.m. Monday morning, and by 9 a.m. I had registered for summer classes...without a glitch. Eight months later, I would be blessed by God yet again.

It was on a cold February evening in the school cafeteria that I would meet a stunningly beautiful girl named Shurla, from the island of Bermuda. Shurla had already received an undergraduate degree from an all-female university in Canada, but had felt that her degree hadn't truly satisfied her vocational yearnings. Interestingly, she felt impressed to go *back* to school, so she enrolled at Andrews to pursue a nursing degree.

Of all the potential suitors she could have imagined for herself, she never dreamed that she would fall in love with a *minister.* (Nor had I ever dreamed that I would marry someone from another country!) But fall in love we did, and two years later we were married in Bermuda. In June 1993, I graduated with a Master of Divinity from Andrews, and Shurla and I moved to Seattle,

WA, where I would begin my pastorate as the Associate Pastor of the Emerald City Community Seventh-day Adventist Church. We had agreed that Shurla would finish her degree after our move, which she did.

Twenty-five years later, Shurla and I are now blessed with two young adult children, a son, Marlon Jr., and a daughter, Reba. We've lived in the Pacific Northwest of the United States, the Midwest, and now Texas. Our ministry has been rich and varied, and as is often the case for most pastoral families, our lives have had their share of indescribable joys as well as inexpressible sorrows. As Madea was fond of saying, "When you get to Heaven, God is not going to look you over for how many stars you have in your crown, but [rather] how many battle scars you have gotten along the way." Just as a rose stem has it thorns, such is the ironic beauty of a purpose-full life!

Wait, There's More...

In discovering my life's purpose, I've learned some other things about purpose that I want to unfold over the remaining chapters of this book. At this point in our journey, though, I think it's important that we pause and reflect over what I call the "anatomy" of purpose. In other words, I now want to focus specifically on *how* purpose is developed in one's life.

Discovering and developing your life's calling, or *central purpose*, can be illustrated by the growth of a tree. First, you have…

The "Acorn, or Seed"

Luke 8[17] records one of the parables of Jesus, the parable of the farmer:

"Soon after this, Jesus was going through towns and villages, telling the good news about God's kingdom. His twelve apostles were with him…(vs. 1)

When a large crowd from several towns had gathered around Jesus, he told them this story: (vs. 4)

*'A farmer went out to scatter seed in a field. While the
farmer was doing it, some of the seeds fell along the road
and were stepped on or eaten by birds. (vs. 5)*

*Other seeds fell on rocky ground and started growing. But the
plants did not have enough water and soon dried up. (vs. 6)*

*Some seed fell among thorny weeds. This seed grew, but later
the weeds choked the good* plants *Some other seeds fell where*
thornbushes grew up and choked the plants. (vs. 7)

*The rest of the seeds fell on good ground where they grew and
produced a hundred times as many seeds.' When Jesus had finished
speaking, he said, 'If you have ears, pay attention!'" (vs. 8)*

Jesus' disciples asked him what the story meant." (vs. 9)

The Interpretation

*"So he answered: 'I have explained the secrets about God's kingdom
to you, but for others I can only use stories. These people look, but they
don't see, and they hear, but they don't understand.'" (vs. 10)*

This is what the story means: The seed is God's message, (vs. 11)

*and the seeds that fell along the road are the people who hear the
message. But the devil comes and snatches the message out of their
hearts, so that they will not believe and be saved. (vs. 12)*

*The seeds that fell on rocky ground are the people who gladly hear the
message and accept it. But they don't have deep roots, and they believe
only for a little while. As soon as life gets hard, they give up. (vs. 13)*

*The seeds that fell among the thornbushes are also people
who hear the message. But they are so eager for riches and
pleasures that they never produce anything. (vs. 14)*

166

*Those seeds that fell on good ground are the people who
listen to the message and keep it in good and honest
hearts. They last and produce a harvest." (vs. 15)*

The 'Planter'

God plants a "seed" in your heart and mind concerning His calling
and purpose for your life… *"For I know the plans I have for you, declares the
Lord, plans to prosper you and not to harm you, plans to give you hope and a
future"* (Jeremiah 29:11, NIV). As mentioned earlier, He may speak
through a book, a sermon, a conversation, or a life experience. Whatever
method He uses, His message will be clear. The "message" that God
implants into your heart and mind is the *seedling* to your life's purpose.
Treat this seedling as if it were as precious as life itself, because it is…it is
vital to your spiritual and emotional well-being.

I believe that the human quest to find purpose in life is so strong that
it can lead one to attempt almost any feat in its pursuit, and when one fails
to attain it, the consequences can sometimes be deadly. Some people find
themselves living a "slow death" when they have never realized any purpose
or direction for their lives.

> *Be not simply good; be good
> for something.*
> – Henry David Thoreau

In *The Brothers Karamazov* series,
a fictional classic written by the
nineteenth-century Russian philosopher
Fyodor Dostoevsky, the Grand Inquisitor
gives this sobering assessment about the importance of understanding one's
life purpose: "For the secret of man's being is not only to live, but to have
something to live *for*. Without a stable conception of the object of life,
man would not consent to go on living, and would rather destroy himself
than remain on earth…"[18] In other words, life lived aimlessly is simply not
enough for most of us.

Just as important as the seedling itself is the soil into which the seedling
is planted. As Jesus explains in His parable, the "seed" is the Word of the
God; the "soil" into which the seed falls is the human heart. As you ponder
the deep significance and spiritual application of this parable, you will want
to ask yourself the questions: *"What is the **condition** of my heart? Am I
receptive to the counsel of God's Word for my life and its purpose?"* This leads
to the next stage in development of the tree –

The "Root System"

In Colossians 2:6, the Apostle Paul comments, "*Therefore, as you received Christ Jesus the Lord, so walk in him, **rooted** and built up in him and **established** in the faith, just as you were taught, abounding in thanksgiving.*" Just as the acorn, or seed, first develops a root system by which to grow, so must we be "rooted" in Jesus Christ. God's word is a revelation of Himself. He is the One who created you and designed you for specific purposes. It is *only* in knowing Him—being "rooted" and "established" in Him—that we can successfully pursue our life's calling. Life is full of uncertainty, and we will have experiences that will test our understanding of anything that is real or true, even our own existence. Therefore, we must understand that our life's purpose is not an *end in itself*, but rather a by-product of a life that is firmly grounded in God's [living] Word – Jesus Christ.

In 2004 I, along with my sisters Marsha and Madeleine, my brother Michael, and my good friend Dennis Baptiste, a CPA, formed a non-profit ministry called Purpose-Full Ministries. Like my current ministry, Purpose-Full Pursuits LLC, PFM was dedicated to encouraging and equipping individuals to discover and pursue their God-given purpose in life.

> *Character is like the foundation of a house—it is below the surface.*
>
> — Author Unknown

In developing the curriculum for our seminars, we resolved early on that our resources, although distinctly Christian-based, would not be intended for Christian audiences only. This firm resolution of ours was made with the reality in mind that there is a temptation many Christian ministries face when wanting to market their products or services to non-Christian audiences: that temptation is to "water down" or "dilute" the Christ-centered, biblical focus of their products or services in the attempt to be more attractive (so they think) to non-Christian audiences.

For a ministry like Purpose-Full Pursuits whose subject matter, purpose, is covered by a broad spectrum of philosophical viewpoints, Christian and non-Christian, the temptation can be greater because of the intense competition between viewpoints, and the respective organizations they represent, for potential customers. Sadly, even some Christian notions about God and Jesus are so broad today that many people profess to believe in God on one hand, but on the other hand they completely discredit the truth, authority, and trustworthiness of the Bible as the revealed Word of God. I think it is extremely dangerous and unconscionably unethical for me as a Christian to intentionally, or unintentionally, lead someone down a philosophical path of discovery of their life's purpose that is not Bible-based. *"Your word is a lamp to my feet and a light to my path"* (Psalm 119:105, ESV).

The "Trunk"

Dr. Myles Munroe in his book, *In Pursuit of Purpose*, writes: "Your fulfillment in life is dependent on your becoming and doing what you were born to be and do…Your purpose is the key to your life. It tells you *what* you are supposed to do and *why*."[19] Pablo Picasso, the famous painter, once wrote: "My mother said to me, 'If you become a soldier, you'll be a general; if you become a monk, you'll end up as the Pope.' Instead, I became a painter and wound up as Picasso." "Do What You Are" is a chapter title in a book written by Os Guinness, *The Call: Finding and Fulfilling the Central Purpose of Your Life*. This chapter title sums up the main idea of what I wish to get across in this section…yes, even this entire book; that is, God has a *central* purpose for your life.

When thinking of your life, of what activity or endeavor can you say, "this *one* thing I do?" In other words, out of all the things that you do in life, can you say, "this one thing is not only what I do best, but is also who *I am*"? Just as the trunk of a tree is the *singular* base of the tree, your trunk becomes the "one thing" that characterizes the vocation of your life. We call the trunk the "Big 'P'" because of its reference to your central purpose. (We'll talk about the "little 'p' " in the next section).

"In botany, trunk…refers to the main wooden axis of a tree which is an *important diagnostic feature in tree identification*…The trunk is the most important part of the tree for timber production".[20] Likewise, once you discover and pursue your life's central calling or purpose, you will not only have a clearer sense of your personal identity but you will also realize that the majority of your life's productivity will come from faithfully fulfilling your central purpose.

At this point, you may be asking yourself the question, "what is the "trunk" of my life?" For instance, are you a—

- *Homemaker*

- *Teacher*
- *Fireman*
- *Policeman or Military Member*
- *Doctor or other Medical professional*
- *Attorney*
- *Minister or Cleric*
- *Architect or Construction Worker*
- *Administrative Assistant*
- *Businessman, Businesswoman, or Politician*

These are just a few suggestions; the possibilities are numerous, especially in the twenty-first century where, because of technological advancements and the ease and mobility with which commercial activities can be transacted, one's vocational fulfillment in life (as well as wealth accumulation) is no longer limited to 'traditional' lines of work such as a doctor, lawyer, businessman, etc. Can you imagine a tree without a trunk? Sure you can...the problem is, it would no longer be a tree, it would be a *stump*! Now, imagine your life along the same lines. What is your "one thing?" Please, before you read any further, take the time to ponder (and pray over) this question. You may want to grab a pen and paper and write down your thoughts.

> *Above all be of single aim; have a legitimate and useful purpose, and devote yourself unreservedly to it.*
> – James Allen

The "Branches"

Many years ago, when I was still in seminary, I had lunch one afternoon at the home of some friends, who were married. A friend of theirs was visiting from out of town. As his wife finished preparing the lunch, the husband and I sat on the balcony of their apartment and talked with their visiting friend. Their friend began airing her frustration with her current job. She was a young professional who worked in a major city where she earned $60,000 per year.

As I listened to her, I couldn't figure out why she didn't like her job. I don't recall her saying that she had an overly demanding boss, or a hostile work environment, or was constantly working long hours; she just wasn't happy with her job—period. At the time, I was not employed in a local church; I was in graduate school where I had a full load of classes. I worked, on average, 35-40 hours per week at *two* jobs, where I only made $5.75/hr at one job (which was one of the highest-paying student jobs on campus) and $3.35/hr (the minimum wage at the time) at the other. I *drooled* over the prospect of earning $60,000 a year and I couldn't understand how a person could *not* like such a job, regardless of how unfulfilled it may have made them feel! Years later, I would find out that the same woman had gone on to work in two other unrelated professions, and she still wasn't happy with her vocation. I concluded that she just hadn't found her niche...her "trunk" in life. Like a squirrel in a tree, she was busy scurrying from "branch" to "branch."

Branches are important to a tree. In addition to giving the tree shape and definition, they also provide stems from which leaves grow. Living in Texas, I can appreciate a nice shade tree during summer when temperatures can reach in excess of 115 degrees! When considering your life's purpose, "branches" serve a God-given purpose too. The branches, or little "p's" as referred to earlier, are the opportunities, projects, or other endeavors that God brings into your life as a way of further using you for His kingdom. Like the branches of a tree, they are connected –or linked–to the "trunk" of your life (your calling or central purpose). They do *not* exist on their own. Rather, they are important for the overall *continuity* of purpose in your life.

> *No one rises so high as he who knows not whither he is going.*
> – Oliver Cromwell

Good vs. Best

When you understand your central calling in life, the "trunk" of your life, it allows you to prioritize some of the major (and not-so-major) choices, or "branches," of your life. "Recognizing that the good is ever the enemy of the best," as Charles E. Diehl once said, your calling helps you to say "no" to the good and "yes" to the best in your life. When we are intentional about choosing the opportunities which avail themselves to us– choosing *only* those that are consistent with and will only advance our *own* internal sense of calling or purpose, discarding all others– then we help to protect ourselves against the inevitable internal fragmentation that is the sure result of a life unfocused and undirected. Less fragmentation in our vocational lives equals more—

✓ *Coherence*
✓ *Congruence*
✓ *Continuity*

in our vocational lives.

One more note about the "branches" of our life's purpose: because I understand my life's central purpose or "trunk," pastoral ministry, I can better choose among the potential opportunities that may present themselves to me. For instance, I want to continue writing and publishing more books. I also want to eventually teach courses to students of various ages about discovering your God-given purpose. And I want to share my vocal talent on a wider scale by producing CDs. Although all of these endeavors could easily be the "trunk" to someone else's purpose, for me they are only branches in that they compliment my trunk—they don't *compete* with it.

> *Patience and tenacity of purpose are worth more than twice their weight of cleverness.*
> – Thomas Henry Huxley

Stuck in the Branches

Early in my ministry and in my marriage, though, I struggled with the branches. At various times, I was presented with business opportunities that I thought were attractive, lucrative, and complementary to my work as a pastor. When we started having children, I wanted to earn additional income so that Shurla could stay home and raise our children. With our household expenses, we were dependent on two incomes, and even though we made enough to take care of those expenses, we didn't have much left over. I wanted more financial flexibility in my life without feeling that I was merely "getting by." So, I decided to dabble in a few business enterprises.

With each different business opportunity, I initially felt good about it and thought that I could earn the additional income I could only dream about. Then, my conscience would begin to bother me and I would get a gnawing sensation in my stomach. I felt as if God was trying to tell me that

I wasn't doing His Will. I would try to dismiss these thoughts as nothing more than negative thinking on my part. But the troubled conscience and the gnawing sensations in my stomach would continue. I became frustrated.

"*Lord,*" I would cry out to God, "*I'm trying my best to provide for my family as I believe you would want me to. But now I feel as if you're trying to discourage me from pursuing this business opportunity. Why?*

What's wrong with it? I can earn a decent living like other people, and I won't have to struggle as much financially. Why are you trying to discourage me from doing this?

Why can't Shurla and I finally have enough money in the bank so that we can take a trip to Disney World, save up for a new home, or buy a new car like other people? Will we always have to struggle to make ends meet? You've given me the ability to know how to earn extra income but I feel as if you're holding me back. Why?"

> *To give anything less than your best is to sacrifice the gift.*
> – Steve Prefontaine, Olympic runner

I felt that God was telling me to stick to pastoral ministry and to trust Him for my family's financial well-being. Through painstaking struggles with my own fleshly desires, I had to learn to once again surrender my will to God and trust Him, even when I couldn't "see" how things would work out. Plus, God knew, as I would later come to find out, that the ministry is too important of a calling for me to confuse other people by making them question whether I was a pastor or a businessman. I'm glad that God, once again, saved me from myself.

Your "trunk" or central purpose may not be pastoral ministry like mine, but you still have to watch the "branches" of your life to make sure that they are truly connected—spiritually and philosophically—to your trunk. "*Trust in the LORD with all your heart, and do not lean on your own understanding. In all your ways acknowledge him, and he will make straight your paths*" (Proverbs 3:5-6, ESV).

The "Leaves"

Just as leaves are the natural offspring of a healthy, growing tree, so the natural offspring of a balanced, focused life is seen in its **production**—quantitatively *and* qualitatively, speaking. Our lives will bear fruit, whether for good or for bad. The difference between the two is solely determined by the quality of the lives which we live. Psalm 1:1-3 (ESV) gives us further insight into this idea:

Blessed is the man who walks not in the counsel of the wicked,
nor stands in the way of sinners,
nor sits in the seat of scoffers;
²but his delight is in the law of the LORD,
and on his law he meditates day and night.

*³ He is like a **tree***
planted by streams of water
that yields its fruit in its season,
*and its **leaf** does not wither.*
In all that he does, he prospers.

A "blessed" person is someone is who is obedient to God's Will and God's Word. This obedience equips a person to prosper and live a productive life, so much so that verse three declares that the

> *The place God calls you to is the place where your deep gladness and the world's deep hunger meet.*
> – Frederick Buechner

blessed person's "leaf" does not wither. What does this mean? It means that the productivity of our lives that is manifested as a direct result of our obedience to God's leading in our lives has benefits that will not be easily swept away by the sands of time.

In my twenty-four years of ministry, I have served as the pastor of eight different churches. I always get a tingling sensation inside of me when one of my former parishioners calls me just to let me know that they were thinking of me and wanted to, once again, praise God with me for the impact that my ministry had on their lives. I give God all of the glory because I know that any good thing my life produces is because of His love and grace being active in my life. For me, the "leaves" of my ministry produce a renewed hope and confidence in Jesus as well as personal productivity in the lives of those whom I serve and with whom I interact. This book is yet another leaf on the tree of my life. Perhaps the following story can shed even greater light on how powerfully influential the "leaves" of a purpose-full life can be:

"I'm So Happy You Didn't Sneeze!"

"On a Saturday afternoon in 1958, I sat in a Harlem department store, surrounded by hundreds of people. I was autographing copies of *Stride Toward Freedom*, my book about the Montgomery bus boycott. And while sitting there, a demented black woman came up. The only question I heard from her was, "Are you Martin Luther King?" I was looking down writing, and I said "Yes." And the next minute, I felt something sharp plunge forcefully into my chest. Before I knew it, I had been stabbed with a letter opener by a woman who would later be judged insane, Mrs. Izola Ware Curry.

Rushed by ambulance to Harlem Hospital, I lay in a bed for hours while preparations were made to remove the keen-edged knife from my body. Days later, when I was well enough to talk with Dr. Aubrey Maynard, the chief of the surgeons who performed the delicate, dangerous operation, I learned the reason for the long delay that preceded surgery. He told me that the razor tip of the instrument had been touching my aorta and that my whole chest had to be opened to extract it.

> *You must be what it is that you're seeking – that is, you need to put forth what you want to attract.*
> – Dr. Wayne Dyer

"If you had sneezed during all those hours of waiting," Dr. Maynard said, "your aorta would have been punctured and you would have drowned in your own blood." It came out in the *New York Times* the next morning that, if I had sneezed, I would have died.

About four days later, after the operation, after my chest had been opened, and the blade had been taken out, they allowed me to move around in the wheelchair in the hospital and read some of the kind letters that came from all over the States, and the world. I read a few, but one of them I will never forget. There was a letter from a young girl who was a student at the White Plains High School. It said simply,

'Dear Dr. King: I am a ninth-grade student at the White Plains High School.' She said, 'While it should not matter, I would like to mention that I am a white girl. I read in the paper of your misfortune, and of your suffering. And I read that if you had sneezed, you would have died. And I'm simply writing you to say that I'm so happy that you didn't sneeze.'"[21]

Millions of lives the world over have been impacted for the better because Dr. King didn't sneeze that fateful day!

"Reproducing" Yourself

It is a natural law in the plant and animal kingdoms, as with humans, that we produce after our own kind. As trees that grow to maturity produce acorns—**after their own kind**—so the product of a Christ-centered, purpose-directed life can be seen in the "seeds" we plant in the lives of others, helping them grow and reach their full potential.

In his book, *Living with Your Dreams*, David Seamands shares an inspiring story of the famous runner Charley Paddock, a story which was originally recorded by Olympic medalist Bob Richards in his book *The Heart of A Champion: Inspiring True Stories of Challenge and Triumph*. It illustrates so profoundly how a life that is lived with purpose can drop the "seed" of purpose-full living into the lives of others:

> One day while speaking in the assembly at a Cleveland [Ohio] high school, Charley said, "Who knows, we may even have an Olympic champ right here in this hall!" Afterward, a skinny, spindly-legged black youngster who had been hanging around the edge of the crowd came up and said to him very shyly, "I'd give anything if I could become a championship runner someday." Charley Paddock answered him warmly, "You can, Son, you can, if you'll make it your goal and give it your all."
>
> In 1936 that young man, whose name is Jessie Owens, won gold medals and broke records in the Munich Olympics. Adolf Hitler watched his stunning performance and was

infuriated, for the fulfillment of that dream did as much as anything to smash his idiotic dream of a superior Aryan race.

When Jessie Owens came home they gave him a ticker-tape welcome. That day another spindly-legged black youngster squeezed his way through the crowds and said, "I'd sure like to grow up and become a runner in the Olympics someday." And Jessie remembered and grabbed the kid's hand and said, "Dream big, Son, dream big. And give it all you've got." In 1948, Harrison Dillard won gold medals at the Olympics.[22]

The Power of Personal Influence

The personal influence of my life may never reach millions of people like Dr. King, Jessie Owens, or countless other individuals of world renown, but the *impact* of my influence on the lives of those with whom God allows *me* to come into contact should be no less greater. The same could be said of your life. Why do I say this? Because if I, or you, am living a Spirit-filled and Spirit-led life of purpose, then God can work through us to touch the lives of others for eternity. The impact does not come from our personal influence only, but rather through the influence of the Holy Spirit working through us. True purpose in life is not merely the product of imaginative thinking or personal willpower. It is, rather, a divine summons placed upon the heart and mind of a person whom God chooses to use for His purposes. And if received and executed in faith, it can, like the acorn of a tree, yield a forest of Kingdom-directed lives of purpose.

9

Potholes in the Road

"Ever more people today have the means to live, but no meaning to live for."
– Victor Frankl

Before moving to Dallas in 2011, my family and I lived in Iowa for thirteen years, five of those years in the city of Davenport and eight years in the capitol city, Des Moines. I loved the laid-back lifestyle of this mostly rural state. Spring there was most lovely, as much of the plant life, inspired by warmer temperatures, would shrug off the slumber of winter and give birth to new buds ready to blossom. The humidity of the summers could at times be "breathtaking" (as in literally taking—or sucking—the breath *out* of you!), but then you could always count on a nice, cool burst of fall air around Labor Day to announce that the "dog days" of summer were coming to an end.

And then there were the winters. They could be brutal. The first snowfall of the year could happen as early as October and end as late as April the following year. As much as I love snow and "white" Christmases, by late February I would become weary of seeing dirty snow and ice piled up like miniature mountains along the sides of streets, or shoveling snow from my driveway, or sweeping up salt and sand that had fallen off of our cars onto the garage floor.

Furthermore, the combination of the intense heat of summer and the gripping cold of winter took its toll on the city streets, causing contractions which could sometimes leave behind crater-like holes. Left unattended, these potholes could inflict major damage on the cars of unsuspecting drivers who accidentally drove over them. So, as soon as the weather warmed up enough, street repair crews would be seen all over the city patching the potholes.

Watch Out for the Potholes

Once you have discovered your life's central purpose and have begun pursuing it, you need to think of your journey as similar to that of being

> *Success is never final.*
> – Winston Churchill

on a road that has some dangerous potholes in it; you will need to navigate around them successfully in order to fulfill your purpose, or destiny.

This is easier said than done. Sometimes people, like unsuspecting drivers on a street freshly thawed from winter, will encounter a "pothole" in life. Even if they are able to "drive through" the experience, damage can nonetheless be inflicted on their personal well-being that will need time and painstaking effort to repair.

Take, for instance, the example of teen pregnancies. Although statistics show that the teen birth rate has been steadily declining for more than two decades, having dropped more than 50% across ethnic backgrounds since its peak in 1991,[23] there are other significant factors about this issue glaring enough to warrant our earnest attention.

Consider the following data:

> ➢ Despite declines in rates of teen pregnancy in the U.S., about 820,000 teens become pregnant each year. That means that 34 percent of teenagers have at least one pregnancy before they turn 20.
> ➢ 79 percent of teenagers who become pregnant are unmarried.
> ➢ 80 percent of teenage pregnancies are unintended.
> ➢ Nearly four in ten teenage girls whose first intercourse experience happened at 13 or 14 report that the sex was unwanted or involuntary.
> ➢ The main rise in the teen pregnancy rate is among girls younger than 15
> ➢ Close to 25 percent of teen mothers have a second child within two years of the first birth.

Even more sobering are the social, educational and financial costs of teen pregnancy:

> ➢ The United States spends $7 *billion* each year due to the costs of teen pregnancy.

➢ Only one-third of teenage mothers complete high school and receive their diplomas.

➢ By age 30, only 1.5 percent of women who had pregnancies as a teenager have a college degree.

➢ 80 percent of unmarried teen mothers end up on welfare.

➢ Within the first year of becoming teen mothers, one-half of unmarried teen mothers go on welfare.

➢ The daughters of teen mothers are 22 percent more likely than their peers to become teen mothers.

➢ Sons of teenage mothers have a 13 percent greater chance of ending up in prison compared to their peers.[24]

The issue of teenage pregnancy is like a pothole which, although it can be "driven though", can still cause enough serious damage that it will take painstaking efforts through the grace of God to overcome.

Blowout!

There are times, however, when the pothole can cause an emotional blowout, similar to that of a flat tire, rendering your life (like the car) immobile for a period of time. An example of a "pothole" like this is drug and/or alcohol abuse.

On a visit back to Memphis several years ago, Shurla and I attended a dinner hosted by some of my high school classmates. It was a festive evening, full of laughter and sharing warm memories from our high school days. Some of us hadn't seen each other since we graduated, some twenty-five years before.

There, I reconnected with Adrianna (not her real name). As we talked, she reminded me that we had actually attended the same elementary school, were in the same 6th grade class with Mr. Sheely, and had entered junior high and high school together. Oddly, I couldn't remember Adrianna during any of our senior-year activities, as if she had mysteriously disappeared after our junior year.

She told me that she had indeed "disappeared" and explained why. Adrianna, as it turns out, had begun experimenting with drugs and alcohol while we were in high school. By the end of our junior year, she had virtually become an alcoholic. Her parents, out of desperate concern for her life, decided to have her drop out of high school and checked her into a rehabilitation program. Adrianna shared that this was the darkest period of her life. She knew that her alcohol use was out of control and that she needed help, but the reality of not graduating on time and the shame that came along with her ordeal were equally devastating. The depression she felt was so strong at times that she had even contemplated suicide.

But her family, by the grace of God, offered unswerving support during her recovery. Their prayers on her behalf not only gave her the emotional lift that she needed but also had a spiritual influence on her as well. She committed her life to Jesus Christ. Gary (not his real name), her boyfriend at the time, was there for her at every step. The two married in their early twenties, have been blessed with two beautiful children, and have been by each other's side ever since. For three years, though, Adrianna felt that her life had been suspended in time. The road back to normality was a slow, painful, and very uncertain one. There were times when she questioned if she would ever truly experience sobriety again. She is thankful to God for the transformation in her life because she knows that things might not have turned out as well as they did.

> *The question is not whether we will die, but how we will live.*
> – Joan Borysenko

Repairing the Damage

Perhaps the worst-case scenario of pothole damage is when a driver goes over a pothole that, as it turns out, is wide and deep enough to do permanent damage to the drivability of the car. In cases like this, a new car is the only answer. Suffice it to say, it is far easier to get a new car than it is to get a new *life*. Simply repairing the frame will not be sufficient enough to compensate for the permanent damage done to the car. Can a person caught in such a predicament still have a successful life and realize their purpose?

Yes. It is important to note that God specializes in taking seemingly *hopeless* circumstances and reshaping them into *hopeful* outcomes. A key illustration of this is the story of the potter found in Jeremiah 18:3-4 (NIV): *"So I went to the potter's house, and I saw him working at the wheel. But the pot he was shaping from the clay was marred in his hands; so the potter formed it into another pot, shaping it as seemed best to him."*) God is indeed great in taking dire circumstances and "reshaping" them to suit His purposes.

Still, this is all the more reason to be keenly aware of the potholes that lie in the pathway to your purpose, for although God can reshape a life seemingly irreparably damaged by sinful behavior, this is not *always* the case. The following story illustrates this reality.

Of all the characters in the Bible, Samson is one of the most intriguing to me. Why? Because his life, in all of its colorful and adventurous detail, closely resembles that of a Shakespearean tragedy. His life is an example of a life irreparably damaged by a devastating pothole.

A Noble Beginning

Samson was truly a son of destiny, in that his life had been divinely blessed by God and was pregnant with potential:

"There was a certain man of Zorah, of the tribe of the Danites, whose name was Manoah. And his wife was barren and had no children. And the angel of the LORD appeared to the woman and said to her, "Behold, you are barren and have not borne children, but you shall conceive and bear a son. Therefore be careful and drink no wine or strong drink, and eat nothing unclean, for behold, you shall conceive and bear a son. No razor shall come upon his head, for the child shall be a Nazirite to God from the womb, and he shall begin to save Israel from the hand of the Philistines...[24]*And the woman bore a son and called his name Samson. And the young man grew, and the LORD blessed him"* (Judges 13:2-5, 24; ESV).

For a while, he flourished in his youthful strength and vigor. Not only was he blessed with handsome looks and a strong body, but he was equally gifted with wisdom and judgment. When he became of age, Samson was a "Judge" in ancient Israel—an individual divinely appointed by God to serve as an administrator in the civil and religious affairs of the nation. His gifts, multifaceted though they were, eventually went to his head. As the old saying goes, "beware that your greatest strength can also become your greatest weakness!"

Mingling with Idolaters

His story begins during a dark period in the experience of the ancient

Israelites. Because of their rebellion and disobedience to the commandments of God, God had allowed the Israelites to be oppressed by their enemies, the Philistines, for forty years prior to the birth of Samson. One Bible commentator offers the following summary of this experience:

> "As His people returned to their evil ways, the Lord permitted them to be still oppressed by their powerful enemies, the Philistines. For many years they were constantly harassed, and at times completely subjugated, by this cruel and warlike nation. They had mingled with these idolaters, uniting with them in pleasure and in worship, until they seemed to be one with them in spirit and interest. Then these professed friends of Israel became their bitterest enemies and sought by every means to accomplish their destruction"[25]

Notwithstanding this disobedience, it was still God's design to raise up a "deliverer" for His people. That deliverer was to be Samson. His mother, a descendant from the tribe of Dan, had been unable to have children until an angel of the Lord appeared to her one day and promised that she would soon conceive and bear a son. The angel promised her that her son *"shall begin to save Israel from the hand of the Philistines"* (Judges 13:3-5, ESV). Furthermore, the angel admonished her that she was to observe strict dietary habits as a part of his prenatal care; interestingly, she was also admonished not to cut his hair, for his hair was to be a symbol of his strength. *"And the woman bore a son and called his name Samson. And the young man grew, and the LORD blessed him"* (Judges 13:24, ESV).

The Prostitution of Purpose

Samson took full advantage of his mental and physical gifts. Because of his quick wit and handsome appeal, he was attractive *to* and attracted *by* women of various cultures and backgrounds, especially those with whom he did not share common religious values. In short, Samson was a "lady's man." He took as his first wife a woman *"of the daughters of the Philistines"* (Judges 14:2). This was the first of a series of poor choices that led to his eventual destruction. This untimely and unfaithful union led to an abrupt separation between the two. His wife had become a willing accomplice in a foolhardy game concocted by Samson and directed at thirty of her Philistine brethren, who were serving as groomsmen in a wedding ceremony. The groomsmen had sought to understand the meaning behind a riddle that Samson had given to them, as a game, during the seven-day feast he threw to celebrate his marriage.

With a perverted sense of humor, he had threatened to take their clothes from off of them—which would be humiliating to them—if they could not answer the riddle by the end of the marriage feast. The groomsmen bribed his bride into seducing Samson to tell her the secret of his strength and had threatened violence against her and her family if she did not cooperate. Because of his superior wisdom and powers of discernment, Samson unraveled their plot and ended up killing thirty other Philistine men, taking their clothing and presenting it to his thirty groomsmen. (Judges 14:18-19). And, in a strange twist, *"...Samson's wife was given to his companion, who had been his best man"* (Judges 14:20, ESV).

Samson's superior strength, also a gift from God, gave him the ability to accomplish unparalleled physical feats. He once took a lion by the mouth and ripped it apart (Judges 14:5-6); he single-handedly caught three hundred foxes, tied them tail-to-tail, put a firebrand in each knot and sent the foxes screaming and on fire through the cornfields, vineyards, and olive trees of his Philistine enemies (Judges 15:4-5). In one particularly dramatic showdown with these same enemies, Samson picked up the jawbone of a dead donkey and, again, *single-handedly* killed *one thousand* Philistines! As if these things alone weren't enough to mesmerize the most active mind, the record of his physical feats continues:

> *"Samson went to Gaza, and there he saw a prostitute, and he went in to her. The Gazites were told, 'Samson has come here.' And they surrounded the place and set an ambush for him all night at the gate of the city. They kept quiet all night, saying, 'Let us wait till the light of the morning; then we will kill him.' But Samson lay till midnight,* **and at midnight he arose and took hold of the doors of the gate of the city and the two posts, and pulled them up, bar and all, and put them on his shoulders and carried them to the top of the hill that is in front of Hebron"** (Judges 16:1-3, ESV).

Beauty, wit, and strength...it was the *misuse* of these three God-given gifts that, when combined, led to Samson's final affair which ultimately brought about his downfall. Again, the record states, *"After this he loved a woman in the Valley of Sorek, whose name was Delilah"* (Judges 16:4, ESV). Need I say more? The story of Samson and Delilah is one of those biblical accounts that has transcended the Judeo-Christian tradition and is easily recognized by people—religious, atheist, or agnostic—the world over. Every time I come across a woman named Delilah, I can't help but to think about this story!

Delilah, like her two predecessors—his first wife and the prostitute of Gaza—was part of a scheme to find out the secret of Samson's strength so that he might be captured and subdued: *"And the lords of the Philistines came up to her and said to her, 'Seduce him, and see where his great strength lies, and by what means we may overpower him, that we may bind him to humble him. And we will each give you 1,100 pieces of silver.' So Delilah said to Samson, 'Please tell me where your great strength lies, and how you might be bound, that one could subdue you'"* (Judges 16:5-6, ESV).

On three different occasions, Samson toyed with Delilah, supposedly giving her the secret to his strength, only for her to find out that he had deceived her. Finally, in an emotional fit that only a woman scorned could give, *"she said to him, 'How can you say, 'I love you,' when your heart is not with me? You have mocked me these three times, and you have not told me where your great strength lies.' And when she pressed him hard with her words day after day, and urged him, his soul was vexed to death. And he told her all his heart, and said to her, 'A razor has never come upon my head, for I have been a Nazirite to God from my mother's womb. If my head is shaved, then my strength will leave me, and I shall become weak and be like any other man'"* Judges 16:15-17, ESV.

The Anguishing Aftermath

That was it! Samson had finally relented under pressure from this vindictive vixen who relentlessly and irreverently sought to take his life for her own selfish gain. The words of King Solomon ring especially true here:

> *The tragedy of life is what dies inside a man while he lives.*
> – Albert Schweitzer

"For by means of a whorish woman a man is brought to a piece of bread: and the adulteress will hunt for the precious life" (Proverbs 6:26).

Then, Delilah had his hair cut while he slept, the Philistines came in, blinded him, bound him, and took him off to prison. One can only imagine the thoughts that must have run through Samson's mind during his dark trial of imprisonment, stripped by his hated enemies of everything that was familiar to him—home, family, friends, culture, even his manhood—only to be bound and shackled like a caged animal. I'm sure he reviewed the events of his past in all of their colorful and, at times, lurid detail.

Yes, he was reminded of his miraculous birth, recalling to mind the amazing story of the visit of the angel from heaven to his parents, foretelling his birth and giving specific counsel on how he was to be reared. From there he was also able to recall the follies of his youth, the feats he was able to accomplish through his superhuman strength, and the women he had loved. Now, he was forced to confront, face to face, the cold and cruel consequences of his willful and impulsive acts of disobedience. He had neglected not only the counsel of his parents, but more importantly, the counsel of his God. *"Remember also your Creator in the days of your youth, before the evil days come and the years draw near of which you will say, 'I have no pleasure in them'... (Ecclesiastes 12:1, ESV).*

The final word of his narrative, though, shows that he was repentant. Yes, he sought God's forgiveness and pleaded that God would show His forgiveness by using him, one final time, as an instrument of judgment against the Philistines:

> *"Then Samson called to the LORD and said, 'O Lord GOD, please remember me and please strengthen me only this once, O God, that I may be avenged on the Philistines for my two eyes.' And Samson grasped the two middle pillars on which the house rested, and he leaned his weight against them, his right hand on the one and his left hand on the other. And Samson said, 'Let me die with the Philistines.' Then he bowed with all his strength, and the house fell upon the lords and upon all the people who were in it. So the dead whom he killed at his death were more than those whom he had killed during his life." –Judges 16:28-30, ESV*

Sadly, Samson's full potential would never be reached. Though assured of God's forgiveness for his disobedience, he had nonetheless mortgaged his destiny to the Devil. Here, Samson had become fatally entrapped by the potholes of lust and deceit—potholes he had willfully chosen to fall into—and only upon God's final manifestation of power did he find redemption, which is God's ultimate purpose for all mankind. Yes, his *eternal* life was secured, but his *earthly* life and all the promise that it afforded was willfully, woefully, and worthlessly cut short.

———————

I took the time to relate the narrative of Samson's life because it is instructive for us all as we journey on the pathway to purpose. Let's look now at the seven potholes you *must*, by the grace of God, navigate successfully to fulfill **your** life's purpose.

> *To the question, "What are you?" I could only answer, "God knows."*
> – G.K. Chesterton

1. **FAITH** – *An understanding of or belief in God that promotes a positive set of moral values and responsibilities that govern our personal choices.*

In this instance, it is not faith itself that represents a pothole; rather, it is the *lack of faith* that could be a huge pothole on the road to fulfilling your life's purpose.

Why do I say this? Because the fact is, regardless of our age, we all face circumstances and realities in life—some as a consequence of choices that we have made and some which are not—that will challenge the very core of who we are. Some examples of these realities are the untimely death of a parent, sibling or friend, a life-threatening illness, family breakup because of parental separation or divorce, job loss, homelessness, or criminal activity.

Research has shown that young people who are actively involved in a caring, Christian community (especially where faith is regularly practiced in their home) are *less likely* to engage in at-risk behavior than young people who do not have similar faith values.[26] Although the reasons for this may vary, the reality is that **one's faith often promotes a positive set of moral values and responsibilities that govern the way he or she thinks and acts**. This indisputable principle applies to both young and old. *"I am the Lord your God, who teaches you what is best for you, who directs you in the way you should go. If only you had paid attention to my commands, your peace would have been like a river, your well-being likes the waves of the sea."* (Isaiah 48:17-18, NIV)

On the contrary, what happens to a person's decision-making when he or she doesn't have a code of morality or set of virtues to live by? More than likely, they will make decisions that put their own well-being above *anyone* or *anything* else. This is what happened to Samson. He slowly lost sight of his miraculous birth and the "signs" which God had given to his parents surrounding his life's holy purpose. He did not allow God to develop and strengthen faith in his life, to become his Friend as well as his Counselor and Guide. This resulted in a lifestyle soured by impulsive, quick-tempered, and oftentimes shortsighted thinking.

Selfish thinking like this is likely to lead a person down a dead-end road of morality. Your code of morality or faith values impact your decision-making, whether for good or for bad. As the expression says:

> *Sow a thought, reap an act;*
> *Sow an act, reap a habit;*
> *Sow a habit, reap a character;*
> *Sow a character, reap a destiny.*

Don't live your life merely by how you *feel* at a particular point in time. Take the time to nurture and develop your faith in God. Decide to make church attendance *and* participation in the activities of your church a *priority* in your life. Develop a daily routine of Bible reading, meditation, and prayer.

> *Men do not reject the Bible because it contradicts itself, but because it contradicts them.*
> – Author unknown

Ask God to lead you to some good devotional literature that you can read in addition to your Bible reading. Also, pray that God will bring someone into your life who is mature in their relationship with Him and who can "pour" into you, or offer you sound Christian counsel, from time to time. As your faith grows, it will strengthen and deepen your sense of identity, give clarity to your purpose in life, add value to your social relationships, and give you a clear and consistent moral compass.

Left At the Altar

When we lived in Davenport, Iowa, I once taught a continuing education class about purpose for a community college in Cedar Rapids, Iowa. On the opening night of the class, I had the small group of students introduce themselves. I will never forget when we got around to Mary (not her real name). She was the last one to walk in and had apologized for being late. She began with a big smile on her face as she introduced herself. She was a manager at a local restaurant. Then, her countenance changed all of a sudden. Her bright, bubbly smile quickly dissolved into a wrinkled, ashen face with trembling lips. Tears burst from her eyelids like twin waterfalls. Stunned, I asked, "What's wrong Mary?" "I'm sorry," she replied, "but my boyfriend left me at the altar this past weekend. We were supposed to be married and he backed out at the last minute. I'm sorry, but I'm still devastated."

She tried to compose herself as she quickly wiped away her tears and offered a nervous smile. To my surprised delight, the other students, none of whom she had known prior to joining the class, rallied around her and offered their support. Though the class was supposed to be neutral on matters of religious interest, the words of hope and encouragement which were given to her would have made you think you were in a small group Bible study. Mary was able to regain her composure in short order and we continued on with the class.

God's Interpreter

> *Blessed is the one who listens to me, watching daily at my gates, waiting beside my doors...*
> – Proverbs 8:34, ESV

Prior to the start of the class, I had struggled with how I was going to approach the lecture material. The college had made it clear that although I could reference Bible texts in my lectures (after all, I *was* a pastor), I could not directly proselytize, or indoctrinate, the students on Christian beliefs. "How was I going to be able to talk about purpose from a non-Christian viewpoint without diluting the potency of the material that I was going to present, material which clearly was Bible-based," I thought to myself.

Then, I learned a very powerful lesson which has since given me greater confidence regardless of the setting that I find myself in. God spoke to me and said, "What you cannot *say*, my Spirit can *impress* upon the mind of the hearer." In other words, I felt that God was telling me that although I could not teach or instill actual Bible texts, He could still, through the power of His Holy Spirit, impress the *theme* of the text upon the mind of the student.

"With God are wisdom and might; he has counsel and understanding" (Job 12:13, ESV). This is exactly what happened in Mary's case. Six months after the class had ended, I was driving back to Davenport one evening from another class I had begun teaching at the community college. Mary came to mind, so I decided to stop by her restaurant to check up on her. She was surprised and delighted to see me. We sat at a table to talk. She told me how impactful the class had been upon her life. She said that although she knew the class was not necessarily Christian in its orientation, she nonetheless felt that God spoke distinctly to her through the lectures. Mary went on to report that after the class had ended, she had felt impressed to dedicate her life to God, had joined a church, and was now active in the children's ministry at her church!

Faith is the fragrance of hope that overcomes the stench of hopelessness. Don't live without it!

Going Deeper

1) *Have you accepted eternal life through Jesus Christ and surrendered your life to Him? If not, have you thought about it or have questions about it?*

2) *On a scale from 1-10, with 1 being "not comfortable at all" and 10 being "very comfortable," how comfortable are you with sharing your faith in Christ with others? What can you learn from your score?*

3) *What role do you think that faith plays in a person fulfilling their life's purpose? Take the time to write down your thoughts, as they may give you deeper insights into yourself.*

2. **FRIENDSHIP** – *A relationship between two or more individuals built on mutual respect, honesty, trust, common beliefs, and concern for the overall welfare of the other person.*

During your teen years, your mind and body undergo tremendous changes as you transition from being a child to becoming a young adult. Part of the emotional changes many youth experience during their teen years involve their self-esteem, or self confidence.

Basically, self-esteem is how you perceive yourself to be, how you *feel* about yourself. Whether you're a teen, young adult, middle-aged or elderly, you may ask yourself the following questions over and over: "Am I attractive?"

"Am I too short or too tall?" "Am I too skinny, or am I overweight?" "Do other people think I'm 'cool'?" "Am I smart or not?" "Do I make friends easily or is it difficult for people to like me?" How you answer these questions will determine the level of self-esteem you have, how good or how bad you feel about yourself. The explosion in plastic surgery services makes it clear that many people, especially those in the later years, are keenly in tune with how they look and feel.

This, however, was not a problem for Samson. As stated before, he had incredibly handsome looks and an infectious charisma to go along with it. We know that these features made him attractive to those of the opposite sex. No plastic surgery needed there! What the Biblical record does not offer much information on, however, are the friends that Samson made as he grew from a child to a teenager and then into young adulthood. We do know that the close proximity in which the Israelites and Philistines dwelled presumably afforded him the opportunity to frequently mingle with his heathen counterparts and to thus make friends. When he married his first wife, as discussed earlier, the Bible says in Judges 14:11 that the townsfolk *"brought thirty companions to be with him."* When Samson separated from his wife behind her deceptive scheme with these groomsmen, she was eventually "given" to his best man. With friends like this, who needs enemies, right?

The Foundation of Friendship

Friendship is a relationship between two or more individuals built on mutual respect, honesty, trust, common beliefs, and concern for the overall welfare of the other person. Who you associate with *will* have a significant impact on your life. Our friends, or close associates, influence us for good or for bad.

> *"He that walketh with wise men shall be wise: but a companion of fools shall be destroyed."*
> – Proverbs 13:20

Does your association with your friends make you want to strive for excellence in your work or to become a better person? Are you able to laugh and have a "good time" without using alcohol or drugs, or engaging in promiscuous behavior? Does your association with your friends cause you to respect yourself and others more?

If you have a close friend, someone with whom you could confide your innermost thoughts and feelings, someone who has your implicit trust, and someone who, overall, has an uplifting influence on you, then you know the value of such a friend. I, too, am blessed with such friends. So was my younger brother Chris. I want to share with you an experience from his life that shows the power of true friendship.

An Odd Couple

When we were in high school, Chris developed a friendship with a guy named Carlos Nelson. Carlos was a colorful guy, to say the least. He could be quite a prankster at times, and a mouthy one at that. Standing about 6'2", Carlos was a slender, athletic guy with large bony hands, a square jaw, and sort of a box-shaped head. Though most of his African-American male peers were sporting low-cut, wavy hairstyles at the time, Carlos bucked that trend by keeping a low-cut version of the afro. His smooth, dark facial skin tone was accented by a nice set of bright teeth, which made up an incredibly inviting and confident smile which he could flash with ease.

For someone with such a slender frame, Carlos was also blessed with a strong set of windpipes, which could bellow out a hearty laugh from time to time. He, Chris and their other friends would sometimes tease each other so hard you would think that they would come to blows at any moment. Their smiling faces would give way to menacing looks and a few sharp words. This tension, though, would be short-lived, for soon after they would continue their regular laughter and conversation as if nothing serious had happened. Neither Chris nor Carlos were known for their academic achievements per se, but when it came to making others laugh, they had few rivals. For anyone who dared to look beyond the "class clown" personas they both could have, though, you would notice a deeper character element at work. Both of them were determined and highly driven young men with regard to their career pursuits.

> *Outstanding people have one thing in common: an absolute sense of mission.*
> – Zig Ziglar

After graduation, Chris and Carlos maintained communication between them, though distant. Chris attended college in Memphis and Carlos joined the Air Force. After a four-year stint in the Air Force, Carlos took a job with Federal Express Corporation in Los Angeles, California, as an aircraft maintenance mechanic, a skill he had developed while in the Air Force.

Chris, after graduating with a business degree, moved out to San Diego, California, for a short while, before finally joining our older brothers Maurice and Michael in the San Francisco, California, Bay area.

There, he met the true love of his life, Melissa, who happened to be the younger sister of Michael's wife Lorraine. After a couple of years of dating, Chris and Melissa married in a beautiful ceremony in 1994. The two settled just outside of San Francisco in Pittsburg, California, and started a family. (The irony of this union is that Melissa, Lorraine, and their family were loyal fans of the San Francisco Forty-niners, and Chris, Michael, and I were loyal fans of the Dallas Cowboys—two football teams which happened to be fierce rivals during the early 1990s. Can you imagine the trash talk that took place between us whenever the Forty-niners and Cowboys played each other? Chris, to his credit though, won the day…he had a sign made which hung above the entrance to their home. It read "Perkins Ranch," an ode to "Valley Ranch", which happened to be—at that time—the official name of the Dallas Cowboys training facility near Dallas!)

The next several years saw both Chris and Carlos flexing their entrepreneurial muscles. Chris and Melissa opened up an ice cream and deli shop in San Francisco. Melissa's parents had owned a similar store for years and helped them to get started. Carlos left Federal Express and Los Angeles and moved to Anchorage, Alaska, where together with another

> *Ordinary people think merely of spending time. Great people think of using it.*
> – Author unknown

friend of his, he opened up an aircraft repair and maintenance business. This business flourished, rapidly growing to the point where it became the largest privately owned aircraft repair and maintenance business in the entire state of Alaska. Though Chris and Melissa would close their ice cream and deli shop within two years, Chris maintained the same drive that led him into business. He and Carlos encouraged each other greatly during this time, a fact that was stunningly revealed a few years later.

The Challenge of His Life

In 1999, Chris was laid off from his job, and went into a deep depression. He would eventually be diagnosed with bipolar disorder. Over the next four Years Chris worked several temporary jobs; he struggled with accepting his condition, though, and would stop taking his medication from time to time. Each time he stopped taking his medication, he suffered a severe mental breakdown, requiring hospitalization. By August 2002, Chris had landed a job with an insurance company and flew to Chicago, Illinois, for training. I drove over from Des Moines and we spent a day together. It was good to see him again. We talked and had a great time. Over dinner, I could tell that although he was genuinely pleased with his new job, he still faced a lot of self-doubt. He was struggling emotionally. I tried to encourage him and reassure him, and for a moment his face would light up with a ray of hope. But just as quickly, self doubts would arise again and a look of despair would cover his face.

He was concerned, very concerned, about the effects his mental condition was having on him physically and, even more so, on his relationship with Melissa. How he loved her and their two small children, Rubin and Rachel! Once again, I tried my best to reassure him that Melissa loved him just as much and that she had been by his side at every step. I really loved that about Melissa...despite Chris's sickness and the challenges that it brought to their family, she *truly* loved him.

He smiled at this thought and we managed to finish our dinner on a lighter note. Driving back to his hotel room, we laughed out loud about experiences from our childhood and high school years together. He updated me on the lives of some of his friends, including Carlos, of whom he seemed to be especially proud. Those hearty laughs did him some good, and though we continued to laugh and talk into early the next morning, we managed to get some sleep. Chris had classes the following morning and I drove back to Des Moines.

The Last Good-bye

Little did I know at the time, but that would be the last time that Chris and I would ever spend together, alone...just the two of us. Though Melissa, our family, and our friends tried our best to encourage him during this period, the mental anguish that he privately endured took its toll. On the morning of April 22, 2003, Chris dressed, ate breakfast, and kissed Melissa and his mother-in-law good-bye as he usually did before leaving for work. Unbeknownst to them, instead of going to work he checked himself into a nearby hotel room, hung a "Do Not Disturb" sign on the outside of his door, and overdosed on sleeping pills. He would be found dead two days later by a cleaning maid.

I can't begin to describe the pain and devastation which gripped our family. I hurt so badly for Melissa, my little nephew Rubin and my beautiful niece Rachel. Both of them were just two years younger than Marlon Jr. and Reba, who were just six and four, respectively, at the time. Outside of my faith in God, I took solace in the fact that Madea, who had passed away in her sleep nearly two years earlier, did not have to look upon the lifeless form of yet another son. She had already endured such an experience, when in August 1998 my brother Maurice died of a massive blood hemorrhage of the brain. He was just forty-five years old at the time.

Shurla and I quickly made arrangements to fly to San Francisco. It was raining on the day of Chris's funeral. As I walked up the steps to the church where the service would be held, I looked over my left shoulder and to my utter astonishment saw one of Chris's high school friends get out of his car and quickly run to the steps. It was Carlos! We embraced and smiled as we looked each other up and down. I hadn't seen Carlos since their high school graduation. He told me that he and Chris had kept in touch and that Chris would, from time to time, fill him in on the details of my life. After introducing him to Shurla and other members of my family, we went into the service together.

"Your Brother, Marlon, YOUR Brother!"

> One of the most beautiful qualities of true friendship is to understand and to be understood.
> – Seneca

The depth of Chris's and Carlos's friendship, however, wasn't revealed to me until the graveside service. After the minister had spoken his final words, and those gathered had begun to disperse, I stood there alone, in the rain, crying and just reflecting back over our two lives together. Carlos, who had been standing off to the side, himself crying, walked up to Chris's casket, dropped quietly to his knees, and slowly draped his long arms over the casket, as if embracing his friend for the last time. Then, in volcanic-like fashion, he let out a cry that reflected the depth of pain and sorrow he was feeling over the loss of his friend.

I walked up to him and tried to console him. Over and over again, like a scratched record, he kept saying, "Marlon, you don't understand! You just don't understand!" Softly, I asked, "Understand what, Carlos?" "Your brother," he cried, "*your* brother!" He shook his head from side to side as if struggling to find the right words. "Your brother, Marlon…Chris Perkins…is responsible for where I'm at today. You don't know where I've come from. Carlos Nelson…the class clown…from little old Memphis, Tennessee. In high school no one would have dreamed that *I* would one day own a *multi-million-dollar* business! If anything, they would have thought that *you* would have achieved this before me. You were the smart one, Mr. Class President and all, not me. I thank God for your brother. If it hadn't been for his constant encouragement, I would have *never* opened up my aircraft maintenance business. Even when I felt like giving up, Chris always encouraged me to keep going. *Your brother* is the reason why I have a multi-million-dollar business today!" Standing there with Carlos, drenched in water, I was stunned by what he shared with me. I never knew that Chris had had such an impact on him.

Choose Carefully

Friendships influence us more than we think. Forming bad friendships can be a "pothole" on the road to your success, if you form the wrong friendships. You will be tempted to make decisions that you shouldn't make, develop a mindset that is contrary to your

> *The righteous should choose his friends carefully, for the way of the wicked leads them astray.*
> – Proverbs 12:26, NKJV

positive development, and ultimately take on a lifestyle that will lead you down a dead-end road rather than onto the super highway of success and fulfillment in life.

Ponder the definition of "friendship" stated at the beginning of this section, and evaluate your current or prospective friendships through that definition. It will give you a baseline from which to judge friendships. Be perceptive of the character traits in others—whether good or bad—without becoming overly judgmental. Avoid close association with others when you perceive them to have questionable conduct or character. Your destiny is too important to sacrifice for a so-called "friendship" that will neither make you a better person nor challenge you to be all that you can be. Choose your friends carefully!

Going Deeper

1) *Do you have a best friend? If so, how would you describe him/her? What qualities about that person do you like most? How are you different, and how do you deal with your differences? Take the time to really think this through.*

2) *Do your close friends share your basic values in life? Do you think that your relationship with them really brings out the best in you?*

3) *How often do you and your friends talk about your life's dreams and goals? What are they?*

3. **FAMILY** – *a basic social unit consisting of parents and their children, considered as a group, whether dwelling together or not.*[27]

All in the Family

> *Many people flounder about in life because they do not have a purpose, an objective toward which to work.*
> – George Halas

Research has shown that the foundation of one's self-esteem is laid during early childhood, most notably by family influences. How you think and feel about yourself is largely conditioned by how members of your family think and feel about you. In Chapters 1-3, I took the time to describe some of my childhood experiences—especially as they related to my family influences—simply because the seeds of who I am today were planted during this period of my life. Samson was no different. He had godly parents who loved him greatly and who surrounded him with godly influences so as to hopefully instill within him a love and respect for God. Tragically, as we have seen, his choices led him through a series of destructive potholes that affected the fulfillment of his life's purpose.

Too Close for Comfort?

For many people, their family is the strongest support group they have.

They love and trust the members of their families more than anyone or anything else. The family unit should serve to nurture, encourage, protect, and promote positive values for each member. Where these qualities are strong in a family, each member of the family experiences a security and personal well-being unmatched by other social relationships.

Unfortunately, this is not always the case in many families. In fact, just the opposite often occurs. Divorce, moral vices on the part of parents, severe financial problems, lack of parental attention or outright neglect, and inappropriate boundaries are present in many families today. These things serve to break down the family unit, causing untold emotional trauma to children and general confusion about the role and function of family relationships. The term used to describe these types of families is "dysfunctional." According to the online resource *Wikipedia.org*, "A dysfunctional family is a family in which conflict, misbehavior, and often abuse on the part of individual members occur continually and regularly, leading other members to accommodate such actions. Children sometimes grow up in such families with the understanding that such an arrangement is *normal*."[28]

Depending on your family history, the parenting styles of your parents, and other habits within your family, the attitude that family members take toward each other can sometimes be negative and counterproductive. Instead of encouraging each other to be all that they can be, many family members tear each other down, through actions as well as words. Perhaps you have heard the words, "you'll never be able to do that." Or, "that's stupid!" Or, "where in the world did you get that dumb idea from?" Again, as negative as these words may be, they often are spoken from one family member to another.

To be clear, your family *should* be one of the most encouraging support groups you will ever have in life. Even if your family is generally supportive of each other and rarely (if ever) hostile towards other family members, there may still exist within your family a mindset that does not believe that individual members of the family will ever achieve anything of great significance. "Greatness," as it may be thought, is something that "other" people achieve, not members of *your* family.

"As A Man Thinketh…"

It is important to recognize that although these words may not be spoken out loud, they are beliefs nonetheless that remain deeply embedded in the back of family members' minds. Our most deeply held beliefs, whether spoken or unspoken, are what control our behavior the most. Yet somehow those negative unspoken expectations become *understood* within the family.

If this is the case within your family, then seek out the counsel of others in whom you have confidence to help give guidance to your dreams and purpose in life. Remember: family influences can either be your biggest dream *builders* or your biggest dream *busters*. Negative family influences can be a "pothole" on the road to your success in life. If you sense that your own family members do not place much confidence in your abilities or possibilities for life, then be careful how much you share your inner thoughts or feelings with them. Negativity breeds negativity.

Don't underestimate the power of negative feedback on your dreams and aspirations. You may well be headed in the right direction in life, but if you're surrounded by negative thinking on a daily basis, then there is a possibility that you will adopt a negative outlook on your own life and thus give up on your life's purpose. This is not to suggest that you only want to surround yourself with people who will never disagree with you or correct you when you are wrong. Good counselors, however, always affirm you as an individual, even if they strongly disagree with some of your ideas. They always look for the *best* in you!

Going Deeper

1. *How would you describe your family situation as it is today? On a separate piece of paper, draw a line down the middle of the page. In one column, list 3-5 things you love most about your family. In the second column, list 3-5 things you like least about your family. Take some time to reflect on your lists.*

2. *How do you think the things you like most about your family can help you be successful in life? In what ways, if any, do you think the things you like least about your family could prove to be a stumbling block to your success in life?*

3. *If you are single, do you want to have a family some day? If so, what are some positive traits you would like to see in your own family? How would you go about making sure that these traits are part of your family? (You will want to begin praying about this NOW, even before that family becomes a reality.)*

4. **FAME** – *The concept of being publicly acknowledged or appreciated over a period of time for a specific ability you possess, action(s) you have taken, or achievements you have attained.*

What would you do if you became an overnight success? Do you think you could handle all of the public attention, money, and other pressures that would suddenly be thrust upon you? Speaking of Samson, the Bible says in Judges 13:25 that *"the Spirit of the LORD began to stir him in Mahaneh-dan, between Zorah and Eshtaol."* Samson made a name for himself because of his unusual physical strength. His strength was evidence of the presence of God in His life. God often blesses His people and brings them into position of stature and/or influence so that they might be a force for good on His behalf. *"A man's gift makes room for him and brings him before the great"* (Proverbs 18:16, ESV). Talent is a gift from God, even though it may not be used exclusively for religious purposes.

Rising Star

In the early 1980s, a teenage girl from Washington, D.C. became a rhythm and blues musical success–virtually overnight. Her name is Stacy Lattisaw. She actually recorded her first song at age twelve. From 1981-1986 Stacy recorded hit song after hit song. Her polished and mature soprano voice, coupled with her youthful innocence, allowed her to attract a cross-section of generations, from small kids to teens to those in their thirties and forties. Perhaps you have heard one of her hit songs, such as "Let Me Be Your Angel," "Love On A Two Way Street," or "Perfect Combination," a hit duet she sang with her neighborhood friend and fellow pop star, Johnny Gill.

Many young people who experience fame at an early age are not able to cope with the pressures: packed daily schedules, early mornings and late nights, demands from family, friends and significant others, sudden wealth, sex, drugs, alcohol, and a host of other things. These things can tax even the most mature person, but they are especially draining upon a young person who is still discovering who they are in this world.

The Choice

Such were the temptations that confronted Stacy. The more famous she became, the greater the pressures she faced. By the mid-1980s, at the height of her popularity, she came to a crossroads: either she could give in to the sexual advances (including the alcohol and drug use that came with them) of powerful music producers who could promote her career, or she could simply say "no" and face whatever consequences such a decision would bring about. Stacy chose the latter. She refused to sacrifice her moral convictions for sex, drugs, and alcohol. (She got these "convictions" largely from her *family* upbringing.) The trappings of fame were not more important to her than her integrity, health, family, and friends.

> *Strong lives are motivated by dynamic purposes; lesser ones exist on wishes and inclinations.*
> – Kenneth Hildebrand

She would, however, pay a painful price for this courageous decision. In short, her career started a sharp decline, and in 1990 Stacy recorded her last R&B song. It was clear to her that she was not going to have a successful career in R&B music unless she played "the game" of sex, drugs, and alcohol. In fact, she decided to leave that industry altogether. She married, started a family, and launched a career recording gospel music. Today, Stacy continues to be content with the life-changing decision she made over twenty years ago.

Fame can be like a seductress: she will tease your wildest fantasies, make you chase her with all of your energy, and cause you to sacrifice your deepest moral convictions. In the end, however, you will discover that she is nothing more than a mirage, like a hollow oak tree or a tasteless lollipop. She can leave you hopeless, senseless, and penniless! *"For all that is in the world—the desires of the flesh and the desires of the eyes and pride of life—is not from the Father but is from the world"* (I John 2:16, ESV).

As you pursue your life's calling, there is the possibility that both fortune and fame may come your way. This is not to suggest that such things come to every person as they pursue their life's calling, because that would not be true. However, if you are good at what you do in life—indeed, if you are great at it—then fame could very well come your way. *"Do you see a man skillful in his work? He will stand before kings; he will not stand before obscure men"* (Proverbs 22:29, ESV). However—remember that you can be *most excellent* and *worthy* of worldly praise, and never receive it. Yet, you continue in your excellence because you know no other way and your praise comes from Above.

Fame is not something that is limited to people who are in the sports or entertainment industries. With the growth of social media outlets such as YouTube, Facebook, Twitter, and other venues, it is much easier for the average person to attract a large following of people—across racial, economic, or cultural lines—in a relatively short period of time.

Fame can be a pothole on the road to your success. If you do not remain humble, make Christ the "author and finisher" of your faith, surround yourselves with well-grounded individuals who have a mature outlook on life and have *your* best interests at heart, then it will be easy for you to get caught up in all of the "hype" surrounding your talents, and therefore get stuck in the pothole of fame. *"The fear of the LORD is the beginning of knowledge: but fools despise wisdom and instruction"* (Proverbs 1:7).

Going Deeper

1. *Have you ever experienced positive publicity for something you have accomplished? What kind of publicity was it and how did it make you feel?*
2. *Do you agree with the idea that fame can be a potential pothole on the road to your success? Write down how you think this could affect you?*
3. *If you were to experience a lot of fame in your life, how do you think you would handle it? List 3-5 ways that you think you could successfully handle fame in your life.*

5. **FINANCE$** – *Resources used to cover expenses associated with our needs and desires.*

Money is a tool or a resource used to supply one's needs and desires. Unfortunately, many people view money as a power in itself, something to be obtained regardless of what you have to do to get it. *"Those who want to get rich fall into temptation and a trap and into many foolish and harmful desires that plunge people into ruin and destruction. For the love of money is a root of all kinds of evil. Some people, eager for money, have wandered from the faith and pierced themselves with many griefs" (I Timothy 6:9-10, NIV).* When we view money from this perspective, it is easy to see how quickly a person's judgment can become clouded. Your values (and integrity) take a "back seat" to the making of money.

Quick Cash

With technological advancements, people in general have quicker access to money, allowing them to make financial decisions that they otherwise would not make if they had to wait. Speedy access to cash credit, coupled with undisciplined habits of spending, often lead to indebtedness. According to student loan provider, Nellie Mae, "more than 54 percent of college freshmen carry a credit card. By [the] sophomore year, the percentage of students who own at least one card rises to 92 percent. . . On average, freshmen *bring* an average of $1,585 in credit card debt to college."[29]

The problem with many youth is that they start making bad financial decisions early in life. Left uncorrected, those bad decisions can quickly become a string of bad decisions, forming an iron-like chain around your financial neck. This is what happened to me. I was a sophomore in college when I, one day, went to my mailbox in the student center on campus to get my mail. Among my mail was a letter from a bank offering me a credit card with a credit line of up to $2,500. In my naïve youthfulness, I filled out the application and mailed it in. On another day, I again went to my mailbox… and among my mail was a letter from the same bank. In that letter was my very first credit card, and I began to use it immediately.

In all honesty, the card was a novelty to me. Growing up, I was accustomed to only using cash to make purchases. I never saw Madea use a credit card to buy food or clothing or anything else. If she wanted to buy something for which she did not have the money, she would simply put it on "layaway," a process allowed by many merchants whereby a consumer could "lay away" an item they desired (meaning that the merchant would place the item on hold for the consumer) and pay the purchase price in installments over a period of time. After the item had been paid for in full, the consumer could then take possession of it.

This process subconsciously taught the principle of *delayed gratification* and protected against runaway debt. One of Madea's "sayings" for directing our attention to the fact that we could count on God to provide was: "God himself will provide a ram in the bush"…referring to the story in Genesis 22:1-12 about Abraham being called to sacrifice his son Isaac. Verse 13 goes on to prove God's provision of need: *"Abraham looked up and there in a thicket he saw a ram caught by its horns. He went over and took the ram and sacrificed it as a burnt offering INSTEAD of his son."* This principle…that God WILL provide for your financial need…"the lamb/ram" you need financially …was a backbone of Madea's beliefs that she impressed upon her children's minds as we grew up.

As I write this, I have been struck with the thought that, today, many parents unknowingly influence the buying habits of their children when their children see them make *everyday* purchases on credit (spending money they do not have), and then they do not pay those purchases off by the end of their credit billing cycle. They are influencing their children to someday become credit purchasers themselves. In fact, it has become an 'accepted' practice for some to intentionally build up insurmountable debt, then declare bankruptcy for a minimal cost, which although damaging and limiting to their future borrowing abilities for a period of years, allows one to keep the items/services purchased on credit *without having to pay for them.* The evolution of this technique is leading to a mindset of wasteful spending without any accountability or consequences that deter further credit misuse.

My New 'Toy'

I was excited by the fact that, with my credit card, I had the ability to "pay" for something that I did not have the cash for. At first, I used it for small purchases, such as gas for my car or eating out, and I would pay off the balance at the end of the month. Then, I began making larger purchases, such as for clothing, and my balance grew to the point where I could no longer pay it all off at the end of the month. I told myself that I need not worry, that if I just managed my credit purchases, that I could *eventually* pay off the balance. Since I never gave myself a hard deadline on "eventually," I kept making monthly minimum payments on my card. "Eventually" I did pay off that card…with another card, one which offered a *higher* credit

> *A fool and his money are soon parted.*
> – Thomas Tusser

limit. And I then ran up the balance on that card. Wash, rinse, repeat…this became the way I managed my credit card debt for many years thereafter, and I became entrapped in perpetual indebtedness at an early age.

It has been only through prayer, faithfulness in my financial stewardship to the Lord's work, and painstaking effort that I have been able to responsibly handle debt. Debt will be a 'cruel taskmaster'…demanding that you become its slave, resulting in untold stress in your life which will affect relationships, career, and future plans. *"The rich rule over the poor, and the borrower is slave to the lender"* (Proverbs 22:7, NIV).

Manager, or **Steward?**

One more thought on finances. Proper money management is much, much more than managing debt. It involves proper management, or *stewardship*, of your overall financial resources. And on a deeper level than this, it involves something much more comprehensive…*total life stewardship*. As someone who is seeking to discover and fulfill your own life's purpose, you *must* understand that living your life's purpose invariably involves properly *stewarding* your overall life—spiritually, physically, and materially. As God prepared ancient Israel to enter into the promised land, Canaan, He gave them this thought-provoking charge:

"And if you faithfully obey the voice of the LORD your God, being careful to do all his commandments that I command you today, the LORD your God will set you high above all the nations of the earth.

²And all these blessings shall come upon you and overtake you, if you obey the voice of the LORD your God.

³Blessed shall you be in the city, and blessed shall you be in the field.

⁴Blessed shall be the fruit of your womb and the fruit of your ground and the fruit of your cattle, the increase of your herds and the young of your flock.

⁵Blessed shall be your basket and your kneading bowl.

⁶Blessed shall you be when you come in, and blessed shall you be when you go out.

*[7] The LORD will cause your enemies who rise against you to be defeated before
you. They shall come out against you one way and flee before you seven ways.*

*[8] The LORD will command the blessing on you in your barns
and in all that you undertake. And he will bless you in
the land that the LORD your God is giving you.*

*[9] The LORD will establish you as a people holy to himself, as he has sworn to you,
if you keep the commandments of the LORD your God and walk in his ways.*

*[10] And all the peoples of the earth shall see that you are called by
the name of the LORD, and they shall be afraid of you.*

*[11] And the LORD will make you abound in prosperity, in the fruit of your
womb and in the fruit of your livestock and in the fruit of your ground,
within the land that the LORD swore to your fathers to give you.*

*[12] The LORD will open to you his good treasury, the heavens, to give the
rain to your land in its season and to bless all the work of your hands.
And you shall lend to many nations, but you shall not borrow.*

*[13] And the LORD will make you the head and not the tail, and you shall
only go up and not down, if you obey the commandments of the LORD
your God, which I command you today, being careful to do them,*

*[14] and if you do not turn aside from any of the words that I command you
today, to the right hand or to the left, to go after other gods to serve them."*
(Deuteronomy 28:1-14, ESV)

God's only requirement for the Israelites to become the perpetual
recipients of His blessings was that they *"not turn aside from any of the words
that I command you today…"* (verse 14). To make sure that His positive
counsels were received with obedient hearts, God also gave the following
promise for *disobedience* to His Word:

*[15] "But if you will not obey the voice of the LORD your God or be careful
to do all his commandments and his statutes that I command you
today, then all these curses shall come upon you and overtake you…*

²⁰The Lord will send on you curses, confusion, and frustration in all that you undertake to do, until you are destroyed and perish quickly on account of the evil of your deeds, because you have forsaken me...

²⁵...And you shall be a horror to all the kingdoms of the earth."
(Deuteronomy 28:15, 20, 25, ESV)

Part of God's commandments to the Israelites also required their faithful financial support of the religious services of the sanctuary:

⁷"Return to me, and I will return to you, says the Lord of hosts. But you say, 'How shall we return?'

⁸Will man rob God? Yet you are robbing me. But you say, 'How have we robbed you?' In your tithes and contributions...

¹⁰ Bring the full tithe into the storehouse [church], that there may be food in my house. And thereby put me to the test, says the Lord of hosts, if I will not open the windows of heaven for you and pour down for you a blessing until there is no more need.

¹¹I will rebuke the devourer for you, so that it will not destroy the fruits of your soil, and your vine in the field shall not fail to bear, says the Lord of hosts.

¹²Then all nations will call you blessed, for you will be a land of delight, says the Lord of hosts."
~Malachi 3:7-12, ESV

If you already belong to a church and faithfully support the ministry of your local church by returning an honest tithe (10% of your gross income) and giving liberal offerings where needed, then may the Lord bless you for your faithfulness and may He continually guide you as you steward other areas of your finances and life in general. If you have not been faithful in this area of your Christian life, or

> *Our sinful natures are so weak, the pull of riches is so strong, and the temptation to parade our prosperity is so intense, that worship is our only safeguard.*
> – Dr. Roland J. Hill

this teaching is new to you, then pray that God will expand your knowledge on this subject and give you the courage to be obedient to His Word. If necessary, seek further counsel on this subject from a trusted Christian friend or pastor, as well as reading other literature on Christian stewardship… or investigate programs on responsible money management, some of which provide classes you can take to learn wise financial management principles.

I know that managing one's personal finances can be very challenging and scary at times, especially when unforeseen circumstances such as a job loss, a serious medical condition, or property damage bring about prolonged indebtedness. God knows this too, and He *wants* to bless your finances. Let Him help you. When you get into debt, without a plan or sufficient income to pay off your debt within a reasonable period of time, you create a financial "pothole" that can severely limit your options in life. Financial problems can overwhelm you, limit your overall perspective on your dreams and aspirations, and keep you from fulfilling your life's purpose. Money is a tool to be used, not a god to be worshipped. Keep it in perspective!

Going Deeper

1. *Do you use a budget as a guide for how you spend your money? Do you have a savings or investment account? What are some of the things you regularly spend your money on?*
2. *Why do you think it's important to use good judgment in spending money? What role does good money management play in one's happiness and success in life?*
3. *Do you understand the concept of "stewardship" as it relates to your finances? List 3 ways that you can become a better steward of your money.*

6. **FITNESS** – *The concept of a physically healthy body and mind.*

Obesity has become an epidemic in the U.S., especially among youth. An article cited in the online resource *Softpedia.com* states that "some scientists believe that poor academic performance among some U.S. youth can be directly linked to "abnormally high levels of obesity among children aged 6 to 11." Furthermore, these same scientists "believe that fitness exercises are the key to reversing this issue, saying that, by engaging in sportive activities, the kids' brains receive numerous good chemical impulses, which trigger the production of various hormones, necessary for a good <u>learning</u> process."[30]

Why am I emphasizing health in this book? Because the fact is that if you are to reach your full potential, developing a healthy lifestyle is vital. Far too many promising people have their lives cut short by health problems, problems which begin while they are *young* and increase with age. What's

> *Physical fitness is not only one of the most important keys to a healthy body, it is the basis of dynamic and creative intellectual activity.*
> – John F. Kennedy

sad is that many of these problems could have been completely avoided had they practiced better health habits. If you do not begin to take control of your health while you are young, chances are you may not do so until you've experienced significant health problems when you're older, some of which may not be reversible. Bad health, whether caused by bad habits or forces beyond your control, can be a "pothole" on the road to your success. It is difficult, though not impossible, to maintain a long-term focus on fulfilling your life's purpose when you have chronic health problems.

How can you develop a healthy, balanced lifestyle throughout your life? Here are some simple steps:

- ➢ **Eat nutritious food–*every single day*!** Nutritious foods include a variety of vegetables, fruits, nuts, whole grains, and a good balance between foods rich in fiber and carbohydrates. Eat sugary foods in moderation. Alcohol, tobacco and drug abuse should be completely avoided!
- ➢ **Try to exercise 5-6 days a week for a minimum of 30-45 minutes per day.** By getting your heart rate up a little, you'll release a lot of stress from your body, promote good blood circulation throughout your body, and feel great overall. Walking is perhaps the simplest exercise you can do and will accomplish all of the above.
- ➢ **Because your body is about 70% water, it is important to keep yourself properly hydrated by drinking enough water.** Many health professionals suggest drinking 8-10 glasses of water per day. Because they are stimulative in nature, caffeinated beverages should be consumed sparingly. Be especially careful of so-called "energy" drinks which are loaded with harmful amounts of caffeine. Learn to

put down the soda can (or that flavored coffee) and grab a refreshing glass of nature's "ale"—water!

> **As the weather permits, get outside and enjoy an abundance of sunshine.** Although it's important to guard against overexposure of UV (Ultra Violet) rays from the sun, nonetheless you will benefit by gaining a healthy dose of Vitamin D. Depression is often linked to a lack of Vitamin D. Have some fun in the sun! It'll improve your mood.

> **Learn to be balanced in everything you do.** Try to avoid going to extremes in anything that you do, whether it be in your studies, exercise, recreational activities, eating, or just lounging around. Balance is key to mental and physical health. So is laughter. *"A joyful heart is good medicine, but a crushed spirit dries up the bones."* (Proverbs 17:22, ESV).

> **Breathe it in!** As you spend time outside, breathe in the fresh air. Breathing in fresh air on a regular basis is key to your health. It expands your lungs and allows oxygen to get into your bloodstream, which is important for good circulation.

> **Take a break.** In order to maintain optimal health, your body has to restore itself on a regular basis. Key to this restoration is proper rest. On average, most people need *at least* 6-8 hours of sleep per night. Have you ever heard of the phrase, "Early to bed and early to rise, makes one healthy, wealthy, and wise"? This is not just for older folks. Turn off your cell phone and other electronic gadgets at night and get some rest. You'll feel much better in the morning!

> **Maintain healthy spiritual disciplines.** The relationship between your mind and body is a delicate one. One affects the other, for better or for worse. Learn to clear your mind regularly by focusing on positive themes, such as Scripture verses, that will encourage you and brighten your perspective on life. I personally set aside a time each day for devotion to God, which includes reading passages of Scripture and prayer. Regular worship attendance at your church is important as well. Because I keep the biblical Sabbath, the seventh day of the week, I am able to "rest" from my regular routine of weekly activities and spend a complete day in worship to God. A clear mind (and conscience) are key to a focused life. Stay positive!

Remember: bad health can be a "pothole" on the road to your success. Appreciate the wealth of your health!

Going Deeper

1. *How would you rate your health condition at this time: good, fair, or poor? Do you exercise on a regular basis, and if so, what type of activities do you do?*

2. *Is there a history of chronic illnesses in your life, like heart disease, cancer, diabetes, high blood pressure, etc.? Do you think that any of these illnesses will affect you? If so, how? What are some things you think you can do to avoid these illnesses?*

3. *What are the 2-3 most important things you have learned from this section? How can you begin to practice these principles in your own life?*

As critical as it is to successfully navigate these six potholes in fulfilling your life's purpose, it is the next pothole, in my estimation, that proves to be *the* determining factor in whether you will or you *won't* fulfill your life's purpose. Don't close this book until you find out what it is!

10

Go to Your Destiny

*"The best way to make your dreams come true is to **wake up**."*

— Paul Valery

Several years ago, I sat in front of my television and listened to an amazing story of two brothers…twin brothers, Alvin & Calvin Harrison. They were guests on *The Oprah Winfrey Show* and were discussing their life's story, chronicled in a brand new book they had co-authored entitled *Go to Your Destiny*. Perhaps the main reason they were guests on the show was because of their recent fame. Both brothers had won gold medals in the Men's 4 x 400 meters relay at the 2000 Summer Olympics in Sydney, Australia. There, they made history together by becoming the first twins ever to compete and win Olympic gold medals together on the *same* relay team since the inception of the modern Olympic Games.[31] As the interview was winding up (I had only caught the last half of it), one of the brothers shared with Oprah and the audience something that really caught my attention. Whenever the two brothers separate, going their own ways, they never say "good luck" or even "good-bye" to each other. They always part with the words, "Go to your destiny," as if giving each other a challenge. These words would take on a deeper dimension of meaning once I understood their background.

"A Warm Blanket and A Hot Bowl of Soup"

Their story, as it turns out, had not begun quite so bright. The twin brothers were born prematurely to their 16-year-old mother in Orlando, Florida. By the time they were teenagers themselves, they were living on their own in Salinas, California. Although track stars in their high school years, the boys were virtually homeless, often hoping simply for a "warm blanket and a hot bowl of soup." By 1995, they were living in a car parked on top of a hill in rural California, praying for a way out of their predicament.

In their book, the brothers describe their situation at that time:

<u>Calvin</u>

"There was a hill a few miles up the road from Marie's house. We decided to park the car there. We sat across the street from a small ranch house that had cows behind it in a field. To our right was a dried up creek bed lined with pine trees and weeds. We chose that spot because hardly anyone drove through that area. We had some blankets and we flipped a coin. Alvin would get the backseat. I would sleep in the front. No big deal, we thought. One or two nights in the car was nothing we hadn't done before. We could handle a couple of days in the car. No problem. At first, it was even kind of fun."

<u>Alvin</u>

"The first night was easy. By the third night it had started to become old. By the end of the first week we didn't know if the situation would ever improve. That's when reality started to set in. Pretty soon three weeks had gone by and we were still sleeping in that Mustang every night. Every morning I looked up at the sky and asked God, 'How much longer?'"

<u>Calvin</u>

"I was praying someone would come along and literally take me out of the situation. I prayed and prayed but I was looking for a miracle. I finally realized that the answer was right in front of me. This mysterious secret to life we are all trying to find begins with the individual. You can gain insight from prayer and studying the Bible, but it was up to me and Alvin to *do something* with that information."

<u>Alvin</u>

"We had to face reality if we were going to get anywhere and that's what reading the Bible helped us to do. Calvin and I read the entire Bible sitting in that car. I had a little green one and Calvin's was red. They were small pocket-sized versions, but we read every page at least once."

Calvin

"Looking through the newspaper one day, I found an ad for a painting job.... it wasn't until I started painting that everything became clear. I realized I was able-bodied. I had arms, legs, feet. I was strong. I was young. It's like I finally understood the answer to all our problems and it all boiled down to us. *We had to create our destiny. No one was going to hand it to us. We had to go out and use everything we had been given to make our life happen. Otherwise, we were going to end up on the street or in that car.*"[32]

Calvin's words, "*We had to create our destiny. No one was going to hand it to us. We had to go out and use everything we had been given to make our life happen...*" underscore a truth that I want to leave with you, the reader:

If you are to fulfill your life's purpose, you must first *choose* to pursue it.

William Jennings Bryan said it well: "Destiny is not a matter of chance, it's a matter of choice; it's not a thing to be waited for, but a thing to be *achieved*." This is not to suggest, as I stated in chapter 8, that your purpose is "*merely* the product of imaginative thinking or personal willpower." As I went on to say, "It is, rather, a Divine summons placed upon the heart and mind of a person whom God chooses to use for His purposes." God reveals your purpose, but you must choose to pursue it. Intuitively, this makes sense, so much so that you may think that it is unnecessary for me to state the obvious. But upon closer inspection, you will discover that the "obvious" is not as simple as it sounds. And this leads me to the seventh pothole:

7. **FEAR...OF FAILURE** – *The concept of not meeting or fulfilling one's personal goals nor attempting to meet a specific goal or need.*

Frozen in Time

"Fear" and "failure" are fraternal twins, meaning that although they are not necessarily identical to each other, they nonetheless have the same effect on people. Fear is a trait that is common to us all, regardless of color, class, creed, or commonwealth. For some, it might be as simple as being in close proximity to certain insects or rodents, such as spiders or mice. For others, it might be the fear of a dog bite, heights, or cramped spaces such as a closet or a small elevator. Regardless of what it is that makes you afraid, the effects are often similar: rapid heartbeat, heightened pulse rate, shortness of breath, and possibly sweat. To these symptoms you could even add the feeling of being frozen in time.

In the Bible, the word "fear" has at least two types of meaning. In one sense, fear can be a good thing in that it speaks of reverence or respect, such as with the oft-used phrase, "the *fear* of the Lord." In another sense, fear carries with it negative qualities, such as prolonged hesitation, tentativeness, or reservation. If left unchecked, these qualities can lead to emotional and functional paralysis, making one feel as if he is virtually *unable* to act.

> *The deepest human defeat suffered by human beings is constituted by the difference between what one was capable of becoming and what one has in fact become.*
>
> – Ashley Montague

When the Bible prophet Jeremiah received his call from God to be "a prophet unto the nations," he met it with trepidation: "*Then I said, 'Ah, Lord GOD! Behold, I do not know how to speak, for I am only a youth.' But the LORD said to me, 'Do not say, 'I am only a youth'; for to all to whom I send you, you shall go, and whatever I command you, you shall speak.'"* (Jeremiah 1:6, 7, ESV). God's directive was meant to save Jeremiah from the "paralysis of analysis."

Proverbs 29:25 says, "*The fear of man lays a snare, but whoever trusts in the LORD is safe.*" Fear can be a 'snare'; it can trap you in a straight-jacket of inactivity. Fear…and more specifically, fear of *failure*…can and *will* prevent you from fulfilling your life's purpose. All too often, this is the case with many people who have a sense of God's calling or purpose in life. They know precisely what God would have them to do—they just aren't doing it!

The No. 1 Barrier to Fulfilling Your Purpose

Then, there are those who don't know what their purpose is in life, neither are they interested in discovering it. Somehow, they are convinced that their lives have little to no real value or meaning. Perhaps they have faced so much rejection in life that they don't want to *risk* any further emotional pain. Although the reasons for both of these cases can be varied, there is a common denominator between the two: both types of people are frozen in fear.

Fear, I believe, is oftentimes the *number one barrier* for many people to achieving success or fulfilling their life's purpose. As such, it is a critical pothole which *must* be successfully navigated if you are to fulfill your life's purpose. People don't like to feel or appear afraid, because they are in overwhelming denial of that "fear"…that it might make them look vulnerable or weak. Rather than acknowledge that fear is the culprit for their inaction, they attribute it to some other reason, such as timing, lack of funding or other necessary resources, job, health, or family constraints. As strange as this may

> *The man who makes no mistakes does not usually make anything.*
> – Edward Phelps

sound, it makes some people *feel* better to think that someone or something else is responsible for their lack of achievement or success. If they can place the blame for their lack of achievement on something else other than their own efforts, then they reason that they have been let off the hook and therefore need not continue to push forward. In the back of their minds is a reassuring voice saying, "Well, you at least tried, but _____ messed up your plans. Don't worry – it's not your fault that you're not happy or fulfilled in life."

It's Always Easy to Blame Someone Else

Please, don't buy into this faulty and fatalistic view of life. Sadly, millions of people do so every single day. Only eternity will afford us the time and mental capacity to fully comprehend the monumental loss of potential that lays untapped in the hearts and minds of those who, under the stifling spell of *fear*, simply give up on their life's purpose. When you acknowledge your fear, you have now labeled an identifiable barrier to your (and God's) success.

No longer can you pass the buck on to some other supposed barrier. The villain has now been unmasked—face your fear! "You are free in Christ," writes author Neil T. Anderson in *The Bondage Breaker*, "but you will be defeated if the devil can fool you into believing you are nothing more than a sin-sick product of your past. Nor can Satan do anything about your position in Christ, but if he can deceive you into believing what the Scripture says isn't true, you will live as though it isn't. People are in bondage to the lies they believe. That is why Jesus said, *'You will know the truth, and the truth will make you free'*" (John 8:32).

Fear Has A Best Friend

Equally powerful in its intimidation as fear is *failure*. In his book, *Failing Forward: Turning Mistakes into Stepping Stones for Success*, best-selling author and leadership expert John Maxwell sheds light on the unrealistic views many hold on the definition of success and failure. He quotes an article written by J. Wallace Hamilton for *Leadership Magazine*: "The increase of suicides, alcoholics, and even some forms of nervous breakdowns is evidence that many people are training for success *when they should be training for failure*. Failure is far more common than success; poverty is more prevalent than wealth; and disappointment more normal than arrival."[33]

Training for failure? That's right! This does not mean that you have succumbed to the idea that you won't succeed, but rather that you understand that *setbacks are part of the pavement on the road to success*. Rather than trying to ignore or even avoid them, you need to plan for them…and learn

> *Success is going from failure to failure without loss of enthusiasm.*
> – Abraham Lincoln

from them. The quicker you learn to deal with failure or setbacks–without allowing them to keep you frozen in a straitjacket of inactivity–the further along you will be in gaining the confidence that is necessary for anyone who is successful in life. Thomas Alva Edison, who in 1880 received a U.S. patent for the incandescent light bulb, once wrote: "Genius is 1 percent inspiration, 99 percent perspiration." When asked by a reporter if he had, in fact, failed more than 1,000 times in trying to create the light bulb, he reportedly responded, "I have not failed 1,000 times. I have successfully discovered 1,000 ways to *not* make a light bulb." Edison's response emphasizes a crucial point: success does not happen automatically; it requires tireless, consistent efforts aimed at a singular goal and applied over time. Even more important, your goal may not be reached on the first, second, or even third try, but this doesn't mean that you have failed. It may mean that all you have to do is to *keep trying.*

Conquering the Foe

When I formed Purpose-Full Ministries several years ago, I tried several attempts to secure money for start-up expenses, primarily through grant writing. Each proposal was denied – and I had applied for *three* different grants. Then, I had another idea. Rather than trying to do it alone, I contacted a friend, Deita, who excels in grant-writing to ask if she could help. She asked me how much we needed. I responded with a five-figure number. As it turns out, she didn't help me write a grant at all – she *gave* our organization the entire amount. What's more, Deita eventually joined the Purpose-Full Ministries board of directors!

Needless to say, I'm glad that we didn't give up. As businessman Harvey Mackay is fond of saying, "Failure is an *attitude*, not an outcome."

———————

Thus far, I have attempted to convince you, the reader, that God has a purpose for your life. That has been my purpose for this book. The world is in dire need of *you* fulfilling your life's purpose. Untold stories of wonderful developments with eternal results are awaiting *your* decision to move forward. Decisions determine destiny. If you trust Him, God's purposes will come to pass, and

> *Every calling is great when greatly pursued.*
> – Oliver Wendell Holmes

He will exalt you in due time. *"If God be for us, who can be against us?"* (Romans 8:34)

Time to Take Action

There has been a guiding theme for this book: my story – my pathway to fulfilling my purpose – was related in order to give just enough color and background to you, the reader, in order that you might be led by the presence of the Holy Spirit to discover your own pathway to purpose. At times, I struggled with how much of my story I should tell, and how much I should leave out. I struggled over whether I should have included more stories from experiences I've had over the years while serving in pastoral ministry, thinking that perhaps these stories would serve to further prove that I made the right career choice when I was a young college student. Maybe this might have been helpful, but that was not how I felt God was leading in my writing. What was more important, I'm convicted, is that you, the reader, be given just enough information to awaken within you, as I wrote in the Introduction of this book, "...a sense of 'specialness' about your own life, and evoke within you a strong desire to seek and to fulfill God's design for *your* life so that you too can begin experiencing a sense of personal fulfillment that will withstand the most severe trials and setbacks one can face in life..." Yes,

> *Opportunity is missed by most people because it is dressed in overalls and looks like work.*
> – Thomas Edison

that has been the purpose for this book – to *inspire* you! As the Danish philosopher and theologian Soren Kierkegaard wrote in his *Journal*, "The thing is to understand *myself*, to see what God really wants *me* to do; the thing is to find a truth which is true *for me*, to find the *idea for which I can live and die.*"

Yet, all of the wisdom I've collected over the years have taught me another valuable lesson:

Inspiration minus *Perspiration* = **FRUSTRATION!**

Unfortunately, it's not enough to merely inspire you. "*What good is it, my brothers, if someone says he has faith but does not have works? Can that faith save him? So also faith by itself, if it does not have **works**, is dead*" (James 2:14, 17, ESV). The difference between a mere dream and a true vision is *work*. For inspiration to work, *you've got to go to work.* You've got to take action on the purpose that God has spoken into your heart, for only in taking action do you show your true faith and belief in the Word of God. Take heart, for God is there to not only guide you but to give you the strength that you will need to fulfill His purpose for your life. Then, our simple formula above will take on an entirely new meaning:

Inspiration + Perspiration = **TRANSFORMATION!**

I want share with you one last story that I think speaks so profoundly to the importance of taking action on your life's purpose.

Purpose – Illustrated

Several years I vacationed on a small island. On a warm, beautiful Sabbath afternoon after church, I was invited to the home of a church member for lunch. There I met Eric Bakerfield (not his real name), the founder and owner of one of the largest medical laboratories on the island. As we visited together, I felt deeply impressed that I was listening to a man whose story needed to be told.

Eric's story begins in 1970, at age 16. Having recently graduated from high school, he quickly found work at the local airport. His job offered him quite a bit of freedom, as he often worked a combination of three days on, three days off. During the four years that he worked at the airport, his salary averaged $2,400 per month. This was a lot of money for a single 16-year old to make in the early 70's. The combination of this large sum of money and his youthful tendencies led him to abuse alcohol and drugs.

> *Every person above the ordinary has a certain mission that they are called to fulfill.*
> – Goethe

The fast and wasteful lifestyle began to take its toll, and Eric felt like he desperately needed to get away from it. He knew the only way to do this would be to remove himself from his friends. He also had a growing conviction that he needed a career change, and thus, in early spring, 1974 he began applying to several colleges in the U.S. He in fact changed his circle of friends, which led him to meet a young Christian girl, Christina (not her real name), later that summer. She invited him to come with her to church, and over the next several weeks, he was convicted to give His life to the Lord and was baptized.

Christina had a brother who attended a small Christian school in Alabama. After meeting and befriending Eric, Christina's brother urged Eric to apply to his school. Although Eric had by now been accepted by another school in Florida, he consented and changed schools in the fall of 1974. What a turning point that summer proved to be in his life!

Eric thought that when he entered college someone *else* would direct his life *for* him. It was a rude awakening to discover that, after arriving on campus, he would have to carve out his own course of direction. After settling into his course schedule, he chose business administration as his major, with a focus in accounting. For a time he privately toyed with the idea of pastoral ministry. In reality, he was searching for purpose. He became frustrated with his major because deep down inside *it really wasn't what he felt that he wanted to do with his life.* He realized that his educational background hadn't given him a broad enough perspective of the many professional choices available to him.

An Encounter with God

One night he was feeling particularly anxious about his situation in school, and he began questioning God as to why He would have him to be there in the first place. His internal ranting led him to go behind the men's dormitory on campus and pray, literally crying out to God. With tears streaming down his face, he cried, "Why am I here at this school? Please give me direction and a purpose for my life!"

> *There is no other truth that compares in importance for successful living with the truth that there is a benevolent God who is working out His plans in the affairs of men.*
>
> – Carlyle B. Haynes,
> *God Sent A Man*

With no direct answer from "above", he went back to his dormitory room, plopped down on his bed, and picked up his Bible. He was not very familiar with the Bible at that time, and not having his mind fixed on any particular passage, the very first text he turned to was Deuteronomy 28:13: *"And the LORD will make you the **head** and not the tail, and you shall only go up and not down..."* After thinking about this text for a few moments, he then put his Bible aside, picked up the college bulletin and began leafing through its pages. He came across a discipline called "Medical Technology". Casually, he read the course description and requirements and he felt strangely impressed that this was what he needed to study. As he lay contemplatively on his bed, God clearly spoke to him and told him that he would become a *leader* in this field, thus fulfilling the promise of Deut. 28:13.

How could this be, though? He had never before considered this profession. Nevertheless, God's call grew more distinct. All of this, however, would be conditioned upon one thing: his continuing willingness to be obedient to God's leading in his life.

Eric pursued his studies in medical technology as if possessed. He eventually transferred to a medical college in Tennessee, where he received his degree as well as three out of the four most prestigious awards that could be granted to a graduate in his field. After graduating from the medical college in 1981, Eric returned to his island home to begin work as a med-tech at the local hospital. Shortly thereafter, he began having thoughts about opening a lab of his own. This idea, however, would ripen within the next few years. Finally, in 1985, Eric, along with his best friend, approached two doctors he knew to share his idea of opening his own lab. The doctors were so excited about the idea that, in exchange for a partnership in the business, one of them offered lab equipment and the other offered to rent a small room attached to his own office for lab space.

Soon after the four men struck a deal, Eric began fixing up the room, hiring construction workers to make the necessary structural changes to prepare the lab for operation. By the end of 1985, the lab was ready to go—except for Eric. Eric was not ready. He was completely frightened by the notion of leaving a secure job with $32,000 in annual salary and benefits, not to mention he, by then, had married Christina and they had started a young family. So, he did nothing with the lab and it sat ready to go for a year and a half.

> *The opportunity of a lifetime must be seized in the lifetime of the opportunity.*
> – Leonard Ravenhill

Wake Up Call!

"Why won't I do it?" "Why can't I do it?" "What's wrong with me?" These questions haunted him like a recurring nightmare. Finally, one night in June 1987, Eric had a dream. In this dream, an English expatriate started a medical lab on his island after which the government immediately stepped in and stopped issuing any more licenses for such labs. To Eric, this was no dream—it was a nightmare! He awoke in a state of shock and fear. With his mind racing, he got up and wrote a letter of resignation from his job at the hospital. *There was no way that he wanted to face the future with the knowledge that God had given him all the tools he needed to make his (and God's) dream a reality, but by his own neglect he would forfeit the opportunity.* He didn't even bother to type up his resignation. He handed it in, hand-written, that very day. Making his newly-founded business a success became the highest professional priority in his life. He spent the next four months finalizing the details of the business, which officially opened for operation in late 1987. The rest, as they say, is history.

Today, as the owner and operator of one of the largest medical labs on his island, Eric is indeed a leader in his field. The breadth of his business affords him influence in many areas of civic life that he otherwise wouldn't have, and all of this because of his pursuit of a dream and purpose that God planted in his heart more than forty years ago. The words of the ancient Roman teacher and philosopher, Epictetus (55-135 A.D.), so appropriately capture the essence of Eric's experience and as such are highly instructive for us all:

> *"Tentative efforts lead to tentative outcomes. Therefore give yourself fully to your endeavors. Decide to construct your character through excellent actions and determine to pay the price of a worthy goal. The trials you encounter will introduce you to your strengths. Remain steadfast...and one day you will build something that endures; something worthy of your potential."*

When we faithfully pursue the purpose that God implants in our hearts, without concern for any power, position or prosperity they may bring to us personally, God can then bless our efforts in ways that prove to be of immeasurable benefit to those around us. This witness is what honors God and brings glory to

> *The secret of success is constancy to purpose.*
> – Benjamin Disraeli

Him. *"And the LORD will make you the **head** and not the tail, and you shall only go up and not down..."*

That's what God wants for you – to be the head, an example, a witness! Personally, I believe it more and more every day, that God wants me—my life and its purpose— to be a witness for Him. This conviction screams from the depths of my soul and from the marrow in my bones! It is like a powerful endorphin that, birthed by the Holy Spirit, energizes every fiber of my being. And, it has become like a consuming fire that, by the grace of God, quenches *every* fear, *every* doubt, and *every* hindrance that would serve only as a "pothole" along the pathway of God's purpose for my life. Your life and my life are proof positive that we were born out of Eternity, that before we were formed within our mother's womb, we were first conceived in the mind of God – the "Alpha and the Omega, the Beginning and the End". St. Augustine, the famous North African theologian and bishop of the ancient Roman city of Hippo, captured the essence of this thought when he wrote,

"You have made us for yourself, and our hearts are restless until they find their rest in You."

So, remain in "restless pursuit" of your destiny, your God-given purpose in life, until you find it and in so doing discover *true* happiness…not being content with a current standard, and constantly striving to narrow the gap between what presently *is* and what is possible.

Now, go to your destiny!

Endnotes

1   Ellen G. White, *The Desire of Ages* (Nashville: Southern Publishing Assn., 1967 ed.), p. 9.

2   Myles Munroe, *In Pursuit of Purpose* (Shippensburg, PA: Destiny Image® Publishers, Inc., 1992), pp 15-16.

3   Carlyle B. Haynes, *God Sent A Man* (Washington, D.C.: Review and Herald® Publishing Assn., 1962), p. 6.

4   Walter Kirn, "Should You Stay Together for the Kids?" *Time*, September 25, 2000, p. 76.

5   Kirn, 76-78.

6   The Holy Bible, English Standard Version. ESV® Text Edition: 2016. Copyright © 2001 by Crossway Bibles, a publishing ministry of Good News Publishers.

7   R. Skip Johnson, *Codependency and Codependent Relationships*, BPD Family: Facing Emotionally Intense Relationships™, https://bpdfamily.com/content/codependency-codependent-relationships. Accessed 11 May 2018.

8   Holy Bible, New International Version®, NIV® Copyright ©1973, 1978, 1984, 2011 by Biblica, Inc.® Used by permission. All rights reserved worldwide.

9   David Blankenhorn, *Fatherless America: Confronting Our Most Urgent Social Problem* (New York: HarperCollins Publishers, Inc., 1995), p. 1-2.

10 David Seamands, *Living With Your Dreams* (Wheaton, IL: Victor Books, 1990), p. 38.

11 James C. Dobson, *Life on the Edge: A Young Adult's Guide to A Meaningful Future* (Dallas, TX: Word Publishing, 1995), pp.1-3.

12 Caroline Myss, *Sacred Contracts: Awakening Your Divine Potential* (New York: Three Rivers Press, 2003), p. 1.

13 Ellen G. White, *Christ's Object Lessons* (Washington, D.C.: Review and Heral Publishing Assn., 1900), p. 355.

14 Scripture taken from the New King James Version®. Copyright © 1982 by Thomas Nelson. Used by permission. All rights reserved.

15 Ellen G. White, *Patriarchs and Prophets* (Washington, D.C.: Review and Herald Publishing Assn., 1890), p. 548.

16 Carlyle B. Haynes, *God Sent A Man* (Washington, D.C.: Review and Herald® Publishing Assn., 1962), p. 26.

17 Contemporary English Version (CEV). Copyright © 1995 by American Bible Society.

18 Fyodor Dostoevsky, *The Brothers Karamazov*, 1879. Translated by Constance Garnett.

19 Myles Munroe, *In Pursuit of Purpose* (Shippensburg, PA: Destiny Image® Publishers, Inc., 1992), Introduction.

20 https://en.wikipedia.org/wiki/Trunk_%28botany%29. Accessed 14 May 2018.

21 Clayborn Carson, ed., *The Autobiography of Martin Luther King, Jr.* (New York: Warner Books, Inc., 1998), pp. 117-18.

22 David Seamands, *Living With Your Dreams* (Wheaton, IL: Victor Books, 1990), p. 52.

23 https://www.thenationalcampaign.org/resources/pdf/Fast-Facts-2012-NCHS-Preliminary-Birth-Data-Summary.pdf. Accessed 14 May 2014.

24 "Teen Pregnancy Statiscs". https://www.teenhelp.com/teen-pregnancy/teen-pregnancy-statistics.html. Accessed 29 February 2016.

25 (Ellen G. White, *Patriarchs and Prophets* (Washington, D.C.: Review and Herald Publishing Assn., 1890), pp. 558-59.

26 "The Study of Exemplary Congregations in Youth Ministry." https://www.faithformationlearningexchange.net/uploads/5/2/4/6/5246709/spirit__culture_of_ym_essay.pdf.Accessed 14 May 2014.

27 https://dictionary.reference.com/browse/family. Accessed 16 February 2014.

28 https://en.wikipedia.org/wiki/Dysfunctional_family. Accessed 17 May 2018.

29 https://creditcards.lovetoknow.com/Teen_Credit_Card_Debt_Statistics. Accessed 17 May 2018.

30 https://news.softpedia.com/news/Obesity-Causes-Lower-Academic-Performances-for-Americas-Youth-100999.shtml). Accessed 14 May 2014.

31 https://en.wikipedia.org/wiki/Calvin_Harrison. Accessed 14 May 2014.

32 https://www.beliefnet.com/Inspiration/2001/03/Go-To-Your-Destiny.aspx?p=1. Excerpted from *Go to Your Destiny,* by Alvin and Calvin Harrison. Published by Hyperion, New York. Used by permission. Accessed 13 June 2014.

33 John C. Maxwell, *Failing Forward: Turning Mistakes Into Stepping Stones for Success* (Nashville, TN: Thomas Nelson Inc., 2000), pp.4-5.

Made in the USA
Columbia, SC
12 December 2019